Mr

Re
Iter
w/

HAIL! HAIL!

CLASSIC CELTIC OLD FIRM CLASHES

MARTIN HANNAN

MAINSTREAM
PUBLISHING

EDINBURGH AND LONDON

First published in Great Britain in 2010 by
MAINSTREAM PUBLISHING COMPANY
(EDINBURGH) LTD
7 Albany Street
Edinburgh EH1 3UG

ISBN 9781845966331

A catalogue record for this book is
available from the British Library

Typeset in Adobe Caslon and Requiem

Printed in Great Britain by
Clays Ltd, St Ives plc

To my brother Stephen, keeper of the faith our father gave us.

CONTENTS

FOREWORD

Like any Celtic fan, I love it when we beat Rangers. Conversely, I absolutely hate it when we lose to them. It's the same for everyone involved with the Old Firm, no matter what side you are on.

To have played for and managed Celtic in victories over our great rivals has been an honour and a privilege for a fan like myself. It has also been an experience, to say the least. I think I can safely say I have received more abuse from Rangers fans than any other Celtic man in recent history, and I take that as a kind of compliment, because it means that I have done my job well – to win for Celtic is all that I want to do.

I wish that there had not been the unsavoury elements associated with the Old Firm, and I believe the sectarian situation is getting better as both clubs do what they can to tackle the issue. This book addresses those problems, but thankfully *Hail! Hail!* is much, much more about the football, about the Old Firm matches themselves.

Martin Hannan, who helped me with my memoirs *Neil Lennon: Man and Bhoy*, has chosen 20 classic Old Firm clashes as seen from a Celtic viewpoint. All the great victories are there, including my own favourite when we won 1–0 in 2004 to complete a five-timer in a single season.

Some of the 20 will surprise readers, but Martin explains why all the games he has chosen were important in their time. He has also gained fresh reflections from some great Celtic players, and I have been happy to make my contribution.

Hail! Hail! is a fine addition to the growing Celtic library. I am happy to recommend it to you.

Neil Lennon
Celtic Park, July 2010

INTRODUCTION

It may no longer be the biggest derby in world football in terms of attendances – a record it held for decades – but, for anyone with a genuine sense of footballing history, the Old Firm derby remains the greatest battle between local rivals anywhere on the planet.

It's a true derby, as it features two teams from the same city. Other great rivalries like Barcelona v. Real Madrid and Liverpool v. Manchester United are not derbies as such, as clubs from two separate cities are involved.

You may argue that the Old Firm derby is not even the only rivals match in Glasgow, as Partick Thistle fans would tell you any time they play Celtic or Rangers, but the Old Firm match has long been the most famous derby in Scotland and has fair claim to be the best-known derby in world football.

Let's list some of the most famous 'true' city derbies. England: Liverpool v. Everton, Manchester United v. Manchester City, Arsenal v. Spurs; Italy: Inter Milan v. AC Milan, Roma v. Lazio, Juventus v. Torino; Portugal: Benfica v. Sporting Lisbon; Czech Republic: Sparta Prague v. Slavia Prague; Spain: Real Madrid v. Atlético Madrid, Barcelona v. Espanyol; Greece: the triangular series between AEK Athens, Panathinaikos and Olympiacos in the Greek capital; Hungary: Ferencváros v. Újpest in Budapest; Romania: Dinamo Bucharest v. Steaua Bucharest; Bulgaria: CSKA Sofia v. Levski Sofia; Russia: CSKA Moscow v. Spartak Moscow; Turkey: the triangular series between Beşiktaş, Fenerbahçe and Galatasaray in Istanbul; Argentina: Boca Juniors v. River Plate in Buenos Aires; Brazil: Botafogo v. Fluminense in Rio de Janeiro, Corinthians v. Palmeiras in São Paulo; Egypt: Al-Ahly v. Zamalek; and in Casablanca, in Morocco, the derby that many experts rate as the fiercest anywhere, with two sets of utterly fanatical followers, Raja v. Wydad. It's an impressive list, and there are many other great rivalries in world football, but the Old Firm derby beats them all because it is unique in several respects, not all of them pleasant.

The Old Firm series has the longest history of any derby, and, crucially, it is an unbroken one, as both clubs have always competed in the top division of the Scottish Football League. Counting friendlies in the early years and minor tournaments such as the long-defunct Glasgow Charity Cup, they have played each other nearly 600 times, a record for any senior derby. Rangers have the most wins, and about a quarter of the matches have been draws.

The Old Firm match is also almost invariably the battle to be the top team not just in Glasgow but in Scotland as a whole. In no other derby can it be said that the winners are usually guaranteed to be en route to a trophy. For between them the Old Firm have dominated Scottish football, with 95 league championships, 67 Scottish Cups and 40 Scottish League Cups between them.

The teams' supremacy in league football in particular is astonishing. Since the foundation of the Scottish League in 1890, the longest period without Celtic or Rangers as champions has been just three seasons, namely 1982–83 to 1984–85, when Dundee United and Aberdeen (twice) won the Premier Division. Contrast that with the long periods of Old Firm dominance, such as the record nine-in-a-row titles won by Celtic from 1965–66 to 1973–74 and Rangers from 1988–89 to 1996–97. From the year 1904 to 1947, albeit with the competition suspended during the Second World War, only one other team won the league: Motherwell in 1931–32.

It's because they have been consistently the two best teams in Scotland that Celtic and Rangers make a derby that is passionate, intense and thoroughly engrossing, but there are other, non-footballing, reasons why the Old Firm derby is renowned. The aim of this book is specifically not to rake over old embers of a history littered with unpleasantness. Sectarianism was and is a blot on the face of Scotland, and only an idiot would deny that, for a century or more, the Old Firm has been an excuse for bigotry and all the dreadfulness associated with it, although it is true that both clubs have profited from that religious enmity.

Thankfully, the efforts of both clubs and the authorities to tackle the bigots have begun to pay off in recent years. Sectarianism has not been eradicated, however, and in certain parts of Scotland and

Northern Ireland it is still not safe to walk particular streets wearing the colours of Celtic or Rangers. There may come a day when all Celtic and Rangers fans will happily mingle in downtown bars after an Old Firm match and swap cheery anecdotes, but it is so far in the future you would need Doctor Who's Tardis to find it.

This book will mention controversies such as sectarian issues when appropriate, and indeed one chapter will be devoted to the match that changed Scots law and really began the long process of tackling bigotry: the Scottish Cup final of 1980. Be assured, however, that this book will be first and foremost about football, about the greatest Old Firm matches as seen from a Celtic FC point of view. (Neutrals should be aware that Mainstream, the publishers of this book, are bringing out a companion volume, *Follow, Follow*, written by Iain Duff, which will tackle the subject from an Ibrox viewpoint. Buying both would be doubly instructive, and, for the record, neither Iain nor I has a clue at the time of writing as to which games the other is choosing.)

I have taken 'classic clashes' to mean the most significant and important matches. It would have been very easy to start with the 7–1 victory by Celtic in the 1957 Scottish League Cup final – unsurprisingly, it is one of the longest chapters in this book – and work down the scorelines, such as 6–2, 5–1, 4–0 etc., to arrive at the twenty best performances by Celtic in terms of goals, but low-scoring matches have been just as vital and important; there are even four draws in the selection of twenty, one included because of matters both on and off the field – fans will guess that means the so-called 'Battle of Ibrox' in 1987.

It was, therefore, no easy task to choose the twenty most significant Old Firm matches from a Celtic point of view. In my opinion, only five were automatic choices, and every Celtic fan would surely agree that the matches of 1888, 1905, 1957, 1979 and 2000 would be in anyone's top ten of Old Firm games as seen from a Parkhead standpoint.

It could be argued that the Ibrox Disaster of 1971 was very significant for the Old Firm. Indeed, it was massively traumatic for Scottish society as a whole. But I did not feel it was right to include the match, as I know there are some families of the victims and other people connected with both clubs for whom the memories are still too raw after nearly 40 years. To feature that game and those utterly tragic events in what is largely a celebration of Celtic's achievements would be inappropriate, but it is correct to acknowledge the disaster as by far the worst event associated with the Old Firm. This book is being published in 2010, and I can only hope that, when the 40th anniversary of the disaster occurs on 2 January 2011, the people of Scotland and Old Firm fans everywhere across the world will take the opportunity to remember the dead and act accordingly.

The more you know the history, the more you realise that certain Old Firm matches came to define an era, such as the 6–2 victory that kick-started Martin O'Neill's reign at Celtic Park. Others were just completely odd occasions, victories attained against all current form, and that is why they are so memorable. There is a mixture of both categories in this book. In each chapter, I will give the background to the match and convey a flavour of the wider events of the time, the better to put the matches in context. Since most readers will be well aware of recent history, it follows that the chapters dealing with earlier Old Firm matches are rather more explanatory. It stands to reason that, with four league games per season and both clubs much more dominant than in the first seven decades of Celtic's history, there are now many more Old Firm matches, certainly than before the 1960s, which is why the majority of chapters are from the Stein era on.

Earlier chapters must rely on accounts such as newspaper reports, since Old Father Time has long ago robbed us of live witnesses to the events detailed here. In naming teams, I have also used the style and formation of the time, so that 2–3–5 is used right up until the 1970s.

I gratefully acknowledge the work of historians and authors Willie Maley, Brian Wilson, David Docherty, David Potter, Pat Woods, my *Scotland on Sunday* colleague Andrew Smith and the people behind the marvellous website www.kerrydalestreet.com, whose efforts to build a comprehensive Internet history of Celtic should be applauded and supported.

I would particularly like to thank all the great Celtic players who gave freely of their time to talk to me. As they would not take a fee, I will be donating 20 per cent of any royalties received to The Celtic Foundation. So, dear reader, tell your friends to buy this book, as it's for a good cause!

My thanks go to Bill Campbell, Pete MacKenzie, Graeme Blaikie, Alex Hepworth and all at Mainstream Publishing; my agent, Mark Stanton, whose idea this book was; football agent Martin Reilly; my colleagues at *Scotland on Sunday*; my research assistant Shaun

Miller; photographer Frances Anderson; the picture archive and library staff of the Daily Record and Sunday Mail Ltd and The Scotsman Publications Ltd; and a special mention to the staff at Dumbarton and Edinburgh Central libraries and especially the Mitchell Library in Glasgow.

My special thanks go to Neil Lennon, a wonderfully intelligent and courageous man whom I am proud to call a friend.

My greatest debt of gratitude goes to my wife and children for putting up with me in writing mode and to my mother for the use of the office and her unflinching support these last 51 years.

Thank you most of all to Celtic Football Club for nearly five decades of a roller-coaster relationship between us that has never been anything less than passionate. Long may it continue.

Martin Hannan
The Westbury Hotel, Dublin, April 2010

I

A Very Good Start

28 MAY 1888
FRIENDLY FIXTURE
CELTIC 5, RANGERS 2

Looking back over more than 120 years of Celtic's history, it seems highly appropriate that the club's first-ever match was played against Rangers. For good or ill, the fates of the two clubs have been interlinked ever since. It is simply unimaginable to think of Scottish football without the Old Firm, and while there have been all manner of problems associated with the matches down the decades, there has also been a genuine sporting rivalry between the two great clubs.

At the heart of the Old Firm story is the world's most popular team game, Association Football. Ged O'Brien, former curator of the Scottish Football Museum and a Celtic fan, maintains that Scotland invented modern football, as the passing game originated here in the 1880s and was exported around the world by Scottish players and coaches. It's a convincing theory when you read how the English teams at the time emphasised individual play.

As the sport exploded onto the world scene in the late Victorian era, Celtic and Rangers were already pre-eminent in a country that really was pioneering football. Their encounters down the years have involved some of the most memorable matches ever played in Scotland. Not for one moment, however, can it be stated that every Old Firm match was an exemplar of the highest qualities of football. It's because they have been so competitive and too often played by tense men fearing defeat that many Old Firm matches have been deficient in skill – yet not one has ever been anything less than exciting, especially for the fans of both sides.

The 1880s was a time of change in Scotland, and the Scottish nation as a whole was getting massively into sport. Football in particular was slowly but surely becoming a national obsession. The expansion of railways, plus industries conceding time off to their employees, meant the ordinary worker, if not himself playing, could spectate at the increasing number of matches.

Glasgow was booming as the powerhouse and Second City of the Empire, providing ships, engines and locomotives for the world. Mines and steelworks across the Central Belt provided the raw materials for this concentration of heavy industry, while there was great demand for labourers on farms and in road and railway construction. Irish immigrants were numerous in the labouring and unemployed classes, as many other jobs and the professions were closed to them. It was from these immigrants and their families that Celtic drew their initial support, creating a bond that has been handed down from generation to generation.

In 1883 the Boys' Brigade had been founded in the city by William Alexander Smith to encourage healthy activities and already numbered membership in the thousands, most from a Church of Scotland background. Many Catholic priests and monks also sought to engage their boys and girls in similar healthy pursuits, and, as we shall see, two of Scotland's top clubs of today owe their existence to the clergy.

There was, however, no religious connotation involved in the founding of Rangers. In 1872, a group of four friends who rowed together on the Clyde, Peter Campbell, William McBeath and brothers Moses and Peter McNeil, decided to put together a football team after seeing matches played at Glasgow Green. They called themselves Rangers, having seen the name in an English rugby book. Peter McNeil, whose family hailed from Rhu in what is now Argyll and Bute, was probably the driving force, as he owned a sports equipment shop. His brother, Moses, was just 17 at the time. They played only a couple of matches that year, but in 1873 the quartet decided to formally establish Rangers FC, though they were too late to join the Scottish Football Association (SFA), founded earlier that year. They were not very successful as a team at first, but Moses McNeil was selected to play for Scotland in 1876 and thus became Rangers' first internationalist.

By 1888, Rangers were well established as one of the bigger clubs in Scotland. They had reached two Scottish Cup finals, losing both to Vale of Leven, and in 1887 they competed in the English FA Cup – a not unusual occurrence at the time – and reached the semi-final. The rumoured arrival of a new club in Glasgow, in the shape of Celtic, was not seen by Rangers as any sort of threat. Indeed, Rangers actively sought to help the new club by agreeing to be their first formal opposition.

At the outset, the relationship between Rangers and Celtic was very friendly, a situation that lasted for a good few years, as Celtic were to find sterner competition at first from nearer neighbours in the east end of Glasgow. Rangers' diligent historian David Mason has in his possession a newspaper cutting from that era that talks of Celtic playing a friendly against Rangers as preparation for a match against their great rivals, Clyde FC. Along with Queen's Park and Third Lanark on the south side, Clyde had been among the main competitors for Rangers in Glasgow for some years before 1888 and remained so for several years after Celtic started playing.

Clyde were well placed to snap up footballing talent on the east side of the city, but the private nature of the club and its involvement in other sports left the way open for another club to come into the area, concentrating on football. The history of the founding of Celtic has been told many times, but it is worth recounting the earliest days, as they form the backdrop to the first match. It also needs to be explained why a club that was formally constituted in 1887 has always held 1888 to be its year of foundation. Simple answer really: that is when Celtic first played football, and in 1936 the club's directors decided once and for all that the 'foundation' date was 1888.

On the initiative of Brother Walfrid of the Marist order, born Andrew Kerins in County Sligo in Ireland, The Celtic Football Club was formally established in November 1887 by a group of Scottish-Irish businessmen meeting in St Mary's Church hall, Glasgow. The club would play principally to raise money for The Poor Children's Dinner Table, a sort of soup kitchen that provided food mainly for the children of Irish immigrants, who found it tough to get work in those days when anti-Catholic feelings were openly voiced across central Scotland. The Great Famine, which had caused the largest wave of emigration from Ireland some 40 years previously, was still burned into the memory of the Irish Catholics of Scotland, and putting food on the tables of the poor was the biggest concern of their clergy and leading figures.

Led by Glasgow-born builder John Glass and a tailor called Pat Welsh – more about them in the next chapter – the founders took their inspiration from Edinburgh Hibernians, founded by Canon Edward Hannan, a cousin of the author's direct ancestors. That club had originated out of St Patrick's Church in the Cowgate in 1875 and was an exclusively Catholic young men's club. Hibernians had overcome sectarian opposition to join the SFA and won the Scottish Cup in 1887, the first club from the east coast to do so. They were given a hero's welcome by the Irish community in Glasgow for their achievement. One member of Hibernians is supposed to have said, 'Why not start a similar club here?' And that's what happened.

Despite the changing scene in football, the Hibernians remained resolutely Catholic and amateur. However, while Irish Catholicism underpinned the Edinburgh club's founding, Celtic of Glasgow – note, the club's name has never formally been Glasgow Celtic – had no bar on any other religion from the start, even though the club's first patrons were the Catholic archbishop of Glasgow, Charles Eyre, and local clergy. His Grace even contributed £1 to the coffers, as did other clerics.

As with other sports at that time, football was supposedly amateur. The Celtic players were also amateurs at first, but the majority of the committee was prepared to go along with the 'shamateurism' practices of the day and pay 'gifts' and 'expenses' that were nearly as notional, and perhaps nearly as valuable, as those of some Westminster MPs of recent times. Having seen developments in England, John Glass was happy with the idea of a football club where players were professional in the sense that they would be provided with jobs and 'rewards' or 'expenses' in compensation for playing for Celtic. But full professionalism would come; Glass was sure of that.

Glass's argument was that better players would make for better entertainment, bigger crowds and thus more money to feed the poor. The contention that Glass and his associates later saw the possibility of gaining rewards for themselves from a professional club is unanswerable, but at first their motives were mostly selfless.

The name of Celtic was suggested by Brother Walfrid himself to emphasise the links between Scotland and Ireland. At that time, Hibernians linked up with other 'Irish' clubs, such as Dundee Harp, and played many fundraising friendlies to aid charities and the other Catholic teams. One of these was the first-ever match played under Celtic's auspices, on a pitch created by the club members and hundreds of volunteers at a site in Parkhead about 100 metres east from where Celtic Park now stands. The original pitch was on vacant land adjacent to the Eastern Necropolis, the cemetery for the area, at the corner of Janefield and Dalmarnock Streets, the latter now known as Springfield Road. The six acres or so were leased for £50 per year, and it's possible that the ground's nickname of 'Paradise' was gained from the fact that it was next door to the cemetery.

The opening match at Old Celtic Park on 8 May 1888 was between Hibernians and Cowlairs and ended 0–0. The gate receipts were put towards funds for the new club, and on 28 May 1888 Celtic FC were able to play their first-ever match. Their opponents would be a Rangers XI, that club being caught up in the missionary fervour to spread the word that Association Football was the best sport around.

Probably caused by the confusing existence of the previous match at Old Celtic Park, it is a myth encouraged to this day in Edinburgh and elsewhere that the first players for the new Glasgow club were all from Hibernians. That is just not true. Only one player in the original Celtic XI, Michael Dunbar, was listed as then playing for Edinburgh Hibernians. The other ten came from west-coast clubs with Irish followings or connections, such as Carfin Shamrock and Govan Whitefield. Yes, as many as seven of the team had played for Hibernians in the past, but that was a time when players frequently changed clubs, even during the season, as did many other Catholic footballers in Scotland.

It remains a curiosity of the club's history that the very first Celtic team did not have any players who had actually 'signed' to Celtic, such considerations as registrations and contracts being ahead of them at that time. The most important recruit to the immediate cause was the man rated as the outstanding Scottish footballer of the era, James Kelly of Renton. A Scot of Irish parentage, Kelly came from an area that could arguably be called the cradle of true Scottish football. In what is now West Dunbartonshire, between Loch Lomond and the River Clyde, there were three teams, all founded in 1873. With their revolutionary passing game and quasi-professional approach to playing football – they had organised training sessions, which caused much mirth at other clubs until they started winning everything – Renton, Vale of Leven and Dumbarton would dominate the early years of organised Scottish football along with Queen's Park.

It was a local approach that reached its peak in 1885, when Renton played Vale of Leven in the Scottish Cup final at Hampden, the former club winning 3–1. The commitment to individual and team improvement had rubbed off on James Kelly, who was the stalwart of the Renton side that in 1888 pulled off a remarkable Double. They won the Scottish Cup by beating Cambuslang 6–1 in the final in February, then played English FA Cup winners West Bromwich Albion in a challenge match for the 'World Championship' – well, only England and Scotland played serious football at that time. Renton won 4–1 in the match played at Cathkin – known as Small Hampden – in Glasgow, and thus the village club became football's first world champions.

Dunbartonshire's supremacy wilted as footballing resources gravitated to the cities and bigger towns. James Kelly was a case in point. Luring Kelly to Parkhead and making him the fulcrum of the new team was John Glass's main aim in 1888, and he succeeded by practising a fine disregard for the rules on amateurism, Kelly being paid considerable sums in a roundabout fashion. Kelly played a crucial part in that first Celtic match, not least because he brought his Renton colleague Neil McCallum with him, but his transition from Dunbartonshire to Glasgow was not made official until later.

Another target for Glass was Tom Maley, a teacher who had played for Third Lanark and Hibernians and was a noted inside-forward. With Brother Walfrid, Glass and Pat Welsh set out to recruit Tom at his family's home in Cathcart, which was well known to Welsh, who was friends with Tom's father. Good looking and dashing, with an eye for the ladies, 'Handsome Tom' was out, but Willie, his younger brother, was in, and he was also on Glass's list. We'll learn more about him in subsequent chapters because that young man was to become the dominant, and often dictatorial, figure in the first 50 years and more of Celtic's existence. The Maleys agreed to play, and the game against Rangers was on.

That first historic Celtic team consisted of Michael Dolan of Drumpellier in goal; Eddie Pearson of Carfin Shamrock and James McLaughlin of Govan Whitefield at full-back; Willie Maley of Cathcart, James Kelly of Renton and Philip Murray of Cambuslang

Hibernian; Neil McCallum of Renton, Tom Maley of Cathcart, John Madden of Dumbarton, Michael Dunbar of Hibernians and Harry Gorevin of Govan Whitefield. It was a scratch team, composed entirely of guest players, and history does not record if they ever played or trained together before the match.

It should be noted that Rangers were represented by their 'Swifts', a sort of young reserve side. Their line-up of Nicol; McIntyre and McPherson; Muir, McFarlane and Meikle; Soutar, McKenzie, McLaren, Robb and Wilson contained several members of their regular first-team squad but was by no means the strongest side they could put out. Any Rangers fan reading this may well be comforted by the fact that Celtic did not beat their best team, but Celtic fans will no doubt think, 'Typical, they always underestimated us.'

Plenty of historians have unearthed the facts of that first match from the various journals that covered football at the time. A crowd reportedly in excess of 2,000 gathered around the pitch that late spring evening to watch the action, bringing in gate receipts that gladdened Brother Walfrid's heart: his charitable concept was going to succeed. Celtic took the field in white shirts with green collars and a red Celtic cross on the breast, black shorts and black-and-green hooped socks. The strips had been donated by Penman's, a drapery in Bridgeton. Rangers wore their light-blue shirts, having rejected their own 'hoops' some time previously.

The first man to score a goal in any shade of Celtic shirt was Neil McCallum, the right-winger from Renton whom James Kelly had brought with him. Just a few minutes into the match, he gained his place in Celtic's history thanks to an error by Meikle, who conceded a corner. The kick was taken by Michael Dunbar – the first 'assist' in Celtic's history – and McCallum headed home from directly in front of goal.

The crowd cheered politely but were stilled after ten minutes when Rangers equalised through Soutar. With wind advantage, Celtic continued to press, and goalkeeper Nicol, the Andy Goram of his day, defied the Celts with a series of saves. From a free kick late in the first half, James Kelly's header was put behind for a corner, and the Rentonian then gleefully rose to head home the corner kick and notch Celtic's second.

Leading 2–1 at half-time, Celtic turned to play into the wind, and it was presumed that Rangers' greater experience would tell in the second half, which they began in energetic fashion. Celtic's defence held out, however, and Tom Maley put the new team further ahead, only for Soutar to clinch a second for Rangers.

With the match nicely poised, Tom Maley grabbed the fourth goal, and, assisted by the tricky McCallum, Handsome Tom then earned his hat-trick by scoring Celtic's fifth. McCallum had a goal chopped off for offside, or the result might well have been 6-2, a scoreline that was eventually achieved against Rangers in the next millennium.

Rangers did not give up and were threatening the Celtic goal when the final whistle was blown. Celtic's first match was completed, and the team that would become their greatest rivals had been comfortably beaten 5–2. The bitterness of the rivalry lay in the future, however, and on that evening the players of both teams went off with the Celtic committee, who hosted them for a most convivial evening of eating, drinking and entertainment.

Over the following ten months, Celtic would play their first full season, including competitive matches. The basis of that first Celtic squad comprised Kelly and McCallum, the two Maleys and players imported en masse from Hibernians. Just as it is false to say the first Celtic team was made up of men from Hibernians, so it would be equally false to say that Celtic's first competitive season was accomplished without their imports from the east, all of whom had been induced to join Celtic by Messrs Glass and Welsh. The new club was ambitious, and the 'rewards' it offered were not unattractive to Hibernians' young men, many of whom were originally from the west coast in any case. James Kelly and 1890s hero Dan Doyle were both 'gifted' public houses by admirers. Nice 'presents' if you can get them.

With their strict amateurism, their bar on non-Catholics and denuded of their best players by Celtic's raids, Hibernians swiftly crumbled, and the death from pneumonia of Canon Hannan in May 1891 effectively ended the club. Some months later, thanks to Catholic leaders in Leith, a new club was born and based at Easter Road, where they played their first match in February 1893. Hibernian FC was, from the start, an open club with no religious bars, which did the Leith club a huge favour. The two clubs founded by Catholic clerics have long been friendly rivals and, perhaps more importantly, have both always tried to play attacking football, leading to some classic encounters over the years.

Of that first Celtic team, James Kelly, the Maley Brothers and Michael Dunbar would all have long connections with the club.

Goalkeeper Michael Dolan stayed on but spent most of his six years in the reserves. Neil McCallum was a vital player for a few years before going south as a professional to Nottingham Forest and then returning to play for Rangers, the first man to play for both Old Firm clubs and the first Catholic to play for Rangers. It perhaps says something about the respect in which he was held in his native Vale of Leven that, when he died in 1920, he was given a grave in Bonhill Church of Scotland's kirkyard with a funeral service conducted by a local Catholic priest.

Eddie Pearson returned immediately to Carfin, and Phil Murray and Harry Gorevin played a few more games but did not survive the influx of Hibernians. John Madden did not score in that first match, but he made up for it with plenty of goals in a fine career at Celtic, though he briefly returned to his native Dumbarton to play for the local side. By late 1889, he was Celtic's leading forward, and in total, in nine years off and on with Celtic, he scored forty-nine goals in one hundred and eighteen appearances. He also played twice for Scotland, both matches being against Wales, and in the second of those, an 8–0 drubbing of the principality, he scored four. His nickname was 'the Rooter' because his shot was so strong it threatened to knock the posts out by the roots. After a spell with Dundee United he moved to Prague to coach Slavia, where he enjoyed such success that he is revered as one of the fathers of Czech football and there is a statue to him in the city.

The first Celtic team will never be forgotten, not least because they won the first Old Firm match. It heralded a bright new dawn for a club whose name would soon be heard around the world of football. Celtic had arrived, and a great history had begun to be written.

THE FIRST OLD FIRM
CUP FINAL WIN

22 APRIL 1899
SCOTTISH CUP FINAL
CELTIC 2, RANGERS 0

In the years that followed Celtic's first Old Firm victory, the club expanded fast and enjoyed immediate success with huge crowds at their matches – in some seasons they had the largest average attendance, beating even Queen's Park. They were soon admitted to the SFA, as the other clubs needed the cash from Celtic's following, a situation that continues to this day.

Newspaper reports of the era frequently referred to the team as 'the Irishmen', which was inaccurate, as only a few Celtic players at that time had been born in Ireland. As early as 1893, a newspaper carried an item questioning the right of 'Irish' players from Celtic to represent Scotland. The barbs were anti-Catholic as much as anti-Irish, and, led by Willie Maley, the club did everything it could to emphasise that it was a Scottish club with an Irish heritage.

From the start, people from outside the immediate area of east Glasgow began to follow the fortunes of a club that represented dignity for Catholics. Celtic acquired the permanent services of James Kelly, Neil McCallum and several well-known players from Edinburgh Hibernians. Most vital of all, they had a team that played good football.

James Kelly was the rock, but the irrepressible Dan Doyle became the talisman. He had played for Hibernians in the 1888 match that opened Celtic Park, then made his name in England as a professional, where he was unfortunately involved in an onfield accident that led to an opponent's death. His return to 'amateur' Celtic from professional Everton in the early 1890s was a cause célèbre, but his talent as a defender was undeniable and he later captained Celtic and Scotland.

The Maley influence began to tell on the Celtic style of play – both Tom and Willie being noted athletes and champion sprinters – as they preferred fast passing movements, and with Doyle at their heart, Celtic had a solid defence. They also had an ability to turn defence into attack quickly, constantly pressurised opponents and had the determination to score by a variety of means. Pundits regularly denigrate 'the Celtic way', but it was no myth. It was how the first Celts played the game, and thankfully many since have embraced the culture.

In their first competitive season of 1888–89, Celtic entered four tournaments and reached the finals of them all, and, judging by reports in the *Scottish Umpire* journal and elsewhere, the new club had swiftly become one of the most feared, as well as one of the most entertaining, teams in Scotland.

In the Scottish Cup final that season Celtic lost to Third Lanark – but only after bad weather at the first match forced a replay. Celtic won their first trophy in their inaugural season, beating Cowlairs 6–1 in the Glasgow North-Eastern Cup final at Clyde's ground, Barrowfield. The Celts also reached the finals of the Glasgow Charity Cup, losing 2–5 to Renton, and the Glasgow International Exhibition Cup, which they lost to Cowlairs 0–2. Four finals with a trophy won out of four tournaments entered in their first season – no wonder Celtic were in demand wherever they went, including England, where they played several matches.

Off the field, both within and outwith the club, there were significant developments in 1890, the most important being the start of the Scottish Football League in the summer of that year. Even before the league arrived, Celtic were making serious money: their annual income by 1890–91 was around £5,000, making them the wealthiest club in Britain, according to figures held at the Scottish Football Museum.

The better-established Scottish clubs had looked with envy at the formation of the Football League in England in 1888 – the idea of a Scot, William McGregor – the FA having legalised professionalism some years earlier. Anybody with half a brain in Scottish football – there have been many of those down the years, usually wearing blazers – knew that a league and professionalism were coming, and some looked forward to it, especially Celtic, though no one dared voice such sentiments for fear of the SFA's inquisition.

In alphabetical order, the following ten clubs joined Celtic in the original Scottish League: Abercorn, Cambuslang, Cowlairs, Dumbarton, Heart of Midlothian, Rangers, Renton, St Mirren, Third Lanark and Vale of Leven. Only Celtic, Rangers, Hearts, Dumbarton and St Mirren still survive in the senior ranks, and only the first two of those have never been relegated. Hibernians were in some disarray, and their secretary 'forgot' to attend. Queen's Park would have nothing to do with it.

Season 1890–91 thus saw Celtic play their first league matches, with the very first game being against Renton, who won 4–1 at Parkhead. Later in the season, Renton committed the ultimate sin, in those amateur days, of playing against a team of 'professionals' from Edinburgh who had been expelled from the league. As a consequence, Renton were also expelled and all their results declared void, which is why some histories of Celtic do not include that original fixture. Celtic were also deducted four points for fielding an ineligible player in that match, but it would have made no difference to their final placing, as Dumbarton and Rangers both ended on 29 points, with the Celts in third on 21. The Sons of the Rock and Rangers were declared joint champions after a 2–2 draw in a play-off, though Dumbarton had the superior goal difference and by today's standards would have been sole champions.

Celtic did win the Glasgow Cup in 1891, their first major domestic honour, but the following season they would eclipse all their achievements by winning the Scottish Cup, beating Queen's Park 5–1 in a replay after the first match was declared void owing to crowd problems. The east end of Glasgow became a scene of riotous celebrations for the next few days, as the Irish community, who have never been known to need an excuse for a party, rejoiced in the victory of their team. Less than four years after their first match, Celtic had won the Cup – could they now go on to win the new league?

Season 1892–93 saw Celtic, playing now in green and white vertical stripes, installed in a new home not far from their original pitch. The club committee had been held to ransom by the owner of the original Celtic Park, who wanted to increase the rental fee astronomically – reportedly from £50 to £450 or £500 per year. With John Glass and Pat Welsh to the fore, the club committee decided to lease another plot with a view to eventually buying their own ground and making it the best around. What we now know as Celtic Park was formerly a brickyard. A new pitch, terraces, a running track with cycling banks and a pavilion with dressing-rooms were built on the site, largely with volunteer labour, in time for the start of the 1892–93 season.

It must have been an interesting scene when that turf was laid, as it was done by the famous Irish nationalist and proto-socialist Michael Davitt, who had served time in British jails for his activities against the Crown but had renounced violence and was now a political force. Celtic committee-man Pat Welsh was also a former republican fighter and had been shown mercy by a Catholic soldier in the British Army and been allowed to flee Ireland. That same soldier was now Welsh's good friend from Cathcart, former sergeant Thomas Maley, father of Celtic players Willie and Tom.

By bringing in Davitt, the Celtic committee made their stance on the fractious issue of Irish politics abundantly clear: they wanted no truck with violence. The likelihood is that Davitt's involvement was largely John Glass's doing. A shrewd politician, Glass was in overall charge of Celtic but had the good sense to let Willie Maley, as match secretary, run the football side of the club. In later years, Maley would declare that the club owed its existence to Glass.

By the early 1890s, Willie Maley was a trained accountant and Handsome Tom was a teacher. Both men were fitness fanatics and had loved football from the start. For Willie Maley, however, the real developing love affair was with Celtic, and he worked closely with James Kelly to take charge of onfield events and built a strong relationship with club president Glass.

In 1892–93 Celtic won their first Scottish League title, not long after Brother Walfrid departed from Glasgow to try and repeat his feats with another large Irish population, this time in London. He left knowing he had created champions for a community he had served so faithfully for 25 years.

His was not the only talent going to England. With Scottish footballers flooding south for money, the SFA finally allowed professional football in Scotland. Celtic secured their own players, captured some new ones and went on to win the league again the following year, with Hearts in second this time – though the next season it was the Edinburgh club's turn to win its first title. With a Division Two now formed, the league was firmly established, and of the senior clubs only Queen's Park stubbornly refused to join.

Celtic and then Hearts won the title in 1895–96 and 1896–97 respectively before Celtic recaptured the championship in 1897–98. By that time, Celtic FC had taken steps to formalise its professional existence by reconstituting itself as a limited company, though some members objected to the new structure and left the club.

Willie Maley was now the club's driving force. In 1897, he and former player Michael Dunbar, by then a successful wine and spirit merchant, were elected to the board of the new company, called the Celtic Football and Athletic Company Limited – Maley was a champion Scottish sprinter at the time, perhaps explaining 'Athletic'. He was in almost complete control, on a salary of £150 a year as manager and secretary, and was a strict disciplinarian.

With the events of the previous months having spread the honours, season 1898–99 was set up for a battle between the country's four best clubs, Celtic, Rangers, Hearts and Hibs. They would duly fill the top four places in the league, Rangers running away with the title ahead of Hearts, Celtic and Hibs, in that order.

The year 1899 began disastrously for Celtic, with a 4–1 thrashing in the league away to Rangers, which followed the first Old Firm match of the season the previous September, when Celtic had collapsed almost unbelievably to a 0–4 hammering at Parkhead. Rangers also put Celtic out of the Glasgow Cup at the semi-final stage, so only the Scottish Cup remained for the Bhoys if they were to avoid a blank season. Fortunately, Celtic's progress in this, the most important tournament, was serene, and victory in the semi-final against Port Glasgow Athletic put them into the final against Rangers, who had a 100 per cent record for the season behind them. Predictably, Rangers were hot favourites.

Maley had been busy with the chequebook, however. Between the start of seasons 1896–97 and 1898–99, he had acquired John Reynolds and James Welford from Aston Villa as well as Jack Bell and Davie Storrier from Everton. He also brought back Johnny Campbell from Aston Villa, the player having left following an argument with a committee man. Former Hearts man 'Big' Barney Battles had left Celtic for Dundee after a players' strike over press reports, but he too was brought back by Maley in 1898, as was striker John Divers – the first of three men of that name to play for Celtic – after a brief sojourn at Everton.

The goalkeeper through all this time was Dan McArthur, a Celtic hero on account of his willingness to suffer being knocked unconscious for the cause at a time when barging keepers with ball in hand was seen as fair play. Dan Doyle had all but retired, but the other big club hero of the day was Sandy McMahon, and if any player could claim to be the first great Celtic striker then it was he. The Selkirk-born former Hibs forward scored two goals when Celtic won the Cup against Queen's Park in 1892, and he was anxious to repeat the feat against Rangers seven years later.

This final was very special in many ways. It was a contest for the last major trophy of the century and came at the end of what had in retrospect been ten good years for Celtic, with their four league championships and numerous other trophies, including the Scottish Cup of 1892. There was also the question of revenge: in the only previous Scottish Cup final between the two sides, in 1894, Rangers had beaten Celtic 3–1 to deny the Parkhead club its first Double. Now, five years later, it was Rangers who were going for the Double, which they had never managed to achieve either. Rangers were also going for a hat-trick of cup wins and would become the first club in the professional era to achieve the feat that only Queen's Park and Vale of Leven had previously accomplished as amateurs. With the league already lost, Celtic also knew that they had one last chance to end the century with a bang.

Celtic were already looking to expand Parkhead to accommodate bigger crowds, and that year Rangers were about to become a company like Celtic and move just along the road to Ibrox Park. They appointed Archibald Leitch to design their giant new stadium with a stand seating 4,500 spectators – it was the first of many designed by Leitch, who also later worked on Celtic Park, Hampden and almost every major ground in Britain.

Rangers also appointed their first formal full-time manager, William Wilton, who, like Maley at Celtic, would leave his stamp on his club. Unlike Scottish-cap Maley, Wilton had been no great shakes as a player, but, just like the Celtic manager, Wilton laid down very strict discipline, including dress codes. Wilton and Maley became good friends and enjoyed many a sporting joust until the former's death in a boating accident in 1920.

Interestingly, in 1899, the *Scotsman* described the two teams as 'the famous Glasgow combinations' and added that Rangers 'next perhaps to the Queen's Park, may be put down as the popular favourites of the Glasgow football public'. Celtic, however, had the concentrated support of a large community of an estimated 400,000 people in Scotland who were either born in Ireland or were second- or third-generation Irish.

The day of the match dawned fair, if cloudy at times, and by the kick-off time of 4 p.m., Hampden was full. The crowd was estimated at around 25,000, and, as was usual in those days, the press recounted breathlessly that the gate receipts had totalled £1,134, with the grandstand yielding another £300. A male labourer of the time would be taking home around £1 per week, so you can see that football had become big business.

The two teams were named as follows. Celtic: McArthur; Storrier and Welford; Battles, Marshall and King; Hodge, Campbell, Divers, McMahon and Bell. Rangers: Dickie; N. Smith and Crawford; Gibson, Neill and Mitchell; Campbell, McPherson, Hamilton, Miller and A. Smith. The referee was Scotland's most respected official, Tom Robertson.

Celtic were in the ascendancy for most of the first half, but Rangers were dangerous on the break, though James Welford was particularly strong in defence for Celtic against the tricky duo of John Campbell and John McPherson. The play was scrappy and often downright poor, however, and the *Scotsman* noted disapprovingly that 'neither side was above taking an unfair advantage of an opponent'. Of course, that has never happened in subsequent Old Firm matches . . .

The two teams got to the interval with barely a proper chance created, though John Hodge was unlucky just before half-time when mistakes by the Rangers defence allowed him a shot at goal. Rangers' forward line was normally the key to their success, but most of them were of average height or below, and Maley had packed the Celtic defence with larger, tougher men, such as Battles, who had an outstanding game. The result was that Rangers could never get going up front, and slowly but surely Celtic turned the screw, one reporter noting that, from quite early on, the men in blue had little hope of overcoming their opponents.

Early on, the second-half play was not much better than the first. Celtic faced a serious problem when outside-left Jack Bell was injured in a collision with Rangers right-back Nicol Smith, a noted hard man, and though Bell carried on after treatment, another tackle from Smith appeared to have ended the Celtic player's match. Big Barney Battles was not having it, however, and signalled Bell to carry on playing, albeit bandaged and limping heavily.

Rangers soon had the ball in the net thanks to Scottish international John McPherson, but again Battles would not tolerate matters and appealed to referee Robertson for offside, as players had to do then. The official could hardly fail to agree, as press reports indicate that McPherson had been 'flagrantly offside'. This decision in Celtic's favour appeared to deflate Rangers and galvanise Celtic, and they charged forward.

Overcoming adversity was already established as a Celtic trait, and with just ten effective men on the field the Celts raised their game and won a corner. Hodge's kick was highly accurate, and Sandy McMahon headed home for the opening goal.

The Celtic tide was now irresistible, even with a damaged winger, and any attempts by Rangers were beaten back by a defence described in one report as 'stonewall' – clichés are nothing new in football. The clinching goal came when John Divers broke clear of the Rangers defence and fired in a shot at goalkeeper Matthew Dickie, only for the rebound to be tucked away by John Hodge.

Rangers had no answer, and their heads went down so that they played the last 15 minutes of the match 'in a half-hearted fashion', as one report had it. The *Scotsman* concluded, 'That the Celtic deserved the victory no one could gainsay; they were the more vigorous and deserving side.'

After the presentations, as usual, both teams and their officials repaired to a social function, and, as ever, relations between the two clubs were friendly. Of that 1899 side, James Welford had just set an unbeatable record as the first professional footballer to hold Scottish and English cup medals. A county-class cricketer – his colleague Davie Storrier was a Scotland international cricketer – Welford would go on to join Irish League side Distillery. Remembered as Celtic's first great goalkeeper, brave Dan McArthur played on until 1903, when one injury too many forced his retirement. After scoring 109 goals in 215 matches for Celtic, Johnny Campbell moved to Third Lanark in 1903 and helped them win the league in his first season there.

The versatile Scottish internationalist Alex King – he even played as goalkeeper when required – moved to Dykehead in 1900, the same year that Jack Bell returned south to New Brighton and then Everton. John Divers moved to Hibs in 1901, John Hodge left the following year for Portsmouth, and later played for Morton, and centre-half Harry Marshall moved to Clyde in 1903, the same year that Sandy McMahon moved to Partick Thistle after an extraordinary Celtic career in which he scored 171 in 217 matches – a scoring rate even better than Henrik Larsson's, though not quite as good as Jimmy McGrory's.

Tragedy struck Big Barney Battles, who transferred to Kilmarnock in 1904. A year later, he was dead. Even a man of his stature could not beat the influenza that developed into pneumonia and took him at the age of just 30. Some 40,000 people lined the route of his funeral procession. His son Barney Jr, unborn at the time of his father's death, would play for Hearts and Scotland. Davie Storrier, too, died young, the Arbroath-born player having captained Scotland and then moved to Dundee FC before passing away in 1910 at the age of just 37.

All the outgoings meant that by the time of the match that features in our next chapter, just six years later, not one of the 1899 side was left at Parkhead. As we shall see, that was part of a deliberate policy by Willie Maley, who was determined to create a new Celtic in the twentieth century – which he did, and a rather good team it was, too.

3

START OF THE SIX

Though Rangers won the Glasgow Cup in August 1899, beating Celtic in a replay, the last national trophy of the nineteenth century went to Celtic. It should have been an omen of hope for the club, but behind the scenes Willie Maley was anxious. Celtic were rich enough to go on buying in talent from other major clubs, but such purchases were becoming expensive even for them, and, with an eye on the finances, Maley wanted a system where Celtic could find their own youngsters and train them to play 'the Celtic way' – with passing, entertaining, winning football. He instituted a formal scouting system, which was not unique, as other clubs had scouts, but Maley swiftly made Celtic's the biggest and best system in Scotland, with scouts well rewarded for recommendations.

The manager was also often his own best scout. Players he signed personally included the mighty James Quinn, a miner from Croy who took a lot of persuasion to leave his dangerous trade and his local team, Smithston Albion, to join Celtic, and Willie Loney, Quinn's great friend and, like him, eventually a Celtic legend.

Celtic had started the new century brightly enough, winning their second successive Scottish Cup in season 1899–1900 in splendid fashion against the champions of the amateur game, Queen's Park. John Divers (two), Jack Bell and John Hodge scored the goals in a 4–3 victory that was a close-run thing, Celtic going 4–1 up and having to survive a late fightback.

Queen's Park had already decided to join the league but stay amateur, and such was the confidence of their committee in the club's future that they set about building the biggest and best stadium in the world, which became the accepted National Stadium. Football was no longer just the working man's pastime. Celtic had proved that themselves by allowing director James Grant to build a luxurious private stand at Celtic Park in 1898 – the club bought it from Grant in 1904 after the main stand burned down – and the new Ibrox and Hampden stadiums had similar stands for those who could afford them. Nevertheless, Maley knew his club had risen thanks largely to the pennies and 'bobs' paid by hard-pressed workers, and while he accepted and indeed drove forward the business side of Celtic, he did not want to waste their money.

Maley's search to find the best of – preferably – Scottish talent was accelerated after Celtic drew a blank, trophy-wise, in season 1900–01. As any former Celtic manager will tell you, especially Tony Mowbray, planning for the future is all very well and necessary, but winning every match is still the club's target, and failure to win consistently is unacceptable. Maley was hardly going to sack himself, and no one else had the power to do so, but he was ultra-ambitious for Celtic and keenly felt the events of 1900–01, when the nearest they got to a trophy was losing the Scottish Cup final 3–4 to Hearts. Worse still, he had to watch the team that were now increasingly recognised as Celtic's chief Glaswegian rivals win their third league championship in succession.

There is no single incident that can be said to have sparked off the Old Firm rivalry, but in October 1901 Celtic played Rangers in the Glasgow Cup final at Ibrox and gained a 2–2 draw. When the replay was ordered to be played at Ibrox, Celtic refused to take part for the obvious reason that home advantage had been gifted to Rangers again. The Cup was promptly awarded to Rangers, and everyone at Celtic, from the committee to the players and fans, was incensed. Queen's Park had long been the 'establishment' club influencing the SFA. Was that support now switching to Rangers?

Unfortunately for Celtic, Rangers also went on to win the league, though the gap between the two sides at the top was down to two points from six the previous year. Celtic then lost the 1901–02 Scottish Cup final to Hibs, but, at the time of writing, one of those two finalists has never won it since – put it this way: it's not Celtic.

Hibs went on to win the league the following season, and Celtic again drew a blank. Maley was now well aware that Celtic had not won any major trophies since 1900, though they had gained the second Glasgow International Exhibition Cup in 1901 and also lifted the trophy for the 'British League' four-team tournament organised by Rangers to raise money for the victims of the first Ibrox Disaster in April 1902, in which 25 people died and 517 were injured.

Press coverage was also now a problem for Celtic, who had tried to encourage good relations with the newspapers and sporting magazines of the day and had built the first press box in Britain as early as 1894. Yet still the Scottish press were often sneering and downright rude about Celtic. Published anti-Irish and anti-Catholic sentiment would come to a head a few years later.

Maley's talent search proceeded. He wanted younger players, strong and agile with skill and pace, who were able to take discipline and instruction. As was normally the case, the players could decide the onfield tactics themselves, but Maley knew what calibre of player he wanted in Celtic jerseys and was desperate to get them. As well as Loney and Quinn, he brought in Peter Somers, 'Sunny' Jim Young, Bobby Muir, Alec Bennett, James Hay and Alex McNair. They were all young, keen and willing to learn. They would form the backbone of the team that Maley was creating, the first great dominant side in Scotland in the professional era.

Not that they won the league right away. Season 1903–04 belonged to Third Lanark, who that year won their only league championship and also took the Glasgow Cup, but they met their match in the semi-final of the Scottish Cup, when Celtic edged them out 2–1 after being one down.

In the final, Celtic played Rangers at the new Hampden Park on 16 April 1904. It was a very significant date for Celtic for one particular reason: all season the team shirts had alternated between green and white stripes and a rather fetching new green-and-white-hooped confection. For the final, Maley chose the hoops, and those have been Celtic's first colours ever since. They are unarguably among the most recognisable football colours in the world.

It was one of the best Old Firm matches for years from a Celtic fan's perspective. Beforehand, Maley had no hesitation in dropping striker Alec Bennett after rumours began to circulate that Rangers were keen to sign him. Jimmy Quinn was moved off the left wing into centre-forward, and a legend was born. Barney Battles had also been dropped, and in his place Maley had a new formula of playing 'Sunny' Jim Young, supposedly a natural centre-half, alongside Willie Loney and James Hay. Young, Loney and Hay: serious football historians consider them to be one of the all-time great half-back lines. For with Quinn up front using all his natural strength, the men behind him provided the ammunition for a scoring machine that would last for years, and it all kicked off in that Old Firm final. It was a close-run thing as to whether that match would make the final 20 for this book, but, for various reasons, the events of 1905 were deemed more substantial.

That was a cracking final, however, and set a world-record attendance for a club match, with an astonishing 64,323 people inside Hampden Park, a figure that in one fell swoop confirmed that the committee of Queen's Park had been correct to build big and bold and also proved the SFA's wisdom – there's a phrase you thought you'd never read – in reducing the price of admission by half to just sixpence.

Referee Tom Robertson of Queen's Park was in charge again, and though Celtic attacked from the off it was Rangers who went two up quite early. Finlay Speedie scored both as a result of what were clearly defensive lapses, the hapless goalkeeper Davie Adams taking the blame. But now Maley's wisdom in creating a young, vigorous team was shown to great effect.

For almost all of the next 80 minutes, the Celts tore into their opponents, and the half-back line's flexibility allowed Loney to get forward in attack and support Quinn, who began to take personal charge of matters. He scored a fabulous solo goal that owed everything to his bull-like strength on the charge, and, in those rather more sporting days, Rangers fans applauded the score.

Just before half-time, Bobby Muir crossed from the right and there was Quinn to hit home a first-time shot. Celtic were back from the dead, and the momentum was with the men in the hoops. Despite a flurry from Rangers, Celtic remained in control, and ten minutes from the end Quinn shrugged off a fierce tackle from Nicol Smith and kept his composure to score what proved to be the winner. Rangers just could not get going against the energetic Celts, who continued to attack, and the Scottish Cup was coming back to Paradise for the fourth time.

The match was duly christened 'the Jimmy Quinn Final' – what else could it be called? – and it would be 68 years before another hat-trick would be scored in a Scottish Cup final, achieved by John 'Dixie' Deans for Celtic against Hibs in 1972.

The final also bequeathed Celtic and Rangers jointly a new name. Historians disagree exactly as to when the phrase 'Old Firm' was first used about them, but there is no doubt that the *Scottish Referee*, which had long viewed the two clubs' growing power and commercialism with distaste, featured in its preview of the match a cartoon under the heading 'The Scottish Final'. It showed a fairly grotty pipe-smoking fellow with a billboard on which was written 'PATRONISE THE OLD FIRM', and in case anyone doubted to whom the publication was referring, the cartoon was captioned 'Rangers, Celtic Ltd'. Whether the phrase 'Old Firm' was used before then nobody can say with certainty, but the cartoon's barbed comment was soon taken up by other writers and the phrase entered the language.

Yet still the rivalry was mostly friendly and certainly not bitter. There were small sectarian issues, but Celtic's Maley succeeded in stopping at least one of them by telling Alec Bennett, whose liking for Rangers and problems with Catholicism had become known, that religion played no part in whether he was selected. Maley uttered his famous dictum 'It's not the man's creed nor his nationality that counts – it's the man himself.' Bennett stayed.

By season 1904–05, the realisation had grown that the Scottish League was at least rivalling the Cup, if not exceeding it, in importance. Willie Maley had set his sights on winning the title again, and now he had the team to do it. They proved him correct in the first few months of the season, from August to January losing only one game, away to Hearts, and winning the Glasgow Cup into the bargain, beating Rangers 2–1 in the final in front of another massive crowd.

As the season neared its completion, trouble erupted when Celtic met Rangers at Parkhead in the Scottish Cup semi-final. A pitch invasion after Jimmy Quinn was sent off for allegedly fouling Alex Craig – Rangers were leading 2–0 at the time – led to the match's abandonment, and the SFA duly convened an inquiry. Maley trumped them, however, by conceding the match, but despite Alex Craig himself testifying that Quinn was innocent, the SFA suspended him until the end of the season, about a month in duration. Maley deftly turned this injustice to Celtic's advantage by making the players feel hard done by, a useful trait in all successful Celtic managers, and the publicity around the case raised Quinn's profile still further.

Rangers' quest for the Double ended with Third Lanark soundly defeating them in the Cup final, and when Celtic beat Motherwell 6–2 away from home they and Rangers ended up jointly topping the table with 41 points from 26 matches. The rules still did not encompass goal average or difference – Rangers would have won the title on both counts – so a play-off was arranged to decide the championship.

Originally scheduled as a Glasgow League fixture and hurriedly made into a Scottish League decider, this match would be unique in Scottish football history. Though several Old Firm games would see one or other team clinch the title in the future, this was the only match that would be a play-off for the title *after* the season had been completed. At the time, it was seen by some pundits as an unnecessary affair. Why could the clubs not share the championship, as had happened before – indeed, in the very first season of the Scottish League?

One correspondent wrote of 'the prolongation of the competition beyond the public interest', and he may well have been correct, as only an estimated 28,000, or maybe slightly more, turned out at Hampden Park. The public perhaps had other things to entertain them, with the activities of jolly King Edward VII always a source of interest. A new movement for female emancipation called the suffragettes was making the news – they would hold their first public protests the week after the play-off match. Readers everywhere rejoiced in *The Return of Sherlock Holmes* by Arthur Conan Doyle, published in March and already a bestseller.

Whatever the reason for the relatively poor turnout, it was still a hugely important match, which probably accounts for why it was a dismal affair. Celtic's team consisted of Adams; Watson and Orr; McNair, Loney and Hay; Bennett, McMenemy, Quinn, Somers and Hamilton. Without exception, every one was a Maley signing, and most of them had been found through the scouting system he had devised. In David Hamilton from Cambuslang Hibs and Jimmy McMenemy of Rutherglen Glencairn, he had found in the junior ranks of Scotland two men who would make Celtic's attack feared for years, with McMenemy, nicknamed 'Napoleon', becoming a true legend. Hugh Watson was another recruit from the lower ranks, having played for Trabboch Thistle in Ayrshire, as was goalkeeper Davie Adams, who had played for Dunipace.

Rangers fielded Sinclair; Fraser and Craig; Gourlay, Stark and

May; Robertson, Speedie, McColl, Donaghy and Smith. Robert Smyth McColl, at centre-forward, was perhaps better known as 'Toffee Bob', as he was already the co-proprietor of a newsagent's that multiplied across the country and gained him much greater and lasting fame as R.S. McColl.

A sign of the league's concern about the match was the appointment of a referee from England, Mr Frederick Kirkham of Preston. The league and the SFA were both concerned about the obvious bad blood caused by the events of the Cup semi-final and wanted none of Scotland's umpires to be put into the position of seeming to be less than impartial. No such accusation could surely be levelled at the Englishman, as long as he got the decisions right. Given the events of season 2009–10, it makes you wonder whether the idea is not worth trying again.

Kirkham did not have much to do because the game was largely a bore. Both sides were anxious not to lose, and reports of the match in the newspapers show that even the gentlemen of the press were thoroughly dissatisfied. 'A very poor game, considering the standing of the teams,' wrote one. 'A downright disappointment,' wrote another. Clearly the stakes had been too high, and how many times has that happened in Old Firm history . . . ?

It was Celtic who rose briefly above the mediocrity. Having lost the toss, they had to play with the strong wind in their favour in the first half, but it did them no good, not even when they forced several corners, which were all dealt with by Rangers. Frantic stuff saw frequent offsides, and it was no surprise that there were no goals at half-time.

Celtic improved in the second half, and after an hour or so of play Jimmy McMenemy put them ahead, placing his shot adroitly behind recent recruit Tom Sinclair in the Rangers goal. Two minutes later, from far out on his wing, Hamilton let fly, and the ball went into the Rangers net via the inside of the post and Sinclair's body. Jacky Robertson pulled one back for Rangers inside four minutes of that score, but that brief burst of goalmouth activity was the last significant action of the game. Rangers lost Adam Gourlay to injury, and Celtic were quite content to play out time against the ten men and clinch the championship.

The response outside Celtic's fan base was underwhelming, but that victory proved to be the catalyst for one of the great periods of the club's history. With Young, Loney and Hay usually at half-back and McMenemy, Quinn and Hamilton providing the threat up front, a great side had emerged that would go on to set several landmark achievements and records, not least of which was the club's first Double, in season 1906–07. They were the first Scottish club to achieve the feat, and just to prove it was no fluke they won the Double again the following season and added the Glasgow Cup and Glasgow Charity Cup for an unprecedented Quadruple that would not be surpassed until 1966–67.

In all, Celtic went on to win six league titles in a row – another record – and all the time Maley was taking Celtic across Europe to show off what he called 'the best team in the world'. In the absence of any serious competitors elsewhere, how could anyone gainsay him?

4

THEIR CUP RUNNETH OVER

21 MARCH 1925
SCOTTISH CUP SEMI-FINAL
CELTIC 5, RANGERS 0

Celtic's international reputation was established during the six-in-a-row years and afterwards by several tours around Britain and the Continent. At home they continued to dominate until the end of the Great War. Yet all the time Rangers were growing their support.

That there were still reasonable relations between Celtic and Rangers prior to the war was shown in 1908, when Alec Bennett was finally allowed to move from 'heaven to Govan', as one wag put it, and join the club of which he was an avowed fan. Tom Sinclair had joined Celtic from Rangers two years previously, and Willie Kivlichan also moved from 'Govan to heaven' – we will meet him again in sad circumstances in the next chapter. Players would move from Celtic to Rangers right up until the end of the First World War, and no one suggested they should not do so on religious grounds.

When did sectarianism arise? Not in one instant, not even at the infamous Hampden Riot of 1909, which involved *both* sets of fans jointly scrapping with the police in a furious protest against the decision of the authorities not to play extra time after the second Cup final replay was drawn. Willie Maley and his friend William Wilton both tried to calm the mob, but to no avail. The SFA withheld the Cup, robbing Celtic of the chance to win three Doubles in a row.

The original rivalry between Celtic and Rangers was on purely footballing grounds at first, before it became commercial. In any power struggle, however, there are often interfering outsiders, and in this case there were people in the press whose irresponsibility knew no bounds.

As Maley's Celtic rolled over their opponents each successive season, there were repeated calls in the press for a club to uphold the honour of Scotland and beat the 'Irish' Celtic. Then Harland & Wolff brought shipyard workers to Govan from Belfast before the war, and with them came their extreme tribalism. When the Easter Rising took place in 1916, anti-Irish resentment across Scotland grew exponentially. Add in widespread religious bigotry – 'too many Catholics, too many Protestants, not enough Christians', as that Belfast philosopher Frank Carson memorably described it – and you had a combustible brew that engulfed both clubs in the 1920s.

Celtic FC was by design a leading force in the Irish Catholic community in Scotland, and Rangers, over a period of time, found themselves elected, willingly or unwillingly, as the standard-bearers of Protestantism. What football had to do with religion has never been fully explained, because there is no explanation, so while this element of the history of the Old Firm should be acknowledged, let's stick to the football.

In 1911, Celtic had acquired a Donegal-born player from Clydebank who was only 5 ft 4 in. tall and weighed just over 7 st. when he first arrived at Parkhead. Patsy Gallacher would fill out slightly and grow a little, but not much. However, what 'the Mighty Atom' lacked in physique he made up for in skill, and over the next few years his inspirational play, not to mention his courage in the face of tough tackling, led Celtic to a renewed period of triumph. It would probably have happened even without the interruption of the First World War, but there's no doubt that Celtic prospered in terms of winning tournaments during that conflagration, though sadly they lost the club's founder, Brother Walfrid, who died in 1915 at the Marist retirement home in Dumfries.

By the end of the Great War, during which Celtic players past and present had served with merit – former Celtic player Willie Angus won the Victoria Cross, but his 40 wounds meant he would never play again – there were great gaps in many Scottish squads. Hearts lost seven first-team members killed in action. Men from Hibs and Raith Rovers who had joined them in the famous McCrae's Battalion paid with lives and limbs. Rangers lost at least four killed. The carnage affected every club, just as it brought devastation to almost every family in Scotland.

Willie Maley's team largely stayed together, as most of the Celtic squad were in reserved occupations, as was the case with several other clubs. Coalmining was one such occupation, and on retiring from Celtic in 1915 the great Jimmy Quinn went home to Croy and back down the mines. Maley was particularly devastated, however, by the death in action of Peter Johnstone, a strapping centre-half who insisted on joining up instead of staying behind to work in the mines and play for Celtic.

League football continued during the war, but the SFA cancelled the Cup and crowds dwindled as more and more men were called up to fight. Celtic won the league from 1913–14 to 1916–17, and Rangers won it the season after that. The Old Firm also had a useful role in playing a host of benefit games for service charities. Inevitably, however, football had taken a back seat during the 'war to end all wars', which ended no wars at all.

The 1920s were not to be a golden era for Celtic. Whether it was the failing powers of Maley or the fact that Rangers were now a much richer and more powerful entity, there was a definite shift in the balance of power in the city. Bill Struth took over as manager at Ibrox upon the death of William Wilton – Maley rose from his sickbed to attend his friend's funeral – and Rangers would go on to win nine of the next eleven league championships under the guidance of this stern figure.

In 1922, Celtic axed their entire reserve team, a sign of the economic troubles that were afflicting Glasgow's east end. The wonder was that Celtic won the league at all in the face of Rangers' relentless drive for progress under the ambitious Struth, but the championship was achieved in 1921–22, and the Scottish Cup was won the following season. That Cup triumph against Hibs brought Celtic equal with the Queen's Park record of ten, but the amateurs had long since ceased to be rivals of Celtic, and, despite that Scottish Cup win, Rangers were undoubtedly now the 'other' top team in Glasgow. By the middle of the 1920s, even Celtic's previous financial superiority over Rangers had vanished. The Ibrox club was also now firmly recognised as the 'Protestant' team, because under Struth no Catholics had been signed for several years.

For his part, Maley made some wrong signings, fell out with players, sold several of them for large sums and alienated others by refusing to increase wages and bonuses. Departures included Joe Cassidy, one of the club's best players, the mercurial Tom McInally

– though he later returned – plus club captain Willie Criggan, who was ousted to Third Lanark for having the temerity to point out that the players at Ibrox were getting more in bonuses.

Yet Maley still had formidable talents in Patsy Gallacher – now in the veteran stage – as well as Jimmy and Willie McStay and a young lad who seemed to have an eye for goal, Jimmy McGrory. 'Legend' is not enough of a word to describe what McGrory would become at Celtic. He was to be known as 'the Human Torpedo' or 'the Mermaid' because of his prodigious leaps and heading ability, and he became a byword for bravery and timing in front of goal. Nevertheless, season 1923–24 ended up a complete blank for Celtic, who finished third behind champions Rangers and runners-up Airdrieonians.

Rangers comfortably beat Celtic 4–1 in the final of the Glasgow Cup that October and won the two Old Firm matches in the league, the Ne'erday game at Ibrox being another 4–1 humiliation. Celtic eventually finished fourth behind Rangers, which left only the Scottish Cup.

Progressing smoothly to the quarter-finals, Celtic came up against a determined St Mirren, and it was only in the second replay that Celtic finally prevailed by a single goal. That match had a bizarre ending, with referee Peter Craigmyle of Aberdeen denying St Mirren a late penalty and instead awarding a free kick on the edge of the box. St Mirren refused to take the kick in protest, so Craigmyle took out his watch, calmly waited until full-time and blew his whistle on the dot to end the match, much to the chagrin of the Saints.

Confounding those who say the Old Firm are always kept apart in semi-final draws, out came the names of Celtic and Rangers to play each other, with the encounter to be staged at Hampden on 21 March. On the same day, Dundee would play Hamilton Academical at Tynecastle in the other semi-final, and Rangers certainly fancied themselves strongly to beat the winner of that tie, no matter who won – Dundee, as it happened. The 16th encounter between Celtic and Rangers in the Scottish Cup was thus eagerly anticipated, more so by the blue half of Glasgow, who could see their hoodoo being broken.

Hoodoo was the word. For there was really only one statistic in Celtic's favour: it seemed that Rangers just could not win the Scottish Cup. They had not done so since 1903, despite reaching the final five times and losing to four different teams – Celtic, Third

Lanark, Partick Thistle and Morton – with the 1909 final void. As the *Glasgow Herald* put it, 'Rangers for something like a decade have been a dominating power in Scottish football and their failure to win the leading prize is inexplicable.' Press and public alike openly spoke of jinxes, curses and all sorts of other nonsense, and more than a few people inside Ibrox had let the prattling get to them, while others were desperate to get the Double they had not yet achieved.

There was no denying the prodigious talents that would be on display at Hampden. Celtic's talisman Patsy Gallacher now had Jimmy McGrory just ahead of him in the forward line, and the youngster was making an impact with his eye for goal. Jimmy McStay anchored the defence in front of goalkeeper Peter Shevlin, Peter Wilson was a more than capable right-half and on the wings were Paddy Connolly and Adam McLean, neither of whom was of top quality but who could put in a shift. John 'Jean' McFarlane at left-half and Alec Thomson at inside-left were the link men along with Gallacher, while the task of shackling the main danger men went to right-back Willie McStay, with Hugh Hilley, one of the bravest men ever to wear the hoops, ready to throw himself at everything from his left-back position.

The chief threat from Rangers was the combination of Alan Morton and Tommy Cairns on the left side of the forward line. They had jointly devastated defences all season, though Morton, 'the Wee Blue Devil' himself, was reckoned to be able to win matches on his own. They would be facing Peter Wilson and Willie McStay, and for some reason Rangers considered that Celtic's right was their weaker side. Big mistake.

An astonishingly large crowd made its way to Hampden on that cold and windy but sunny Saturday, and from early on there was speculation that the world-record attendance for a club match might be beaten – a six-figure crowd would be needed to do so. By the time the gates were shut, there was indeed a world-record crowd for a club match inside Hampden, with 101,700 people having paid over £5,000 in total to attend. It was reported that thousands were still outside when the gates were closed. If anyone doubted it, Old Firm fever was here to stay.

Perhaps football was once again acting as a blessed relief for people contemplating a troubled time and a possibly dismal future. In Britain's underperforming economy, industrial unrest was rife and would culminate in the General Strike the following year. In Germany Adolf

Hitler was finalising *Mein Kampf*, while a Scottish inventor, John Logie Baird, was working on a new contraption he would eventually call television. It would surely never be as popular as the movies, though, where Charlie Chaplin reigned supreme in *The Gold Rush*.

In Edinburgh a magnificent new stadium was being inaugurated that very day in spectacular fashion. Murrayfield, soon to become the home of Scottish rugby, hosted the Calcutta Cup match between Scotland and England, and a crowd of 60,000 saw the Scots come from behind to beat the 'Auld Enemy' and clinch the country's first-ever Grand Slam.

At Hampden the teams were announced as follows: Celtic: Shevlin; W. McStay and Hilley; Wilson, J. McStay and McFarlane; Connolly, Gallacher, McGrory, Thomson and McLean. Rangers: Robb; Manderson and McCandless; Meiklejohn, Dixon and Craig; Archibald, Cunningham, Henderson, Cairns and Morton. The referee was the same Peter Craigmyle who had made that call against the refuseniks of St Mirren just a week previously.

Before the off, a leprechaun was up to his tricks. It might seem harmless now, but back then it was daring stuff. In the Celtic dressing-room before the 3.30 p.m. kick-off, Willie Maley gave a short speech and left, followed by captain Willie McStay saying a few words. Then Patsy Gallacher asked for the floor. He exhorted his colleagues to start talking to the Rangers players from the start. They were to be sure to mention hoodoos and curses – a form of sledging, you could call it. Furthermore, contrary to Celtic's usual up-and-at-'em approach, they would pack their defence for the opening part of the match so that Rangers and their fans would get frustrated. That Gallacher should dictate tactics was entirely in keeping with the usual modi operandi at clubs like Celtic and Rangers. Senior players, rather than the manager, decided the tactics, and that was still the case into the 1960s in some clubs.

Gallacher mentioned defensive weaknesses he had spotted in Rangers, pointing out that they had lost 1–4 to Hibs only ten days before. For a final flourish, he worked his way round the team, talking up everybody's strengths, and by the time they headed up the tunnel Celtic's eleven men were ready to take on anything Rangers could throw at them, as well as give them the verbals about the hoodoo.

One wonders what thoughts went through Willie Maley's mind when his team came out and packed back into defence from the start. This was not his way, the Celtic way, but it proved effective. Rangers were playing into the sun but had a breeze behind them and almost took full advantage from the off, Peter Shevlin making a mess of a goal kick into the wind but brilliantly saving Geordie Henderson's return shot. Shevlin defied Morton shortly afterwards, and it looked as though it would be only a matter of time before Rangers took the lead.

All over the pitch, however, Celtic were beginning to win the individual duels. Rangers went to their left wing to attack almost ceaselessly, Tully Craig, Andy Cunningham and even centre-half Arthur Dixon trying to back up Morton and Cairns, but Wilson and Willie McStay soaked up their pressure. Stuck alone on the right, Sandy Archibald had no chance of beating the redoubtable Hilley. Adam McLean took on Bert Manderson in a physical challenge and won it, while McFarlane had bested Andy Cunningham and began to spray passes about. Peter Wilson was in sublime passing form and knew just whom to feed. As he moved stealthily up front, Patsy Gallacher was raring to go, and he had a shot that Willie Robb did well to save at the foot of the post. Just as 'the Mighty Atom' had wanted, Celtic had held Rangers for the first 20 minutes or so, and now they began to break out more from their defensive mould, all the while jabbering about jinxes to their opponents.

Rangers were still dangerous though, and Shevlin saved again from Morton before Henderson and Cunningham sent their efforts just by the post. Shevlin was by far the busier goalkeeper, though Robb in the Rangers goal was happy to see a long-range lob from McFarlane land on the roof of his net. On either side of that chance, Shevlin was busy keeping out Morton, Henderson and McCandless in quick succession.

As the half-hour mark approached, Celtic had managed to force just one real save from Robb, but Rangers had not taken advantage of their pressure. Suddenly Celtic clicked into full attack mode, and Rangers were caught on the hop. Gallacher put Connolly away clear on the right, and he dashed past Billy McCandless to the line and sent in a cross that Jimmy McGrory met on the rush, blasting the ball home for a well-worked opener.

Rangers' defence almost lost the plot at this point, Robb having to save successive miscued clearances from his own players Dixon and Dave Meiklejohn. But Rangers soon recovered their composure and pressed Celtic until half-time, when even the most die-hard hoops fans would have had to admit that their side was a trifle fortunate to be in the lead.

At half-time there was a protest by some fans who wanted their money back because in the tremendous crush they could not see the match from their vantage point on the terraces. The band played 'It Ain't Gonna Rain No More, No More' and were duly rewarded with a snow flurry.

The Celts were even luckier early in the second half when Meiklejohn's shot hit the bar and rebounded straight to Cairns, only for the normally deadly forward to head the ball into Shevlin's arms. But that break seemed to inspire Celtic, and they went two up after an hour of play. Dixon conceded a corner under pressure from Gallacher, and Connolly's cross was headed home by McLean while the Rangers defence was too busy man-watching McGrory.

Six minutes later, the ace striker himself grabbed the third with a virtual replay of his first. He started the move himself, sending the ball out to Connolly before dashing into the area and slamming in an unsaveable shot from Connolly's cross. At the traditional Rangers End of Hampden spaces began to appear immediately, as the match was over as a contest.

Celtic's fans shouted for more, and they got it. Thomson notched the fourth with a simple header for which Robb was at fault, and the Rangers goalkeeper was again partly responsible in the final minute when he and Manderson mixed up a pass back and McLean nipped in to scrape the ball home. Said the *Evening Times*, 'As it trickled across the goal line, the huge crowd could not forbear a mighty laugh.'

The five-goal victory remains to this day the record score by Celtic in a Scottish Cup match against Rangers. It may not have reflected the balance of play over the 90 minutes, but no supporter in the green and white contingent gave a hoot for such niceties. It was a devastating scoreline, one that was all the better for being so unexpected, and the newspapers were merciless about the performance of Rangers: 'Did Funk Beat Rangers?' asked one headline, and football correspondent Clutha of the *Evening Times* suggested they had lost because of an 'unreasonable superstitious fear of themselves, born of their series of Scottish Cup failures'.

The *Scotsman* wrote, 'Opportunism was a factor in the Celtic victory, but the side, if not brilliant, were very good all through, and their go-ahead style invited success.' The *Glasgow Herald* opined, 'That Celtic's victory was cleverly, clearly and on merit obtained is beyond question . . . [Rangers] are temperamentally unsuited for, and unnerved by, what is known as cup tie football.' The *Edinburgh Evening News* noted that Rangers were 'hopelessly outclassed' and added, 'It would be idle to select any particular player for praise. Each man did his bit and did it well.'

Three weeks later, Celtic showed that, unlike Rangers, they most certainly did have the right attitude for Cup football with a famous performance against Dundee in the Cup final. Former Celt Davie McLean put the Taysiders ahead after 30 minutes, and as the match wore on, that seemed likely to be the only goal, as Celtic were lacking inspiration.

A piece of magic that is still talked about brought them back into the game. Patsy Gallacher waltzed through the defence, and when he was brought down almost on the goal line, he somersaulted into the net with the ball between his legs. Perfectly legal, and a goal that earned that match the name of 'Patsy Gallacher's Final'. With seconds remaining, Jean McFarlane floated in a cross and Jimmy McGrory soared to head home the winner, leaping without a care for himself, so that when he fell to earth he was almost knocked out by the impact.

Celtic had won the Cup for a Scottish-record 11th time, and surely now they would end Rangers' domination of the sport in Scotland. That looked to be the case the following season when, with Tommy McInally back, Celtic won the league and Glasgow Cup, though they lost out on the Treble when St Mirren beat them 2–0 in the Scottish Cup final. The truth was, however, that, apart from Jimmy McGrory and the McStays, most of that team had peaked during those two seasons, and they were soon broken up by Maley, who later even contemplated selling the priceless McGrory to Arsenal, though he relented when the player refused to go.

With Patsy Gallacher 'retired' by Maley – 'the Mighty Atom' took the huff and went off to play for Falkirk FC for five more years – Rangers won the league and Celtic the Scottish Cup in season 1926–27 before Rangers finally broke their hoodoo by winning the Double for the first time in 1927–28, beating Celtic 4–0 in the Scottish Cup final. They would go on to win five league titles in a row, and Celtic had to wait until 1931 to win their next Scottish Cup.

It would be a year that would see great glory but also a terrible tragedy, one that Celtic fans – even three generations later – still remember.

5

THE TRAGEDY OF
JOHN THOMSON

5 SEPTEMBER 1931
SCOTTISH LEAGUE DIVISION ONE
RANGERS 0, CELTIC 0

The Pavilion Theatre, Glasgow, on the evening of 4 July 2002. In front of a capacity house in the venerable old theatre the third production of *The Celtic Story*, the musical drama that tells the history of the club from its foundation, is starting. The new cast is led by Celtic fan Tony Roper, alongside the author's brother, Stevie Hannan, the whole show produced by the author's friend Ed Crozier.

The premiere gets off to a slightly shaky start, but as Dave Anderson and Dave McLennan's musical comedy-drama reaches the 1930s in Celtic's story, a truly stunning theatrical moment takes place, one that lives in the memory. Front and left of stage, a 71-year-old woman stands in the spotlight. Her good looks belie her age and well-lived life, but she seems almost frail this night, until she starts to sing a song. The tune and the words are familiar, having been passed down the ages to become part of Celtic's folklore.

For Annie Ross the moment is highly personal. Her brother, Scottish entertainment legend Jimmy Logan, starred in previous incarnations of *The Celtic Story*, first produced in the club's centenary year of 1988. Her own last appearance in Glasgow had been alongside Jimmy on the same stage. Logan had died only the previous year, and now Ross was keen to pay her own form of tribute to her brother in the show in which he had starred.

With her American accent, the legacy of being sent to live in Los Angeles with her aunt Ella at the age of five, Ross's character had to be transplanted to Boston from Glasgow, but in a real sense Annie herself had come home. Now on the stage where Jimmy Logan had so often brought laughter and joy to Glasgow audiences, she begins to sing of tragedy, of a young life snuffed out, of a hero taken in the midst of his prime.

The song is credited to Mick Garngad, aka Mick McLaughlin, a legendary Glasgow street poet of Irish extraction. The words are perhaps banal, the sentiment maudlin, but this is no ordinary singer: this is Annie Ross, a legend of jazz music, the mistress of vocalese who had first cut a record more than 50 years previously and had sung with all the greats. She was also an underrated film actress and friend of the famous, such as Frank Sinatra. In other words: a star.

In front of our eyes Annie Ross transforms herself. Not surprisingly, she had been nervous at the start of the show, but now she slowly builds the song into something far greater than its mere content. It's a fine tune, and with her passionate delivery the words take on real meaning, genuine pathos. In her own inimitable powerful fashion, Ross sings the story of how Celtic's and Scotland's fine young goalkeeper John Thomson made the ultimate sacrifice, killed when his skull was fractured in an accidental clash while saving a certain goal during an Old Firm match at Ibrox Park in 1931. Lumps grow in throats as the Celtic fans in the Pavilion sit spellbound.

The emotion in her voice carries out into the audience, and we are smitten as she builds to the climax:

So come all you Glasgow Celtic,
Stand up and play the game,
For between your posts there stands a ghost,
Johnny Thomson is his name.

As the notes die away, there's an instant of silence before thunderous applause rings out from the audience, many of whom rise to their feet in acclaim. There are grown men with wetness in their eyes. Annie Ross and the cast seem taken aback, almost amazed at the emotions they have unleashed. Perhaps Anderson and McLennan neglected to tell them that when *The Celtic Story* was originally produced in 1988, during the scene where Thomson's coffin passed across the very same stage at the Pavilion, the entire audience rose and stood in respectful silence.

On this night the production is transformed and goes on to be a massive hit. It is a remarkable achievement, one of which Ross would later speak with pride. Somehow, with her jazz-singer's ear for the real feelings in a song, Ross had turned a supporter's standard into a classic anthem for doomed youth and unrequited love. For John Thomson died without really knowing how much he was loved, nor could he have known what a legend he would become. Watching those scenes in the Pavilion, you had to wonder about this man. How could the death of a goalkeeper, more than 70 years earlier, still affect so many people so personally that they would shed tears for him, albeit with the genius of Ross as the instigator? The answer lies in the symbiotic nature of the football club and its support, but more pertinently in the character of the man himself.

The mere fact that Thomson was killed in the service of the club as a result of injuries received on the pitch, the only Celtic player to die in that manner, would have made him exceptional. But there was more, much more, to the tragedy of John Thomson, a cataclysmic event that cast a shadow over Celtic for years afterwards.

It happened at a time when football really was the opiate of the masses. The Great Depression had begun to hit hard, particularly in Glasgow and the Central Belt of Scotland, where the brief post-war boom in shipbuilding had sustained heavy industries such as coalmining and steel production.

By 1931, William Beardmore's great industrial concern, which once employed 40,000 people around Glasgow and was centred on Parkhead Forge, was on the road to collapse, with the company's shipyard at Dalmuir having closed in 1930. Mine owners imposed wage cuts on their employees in the summer of 1931, and unemployment rose steadily: by the end of 1932, some 30 per cent of men in Glasgow would be jobless.

It was a time of restlessness in domestic and world affairs. Mohandas K. Gandhi made headlines with his leadership of India's independence movement. Spain was in the grip of near-revolution, with King Alfonso XIII exiled, and in Germany the Nazi Party's rise seemed inexorable. In America, meanwhile, the Empire State Building had just been completed, becoming the tallest structure in the world and a symbol of that nation's rise to dominance.

The economic crisis loomed over everything in Britain, however. Two weeks before the first Old Firm game of the season, Ramsay MacDonald resigned as Labour prime minister in the face of opposition within his own ranks to the budget cuts he deemed necessary. MacDonald, who was expelled from the Labour Party, then formed a national government and, despite riots in Glasgow and elsewhere, later won a mandate to govern the country with a coalition.

Yet, in the midst of the Depression, football kept attracting huge crowds, never more so than when Celtic and Rangers met. It seemed to be the only outlet of fun for workers or the unemployed, who were given concessions. Despite the tough times, however, some spectators did like their creature comforts. To meet this demand, Rangers had constructed a new main stand in 1928, with seating for more than 10,000 above a standing enclosure with a similar capacity. Celtic had also built a new stand in 1929, after fire destroyed their old pavilion.

New stand or old, it did not seem to affect the results for Celtic at Ibrox. By the start of season 1931–32, they had not won at Ibrox for a decade and, indeed, had only beaten Rangers three times in that period, including the 5–0 Scottish Cup win of March 1925 that featured in the last chapter. It did not seem to matter too much that they could not dominate their old rivals, for after that memorable 1925 Cup triumph Celtic went on to win the league in 1925–26 and then lifted the Cup again in 1927 and 1931, in the latter year foiling Motherwell's bid for the Double, the Fir Park club having ended the Old Firm's 27-year streak of championships shared between them.

In the 1931 replay, which was won 4–2 to take the Cup to Parkhead, John Thomson had gained his second Scottish Cup-winner's medal, having won his first as a mere 18 year old in 1927. By the end of that 1930–31 season, he had also played four times for Scotland and four times for the Scottish League and seemed set fair to keep the international jersey for as long as he wanted, as he had superbly defied England in a 2–0 victory at Hampden Park – it wasn't just to Celtic fans that he had become a hero.

In common with all the other Celtic players, Thomson missed out on Scotland's three-match tour of Europe in May 1931, as the club had embarked on a groundbreaking nine-week visit to the US. Thomson played in all thirteen matches on that tour, with

Celtic winning ten times, making friends wherever they went and beginning strong links with the country, which the club maintain to this day.

Had Thomson gone with Scotland, he surely would have added to his cap tally. Moreover, Austria would not have beaten Scotland 5–0 had Thomson been in goal, as they did in Vienna on 16 May. Such an event would have been unthinkable, because Thomson by then was already seen as the best goalkeeper in Scotland and possibly in the British Isles. And he was still in the early days of his career ...

Born in Kirkcaldy, Fife, on 28 January 1909, Thomson was the son of a strongly Christian couple, John senior and Jean, both members of the evangelical Church of Christ, which their son joined too. That he was not a Catholic made no difference to the Parkhead crowds, who took young John to their hearts after he joined the club at the age of just 17.

By then Thomson had already followed his father into the coal pits of Fife, working from the age of 14 at Bowhill Colliery, where his job was to couple and uncouple wagons deep underground. Perhaps the strength and agility he showed in his all too brief career were developed doing that dangerous job, but the fact is that he had already displayed the natural-born talents of a goalkeeper as a schoolboy.

From an early age Thomson worked hard at improving his goalkeeping skills, and at just 16 he left local amateur side Bowhill Rovers – they are still going today – and moved into junior football with Wellesley Juniors, who are long since defunct. The juniors played in green and white stripes and had a huge local rivalry with Denbeath Star.

Willie Maley had been told about Thomson by a club scout called Stevie Callaghan, who had watched him playing for Wellesley against Denbeath Star. Thomson signed for Celtic for just £10 in October 1926. Peter Shevlin was the man in possession of the gloves at Parkhead, but after Shevlin let in three goals in a 6–3 victory over Brechin City in the Scottish Cup in February 1927, Thomson was given his chance.

The 18 year old seized it gleefully and made his debut against Dundee at Dens Park, Celtic winning 2–1. He was soon the club's first-choice goalkeeper in a season in which Celtic eventually finished second in the league to Rangers. He was also between the posts in the Scottish Cup final against East Fife at Hampden Park, Celtic winning 3–1 and Thomson taking a lot of credit for his performance.

Though not overly tall, standing at just 5 ft 9 in. in his stocking soles, Thomson was a match for bigger forwards because of his superb athleticism and courage. Even in his early days at Celtic he was already showing bravery, particularly his willingness to dive at the feet of opponents or into a melee of players in order to get the ball. As far as John Thomson was concerned, getting hold of the ball in his territory was the mission of his life.

Photographs show that he was a handsome, open-faced lad, and he had a slim and wiry strength, especially in his arms. Unfailingly modest and with a winning charm about him, Thomson soon became the darling of Parkhead, not least because of an outstanding performance against Rangers when Celtic won 1–0 in October 1927. His courage and skill on the pitch were the talk of the press, and flattering profiles of his character also appeared. He practised and truly believed in sportsmanship, and, though humbly born, he had been well raised and at all times conducted himself as a gentleman.

In the days when goalkeepers went for the ball every time it came near them, Thomson's bravery was soon the wonder of the Scottish game. In 1930 he was badly injured in a dive at a player's feet, fracturing his jaw and breaking ribs. He recovered quickly, and it only added to his growing stature in football, though it worried his mother, Jean, who reportedly had a premonition of his death.

Like many people from the east of Scotland, and as a devout Christian, Thomson was mystified by the bigotry in Glasgow. He took refuge in his own religion and became engaged to Margaret Finlay, whose father, a colliery manager, was a leading figure in the Church of Christ as well as being a staunch Celtic supporter.

On the morning of the fateful day, the newspapers were full of reports of a Glasgow steamer, the *Opal*, sinking off Land's End with the loss of the captain and chief engineer. By nightfall the evening papers would carry news of another tragedy, one that happened in full view of nearly 80,000 people.

Celtic's team that day included Jimmy McGrory, then in the middle period of his remarkable goalscoring career and fully recovered from the broken jaw he had sustained on the American tour. Alongside him up front were Charlie 'Happy Feet' Napier, a renowned dribbler of the ball, and Peter Scarff – more about him later – while Jimmy McStay, whose family has had such a long association with Celtic and who later managed the club during wartime, was at centre-half as usual.

The match at Ibrox was, as always, a very competitive affair, but as with many Old Firm games the sheer pace and effort of the players put a premium on skill. Referee W.G. Holborn was also determined to keep strict control of the match, and according to press reports he cracked down on even 'petty infringements'.

The *Glasgow Herald* reported that 'some idea of the drabness of play may be gathered from the fact that the first decent shot to trouble either of the goalkeepers came after 35 minutes'. So, in other words, it was a not untypical Old Firm encounter. Except that a few minutes into the second half an event occurred that made this Old Firm match significant for entirely the wrong reason.

Young Sam English, the Northern Ireland-born former shipyard worker from Dunbartonshire, was playing in his first Old Firm game. Irony of ironies, he had actually been declared unfit to play the day before the match but managed to recover sufficiently to make the team. In the first half he had already shown flashes of the speed and skill that would make him the top goalscorer in Scotland that season, with 44 league goals from 35 games – still a seasonal record in the league for Rangers. The previous month he had scored five goals against Morton, and the Celtic defence knew the centre-forward was the main danger to them.

English had been shackled by McStay in particular, but five minutes into the half he broke free and chased a direct through ball from Jimmy Fleming into the Celtic penalty area. Thanks to newsreel filmed by British Movietone, we can see for ourselves what happened next, and the only conclusion can be that the event was a tragic and terrible accident with no blame whatsoever attached to English.

Quick as a flash, Thomson raced from his goal and hurled himself at the feet of English, who was moving diagonally across the area at considerable speed and attempting to tap the ball beyond Thomson for a certain goal. The goalkeeper won the race, deflecting the ball wide of his goalposts, but at a terrible cost.

Thomson's head thudded into English's knee, sending the Rangers player flying. The goalkeeper had made his final save, as the impact fractured his skull and damaged an artery in his brain. His death was almost inevitable from that moment.

At first Thomson did not lie prone. For a few moments he pointed upwards from the ground with his right hand, as if to say, 'I'm all right.' But, with blood seeping from the wound to the right side of his head, he soon lapsed into unconsciousness, and it was instantly clear to the players who quickly surrounded him that Thomson was in very serious trouble. English himself hobbled over and was one of the first to signal to the bench that help was needed. The Rangers player James 'Doc' Marshall, who had gained his nickname from the fact that he was a medical student, was aghast. He quickly told his colleagues just how bad things were.

Ambulancemen from the St Andrew's Ambulance Association went to work on Thomson, but it was clear that swift hospitalisation was his only hope. In photographs of the scene, which can be found in the records of the Glasgow newspapers in the Mitchell Library in Glasgow, both managers, Willie Maley and Bill Struth, can be seen looking on helplessly as the ambulancemen put Thomson on a stretcher. The players in the grainy picture look deeply shocked.

It was then that something happened off the pitch that has passed into Old Firm legend. Seeing the man who had defied them on previous occasions now out of the match, and perhaps thinking he was timewasting, some Rangers fans behind the goal started to shout and jeer – the exact words are not recorded, but they can be guessed.

The *Evening Times* recorded that the commotion was 'prolonged and loud' until the Rangers captain, Dave Meiklejohn, went over and motioned to the crowd to be silent. Realising that something truly terrible was happening, even the loudest of the jeerers fell quiet.

As Thomson was being taken away, the silence around the ground was eerie. He appeared to regain consciousness briefly, but that sign of hope was soon extinguished. In the crowd, members of his family, his fiancée and his future father-in-law looked on as Thomson was carried towards the main-stand tunnel. As the stretcher approached, a single piercing female scream shattered the silence. It came from Thomson's fiancée, 19-year-old Margaret Finlay, as she saw the crimson-stained bandage wrapped around her man's head.

Dr Willie Kivlichan, one of the few men to play for both Celtic and Rangers in the twentieth century, was the Celtic doctor and had been attending to Thomson. He immediately ordered an ambulance. Margaret Finlay and Thomson's brother James made their way into the dressing-room. Dr Kivlichan did what little he could for the dying young hero. Margaret wept in agony as James Thomson went to his brother. 'When I saw Johnny then I knew he would not recover,' James later told reporters.

Meanwhile, the match went on. Chic Geatons took over in goal, and the match began again with a goal kick – in all the confusion the referee, Mr W.G. Holborn, had not realised that the ball came off Thomson before going behind and that Rangers should have had a corner. No one in blue protested.

In those days of no substitutes, the ten men of Celtic held out for a goalless draw. In truth, most of the players wanted to carry on because, though they knew Thomson was badly injured, no one guessed how seriously hurt he was. In any case, Johnny had always come back from massive hits before.

As soon as the match ended, the players of both sides learned that Thomson's prospects were dire. There were not the usual comments from either manager of 'He'll be fine.' Sam English broke down in the dressing-room and was taken straight home by colleagues. The remainder of the players, like the rest of the country, which rapidly came to hear of the news, could only go home and sit and pray.

This time there would be no recovery by Thomson. Rushed to the Victoria Infirmary, at around 5 p.m. the goalkeeper went into convulsions, and Dr Norman Davidson decided to operate to relieve the swelling in his brain caused by the obvious depression fracture to the skull. The medical records showed later that the operation made no difference to the outcome.

Thomson's parents had been sitting at home in Fife when a policeman came to the door with the news that their son had been injured. John senior and Jean rushed through to Glasgow and reached his bedside in the Victoria Infirmary at 9.15 p.m. A few minutes later, John Thomson of Celtic and Scotland breathed his last. The time on the death certificate was 9.25 p.m. He was 22 years and 220 days old.

Willie Maley, club captain Jimmy McStay and director Tom Colgan were told the news shortly afterwards. Maley's first concern was for Thomson's family, and he went immediately to assist them. It fell to McStay to tell Thomson's fellow players the news, as Jimmy McGrory later recalled: 'I sat with my wife all evening wondering if the phone would ever ring. Then I decided to phone the Victoria Infirmary itself, but the switchboard was jammed with calls. Jimmy McStay phoned me about 10 p.m. to tell me, broken-voiced, that

John was dead – "He died half an hour ago." That's all he said and put the phone down, obviously too choked to say any more.

'I was dazed. I could have died myself. Never in a hundred years did I think he would die – only 22. I went through to the living room and said to my wife, "He's dead."

'"God rest his soul," she said. I remember we sat there in disbelief.'

That was the overwhelming feeling of an entire nation. No one could believe that this young hero had perished, cut down in front of 80,000 people. Until the Sunday papers came out the following morning and confirmed the news, many people in Glasgow and beyond simply refused to accept it, writing off the story as malicious gossip. But it was true, and John Thomson had gone.

Scotland was bereft. The reaction to Thomson's death was extraordinary. No one could remember anything like it. Every newspaper in the land carried fulsome accounts of the match and its aftermath, and the obituaries did not fail to mention his good humour and gentlemanly character. But it was the public reaction that proved just how loved this young man was: an unprecedented outpouring of grief spread across the land.

He was prayed for in churches of all denominations on the Sunday, and a memorial service the following Tuesday in Glasgow's Trinity Church saw the police being called to hold back the crush of thousands of people who wanted to attend. Rangers captain Dave Meiklejohn read the lesson, Celtic's Peter Wilson having been unable to reach the church because of the crowds. Sam English sat in the pews with his head in his hands, crying openly when 'Dead March in Saul' was played.

The *Scotsman* reported that the Rev. H.S. McClelland preached a eulogy and sermon in one. He said, 'What we saw then was an act of superb and uncalculating courage, an act of supreme and unfaltering loyalty, a flash of that divine fire that burns out all thought of self when danger assails that to which we are committed.

'John Thomson did not give his life for a goal. He gave his life for an ideal – the ideal for which every brave life ought to be willing to lay itself down – loyalty to the trust placed in our hands.

'His death is a great loss to British football, for no one has done more than John Thomson to bring honour to the game.'

The Rev. McClelland then went on to excoriate the bigotry surrounding the Old Firm and condemned those who cheered from the Rangers terracing as Thomson lay dying, pointing out that, if it had been a Rangers player injured, the cheer would have been as loud from the Celtic end.

'If the death of John Thomson brings to an end this ghoulish gloating over fallen opponents, his last brave action will have achieved far more than the saving of a critical goal,' said the minister.

McClelland was reflecting the mood of anger that had grown up swiftly against the 'fans' who had cheered when Thomson fell. The editor of the *Evening Times* wrote of the 'sting of shame' that they would feel, provoking a response from some of the perpetrators, which has rarely been reported since. In the *Evening Times* of Tuesday, 8 September the following letter appeared:

> Sir, We of the Bridgeton Rangers Supporters Club wish to offer our apology to the football public and also Celtic and Rangers FCs for the jubilation which was caused at the back of the goal when John Thomson was injured. We really did not realise it was a serious injury until David Meiklejohn appealed to us. This has proved a lesson to us. We hope it will do so to others. Hoping everyone will accept this apology, we are etc. THE BRIDGETON RANGERS SUPPORTERS CLUB

The shamed supporters club bought a memorial wreath, which was displayed in Bridgeton. Nearby another wreath, from the local Sacred Heart Roman Catholic Church, was also displayed to the public. In death John Thomson had conquered the bigotry that so upset him.

The following day, Wednesday, 9 September 1931, Thomson was buried at Bowhill Cemetery in Cardenden, in his native Fife. On a warm afternoon, elder David Adamson of the Church of Christ presided over a small and plain ceremony in the Thomson family's garden. He ended with the invocation 'Good night, dear brother, good night.'

The coffin was carried to the cemetery almost half a mile away by Thomson's fellow Celtic players, each member of the squad taking his turn, always led by Willie Maley walking slowly behind a pipe band and colliery silver band.

The mournful procession made its way through a huge and respectful crowd that perched on every vantage point to catch a glimpse of the flower-bedecked coffin. Estimates of the numbers that lined the streets vary between 30,000 and 50,000, and in places the newspaper photographs show they were certainly packed 40 to 50 deep.

The *Glasgow Herald* reported that among the crowd were miners who had given up a day's pay to attend and 'schoolchildren who had worshipped him from afar who refused to attend afternoon school'. A contingent of unemployed men had walked the 55 miles from Glasgow to be there, while special trains brought thousands from the western city to Fife. Rangers and almost every senior Scottish club were represented, as was the Scottish Football Association and Scottish Football League.

On reaching the cemetery, the coffin was transferred to the Thomson family. His father, brother and uncles joined Willie Maley as pall-bearers. As men and women wept openly, John Thomson was laid to rest.

At the graveside, miner and Church of Christ elder John Howie gave the funeral oration, and Celtic chairman Tom White associated the club with his remarks before thanking the crowd on behalf of the family and club for 'this glorious demonstration of your love'. As if to prove it, hundreds queued to pile flowers in or around the unfilled grave.

A Fatal Accident Inquiry later concluded that Thomson's death was indeed that: a tragic accident. A post-mortem found he had suffered a depressed fracture at a point in his skull that was thinner than normal. No medical treatment could have saved him after such a blow. The only discordant note was struck by Willie Maley, still wrapped in grief, who said at the inquiry that he 'hoped it was an accident', ambiguous words that did not reflect the feeling among Celtic's players and staff – and which Maley regretted afterwards. These words have since been taken out of context many times by people with no understanding of what transpired in court and who, for some reason, want to lace this tragedy with their own bigoted bile. For Maley had been warned to give the truth and nothing but the truth, and the fact was that, sitting in the stand, he could not see what actually happened: 'I did not see enough to enable me to form an opinion,' were his exact words to the court. It is also forgotten that, when Celtic next played Rangers at Parkhead, Sam English was singled out for horrendous treatment by the home fans, including shouts of 'murderer'. The man who made a loudspeaker appeal for respect to be shown to the Rangers player was Willie Maley.

Among the many tributes paid to Thomson, a few stand out. The referee in his final match, W.G. Holborn, wrote to Thomson's parents to say that their son's every action was 'that of a gentleman'. To Willie Maley, Thomson was 'the greatest goalkeeper' Celtic had ever had, and he added, 'They never die who live in the hearts they leave behind.' A journalist called him 'the Prince of Goalkeepers', a name that stuck because he really was a prince among men as well as a fabulous goalkeeper.

On the Saturday after the funeral, Thomson's death was marked at every senior Scottish game with a minute's silence. At Parkhead, where Celtic were playing Queen's Park, the team walked out without a goalkeeper to symbolise their loss, young John Falconer joining the side only when play was about to commence. At half-time a piper played the ancient lament 'The Flowers o' the Forest'. All the solemnities across the land were observed in utter silence.

Margaret Finlay eventually married and had a family. She never once spoke to them of John Thomson.

A few weeks after the burial, Sam English, Bill Struth and Dave Meiklejohn visited the Thomson family at home. Like the true Christians they were, the Thomsons had accepted that John's death was an accident, and their concern was for English, who was already the subject of vilification for having 'killed' Celtic's hero.

English was the other victim of the tragedy. He could not handle the opprobrium that was directed so wrongly at him, and he left Rangers to ply his trade down south. But he told friends the sport had become 'joyless' to him, and he retired at 28. He returned to Celtic Park once, at Willie Maley's invitation, for a memorial ceremony for Thomson. In later life, English was a victim of motor neurone disease, the same affliction that would later kill Celtic's greatest-ever player, Jimmy Johnstone. English died from the disease in the Vale of Leven Hospital at the age of 58.

Another tragedy afflicted a Celtic player from that Old Firm match of 1931. Three months after Thomson's death, Peter Scarff was playing against Leith Athletic when he began to cough up blood. Diagnosed with tuberculosis, he died less than two years later at the age of twenty-five.

In our own time, we have seen the shattering effect that death on the pitch can have. Former Celtic player Phil O'Donnell, then captain of Motherwell, collapsed during a match against Dundee United at Fir Park on 27 December 2007. He had suffered heart failure and died in the ambulance. Just thirty-five, he left a widow and four young children. Scottish football and our small country as a whole mourned O'Donnell, and, just as happened with John Thomson, crowds lined the streets as his coffin went by.

Phil O'Donnell, gentleman and noble soul, was also the first senior Scottish professional since Thomson to die as the result of trauma suffered in a match. Falkirk youth player Craig Cowans was electrocuted at the age of just 17 in an accident following a training session in 2005, a death that yet haunts his club and then manager John Hughes, now with Hibs. Celtic also lost a young player, Brian McGrane, a former schoolboy internationalist from Faifley in Clydebank, in December 1977. McGrane felt severe stomach pains during a match against his home-town team Clydebank, and on examination in hospital it was found that he was suffering from an enlarged spleen. He then sustained a fatal brain haemorrhage. Tests showed he had leukaemia. Brian McGrane died at the age of just 19, leaving a wife, Susan, and unborn daughter, Jennifer.

Let us hope the medical screening that has been brought into Scottish football since O'Donnell's death will mean that he will be the last to die this way. No such improvements were made after Thomson's death. It really was seen as a dreadful, awful 'one-off' accident, and, viewing the newsreel footage, it is impossible to conclude otherwise.

Celtic as a club took a long time to get over Thomson's death. The whole Celtic family was devastated, and fans and players alike spoke of the darkness of that time at Parkhead. Willie Maley, the father figure of the club, felt as though he had lost a son, and though he tried manfully to put a brave face on things, 'Mr Celtic' was never quite the same again. The club would not win the league until 1936, the Scottish Cup win in 1933 being the only major honour achieved in that five-year spell after Thomson's untimely demise.

There are memorials to John Thomson in several places. Celtic Park contains a display cabinet with items relating to Thomson, Kirkcaldy Museum is the venue for a small exhibition about him and Thomson Court in Cardenden is named after him.

After a campaign that even involved a debate in the Scottish Parliament, Thomson was inducted into the Scottish Football Hall of Fame at the Scottish Football Museum in Hampden Park in 2008 after nominations from many people, including MSPs and the MP for Kirkcaldy and Cowdenbeath, Gordon Brown.

To this day, John Thomson's grave remains a place of pilgrimage for Celtic fans. The flowers are constantly renewed, and club scarves and other souvenirs are regularly laid there.

On the memorial stone that was erected by public subscription, it states:

IN MEMORIAM
JOHN THOMSON
SCOTLAND'S INTERNATIONAL GOALKEEPER
who died 5th September 1931
aged 22 years
The result of injuries received at Ibrox Park
Beloved son of John & Jean Thomson
'Honest and upright he played the game
Beloved and respected he made his name.'

Factual and correct, but the greatest memorial of all must be that John Thomson's name is still revered by Celtic fans almost 80 years later. If anything, however, the name of Thomson deserves to be better known.

All who love courage in sport and appreciate the dignity of a good man can find inspiration in Thomson's story. He was a muscular Christian in his own way, showing by his example that courage and daring on the field of play could co-exist with modesty and nobility off it.

That he was taken in a tragic accident at the age of 22 means that the photographs and newsreel footage preserve him as he was: the young 'Prince of Goalkeepers'. At Celtic Park and indeed in Scottish football as a whole, we have never seen his like since, and we probably never will. And it's when you know the history that you realise why Annie Ross brought tears to many eyes that night in the Pavilion.

It seems fitting to end this chapter on the Old Firm match that cost the life of the Prince of Goalkeepers with the words of that song about him:

A young lad named John Thomson,
From Wellesley Fife he came,
To play for Glasgow Celtic,
And to build himself a name.

On the fifth day of September,
'Gainst the Rangers club he played,
From defeat he saved the Celtic,
Ah but what a price he paid.
The ball rolled from the centre,
Young John ran out and dived,
The ball rolled by; young John lay still,
For his club this hero died.
I took a trip to Parkhead,
To the dear old Paradise,
And as the players came out,
Sure the tears fell from my eyes.
For a famous face was missing,
From the green and white brigade,
And they told me Johnny Thomson,
His last game he had played.
Farewell my darling Johnny,
Prince of players we must part,
No more we'll stand and cheer you,
On the slopes of Celtic Park.
Now the fans they all are silent,
As they travel near and far,
No more they'll cheer John Thomson,
Our bright and shining star.
So come all you Glasgow Celtic,
Stand up and play the game,
For between your posts there stands a ghost,
Johnny Thomson is his name.

6

RECORDS THAT CANNOT
BE BEATEN

1 JANUARY 1938
SCOTTISH LEAGUE DIVISION ONE
CELTIC 3, RANGERS 0

By the latter half of the 1930s, football seemed to be taking over the leisure hours of the entire population of Great Britain. Crowds flocked in amazing numbers to watch professional matches. Radio, cinema, newsreels and music and dance halls all had their followers, but only one form of entertainment really held sway over the male half of the nation – though many women were keen spectators – and that was football.

Perhaps people were unwilling to deal with the looming threat of war in Europe. Perhaps they were just glad to be working again in a country stuttering its way back to full employment. More likely they simply loved football, especially in Scotland, where possibly too much of the people's communal store of emotion was invested in what was, after all, just a game.

For the followers of Celtic the 1930s had been hard to bear, starting as they did with the death of John Thomson in 1931. As we saw in the last chapter, that horrific event had long repercussions for Celtic, and there were other deaths, too. James Kelly, the man from Renton who was the first to captain Celtic, died in February 1932 aged 62. Willie Maley, still in anguish following Thomson's death, could scarcely believe his great friend and collaborator had gone. Maley also spent long hours attending to tuberculosis victim Peter Scarff, who died the following year. It was truly a dark time at Parkhead, with the gloom lightened only by a stirring run in the Scottish Cup of 1933, which saw Jimmy McGrory score the only goal in the final against Motherwell.

The next two seasons saw Celtic draw a blank. Even Maley himself came under increasing scrutiny, especially when the O'Donnell brothers, Frank and Hugh, and 'Happy Feet' Napier were sold in the summer of 1935. In the club's defence, it must be pointed out that attendances at Celtic Park had plunged during the worst of the recession and when the team was underperforming. Maley, now in his late 60s, still felt duty bound to balance the books, but much more important was that the old fighting spirit was still in him, as he proved at the start of season 1935–36.

His elder brother, Handsome Tom, died at the age of 70 on 24 August 1935, but, instead of going into a slough of despond, the old Willie Maley came charging out, determined perhaps to commemorate properly the man who, after all, had been indirectly responsible for him becoming Mr Celtic. With new young players like Jimmy Delaney and captain Willie Lyon, and with Jimmy McGrory enjoying an Indian summer in his career, Celtic promptly romped away with the league title, scoring 115 goals for the loss of just 33. It had been a long ten years without the championship, but Maley had yet again built a team to be the best in Scotland.

The following season saw something utterly remarkable. Today's young people, used to seeing football only from the comfort of a seat in a covered stadium, or more usually from the luxury of an armchair in front of a television, would scarcely believe that tens of thousands of people would squeeze up against each other for hours, on terracing open to the elements, just to watch a game of football. But in 1937 Celtic featured in a match that set a world record for crowd numbers at a club match and which is still the European domestic club-attendance record. Since no ground in Europe now holds more than 110,000, that record can never be surpassed. It was set at the Scottish Cup final, when 147,000 people crammed into Hampden to witness Celtic play Aberdeen. Amazingly, just one week prior to the final, the then world record for attendance at any match had been set at Hampden when Scotland played England in front of 149,000 spectators, the vast majority of whom went home happy, as the Scots won 3–1.

No one really knows why that astounding number of people turned out at Hampden, but the thought that it might be the last peacetime Scottish Cup final was in many minds. The vast majority of the crowd were Celtic fans, though a huge number came to support Aberdeen – popular legend at the time was that not all of their fans spoke in the Doric, and Govan was suspiciously quiet that day. Goals from Johnny Crum and Willie Buchan in a 2–1 victory brought the Cup back to Celtic Park, though the league championship had gone to Ibrox.

History was much on the mind of Mr Celtic. In 1936, Maley penned a column in the *Weekly News* about the history of Celtic, and in time for the Golden Jubilee season these jottings were expanded and turned into a book, *The Story of The Celtic* – note the definite article – and, though it was an autohagiography published in 1938, a lot of what we know about the early days of Celtic comes from that source. Double-checked, it turned out to be accurate in most respects, though it often reads like it was written by an accountant, which, of course, was Maley's original profession.

Could Celtic make more history in their 50th year? This was Celtic – of course they could, even though the team was inconsistent at first and lost the Glasgow Cup final to Rangers, meaning there would be no Grand Slam in Jubilee season.

Celtic announced in the November that another big favourite with the fans, Willie Buchan, had been sold to Blackpool, albeit for a Scottish-record transfer fee of £10,000. The fans were universally shocked, however, when it was revealed in the first week of December that McGrory was retiring as a player and going off to manage Kilmarnock. He was 33 and could conceivably have come back and played another season, as Maley wanted, but the chance to manage a club, and with a sizeable increase in salary, could not be refused. McGrory's goalscoring record is simply unsurpassable – his 550 goals in all first-class games is still a British record. He also famously scored eight in one match, against Dunfermline in 1928, and against Motherwell in 1936 he scored three in three minutes. He was the goalscorer supreme and loved Celtic so much that he had turned down a fortune to join Arsenal and even played on for Celtic when others in the squad earned more. It would not be long before he was back at Parkhead.

Celtic were challenging in the league as the turn of the year approached, and on Christmas Day Kilmarnock arrived at Parkhead with their new manager taking his seat in the stand to a rapturous reception. Still miffed that McGrory had left, Maley instructed his men to put everything into the game, this despite the fact that Rangers were due up the following week. The result was an 8–0 thrashing of McGrory's men, with Maley neither able nor willing to conceal his delight. McGrory got his revenge, it should be said, when Kilmarnock put Celtic out of the Scottish Cup later that season.

The scene was set for a Ne'erday clash of crucial importance. Hearts had been going well all season and were level with Celtic at the top on 31 points, Rangers just a point behind them with a game in hand. With Hearts at Easter Road to play Hibs, Celtic had a real chance to go top on their own, but they were up against a side unbeaten away from home all season, and Celtic had not won a Ne'erday Derby for ten years.

There was a lot of sheer giddiness on the part of the British population at that time, not least because of the coronation earlier in 1937 of King George VI and Queen Elizabeth, and Neville Chamberlain's continuing assurances that Herr Hitler was a nice guy, really. The Spanish Civil War and Japanese atrocities in Manchuria were happening far away, and people just wanted to have a good time. Movie magic had come from the US with *Snow White and the Seven Dwarfs*, which was still playing in cinemas nine months after it had opened, while Britain's home-grown entertainment queen, Gracie Fields, was awarded the CBE in the New Year's Honours List, much to the delight of the populace.

Yet another crowd phenomenon occurred. With hopes high, more than 100,000 people converged on Parkhead that Ne'erday afternoon. As the 2 p.m. kick-off approached, it was decided to delay the start to allow more people in, and eventually some 92,000 got in before the gates were ordered to be shut for safety reasons 20 minutes into the match, leaving more than 10,000 disappointed people outside. The original crowd figure was reported as being 83,500, but with the acknowledged ground record being 88,000, and witnesses adamant that it had been easily exceeded, Celtic's infamous creative accountancy with crowd sizes was set aside and the 'true' record figure of 92,000 was later disclosed. It was the biggest attendance at any match on an extraordinary day for Scottish football, which also saw record crowds at Hibs and a Second Division crowd record established at Stark's Park in Kirkcaldy, where Raith Rovers lost to local rivals East Fife.

Celtic's side was little changed from that which had started to pile in goals in previous weeks. Between the sticks was James 'Joe'

Kennaway, the Canadian who had signed for Celtic after the death of John Thomson in 1931 and had kept his place almost from the day he arrived at Parkhead. Bobby Hogg was a classy defender at right-back, while John 'Jock' Morrison had replaced the great Peter McGonagle in 1935 and was a more than capable left-back. Captain Willie Lyon was at his usual berth of centre-half, with George Paterson to his left and utility player Matt Lynch to his right.

The forward line had kept its cutting edge despite losing McGrory, but on this Ne'erday they would have to do without the injured Jimmy Delaney, who was well on his way to becoming a club legend. Joe Carruth, who like Delaney could play at outside-right or centre-forward, was chosen on the wing with prolific goalscorer John Crum in the centre of the attack. Crum and inside-forwards John Divers on the right and Malky MacDonald on the left formed a trio whose interpassing was a treat to watch. Frank Murphy was in his normal berth at outside-left, from where he was deadly with a cross.

The Rangers team was Jenkins; Gray and Winning; McKillop, Simpson and Brown; Fiddes, Venters, Smith, McPhail and Kinnear. Bob McPhail was making his return from long-term injury, and as the club's top goalscorer – he would finish his career at Ibrox with 261 goals, second only to Ally McCoist in the all-time Rangers list – his presence was seen as a major boost. The referee was Mr M.C. Hutton of Glasgow, Scotland's top whistler who had been in charge of the Scottish Cup final and was therefore used to large crowds.

Mr Hutton's main decision was how long to delay the start, given the numbers still trying to get in. He allowed five minutes, and even then, after the teams took the field and got ready to play, a spectator ran on and shook the hands of Paterson and Morrison before the police escorted him away. Kicking off eight minutes late, Rangers went straight into attack, but the Celtic defence held and Carruth broke down the right, but to no avail. The first ten minutes or so was end-to-end stuff, but already the signs were there of a special Celtic performance.

The first real chance fell to John Crum, who headed a low Divers cross past the post. Behind the goal, the Celtic end was just a mass of humanity swaying as one, and there were fears that, if anyone fell, carnage would result. The supporters were in a state of high excitement, because, apart from a couple of brief flurries by the visitors, Celtic made nearly all the running in the first half.

Malky MacDonald fired in a fierce shot, which George Jenkins held, before the increasingly influential Crum shot narrowly wide. Jimmy Simpson managed to divert a goalbound Carruth shot behind for a corner, before Jenkins saved superbly from the same player. The Rangers goalkeeper surpassed that effort with another excellent save, tipping over a shot on the turn by Crum.

Very much against the run of play, Rangers almost scored, the post coming to Kennaway's rescue after James Fiddes had beaten the keeper. Jimmy Smith sclaffed the attempt to net the rebound, and Celtic breathed again.

With people popping out of the convulsing crowd and onto the track every so often, like toothpaste squeezed out of a tube, the match roared on and Celtic finally got their overdue reward after 38 minutes. From a corner by Carruth, the ball was half cleared and made its way to John Divers, who controlled it, beat a couple of defenders and from 15 yards rifled in a shot that somehow found the net but none of the intervening bodies. The Celtic fans were in ecstasy, but more than a few wondered if Rangers would get their act together in the second half, because the men in blue could surely not be so poor again after the interval, during which many more people took refuge on the track from the crush. These scenes would later prompt a review of safety at the stadium, which effectively meant that no similar size of crowd would ever be allowed in Celtic Park again.

It remained 1–0 for only six minutes of the new half. Jenkins's goal came under siege, and the goalkeeper, who was Rangers' hero of the day, foiled Divers after excellent lead-up play by Crum before Paterson lobbed one into the middle, where Simpson tried to stop the ball with his arm. It still found Crum, but, even as he shot past the post, referee Hutton was pointing to the spot. Malky MacDonald stepped up and shot low and hard to Jenkins's left for the second goal.

Rangers rallied, but Bob McPhail was less than match-fit and Alex Venters was well out of form. Celtic's defence contained them easily, and the passing of the forwards should have brought more scores. As it was, McPhail finally found a touch, but Joe Kennaway pulled off a marvellous one-handed save.

After 72 minutes, Celtic deservedly got the clincher. Crum created it with a lob that this time Simpson couldn't reach even with his hands, and Divers ran in to smack the ball home. Two goals in his first Old Firm match – not a bad start to the year for Divers.

Kennaway was determined to keep a clean sheet and did so with a marvellous late save from a Smith header. Still Celtic were not finished, and MacDonald had the ball in the net again only to be ruled offside. It could and perhaps should have been more, but at the final whistle Celtic's fans were delirious about the three-goal thrashing of their old rivals.

Lest there be any doubt that it was a proper trouncing, here's what the press had to say: 'Celtic were sparkling in attack, keeping Rangers running with their craft and versatility'; 'Rangers had never got a grip of things and their attack was very dismal'; 'No doubt about the merit of the Celtic success, they should have been as many goals up at half-time as they were at the end'; 'Rangers never got to grips with Celtic's young forwards, who at times did pretty much as they liked.'

The *Scotsman* was scathing: 'The Light Blues were a very ordinary lot, being but a shadow of former Ibrox teams.' The *Edinburgh Evening News* noted: 'The confident Celtic defence broke up every move of the Ibrox men who were forced to retire baffled.' Alan Breck was prescient in the *Evening Times*: 'The manner of the defeat will revive doubts about Rangers' ability to retain the championship.' And so it proved. On the same day, Celtic's nearest rivals, Hearts, drew 2–2 with Hibs, and then Celtic went to Tynecastle a week later and thumped Hearts 4–2. Despite a not untypical slump after their shock exit from the Scottish Cup at the hands of McGrory's Kilmarnock in early March, Celtic clinched the title on 23 April at Love Street with a 3–1 defeat of St Mirren. Two days later, Willie Maley celebrated his 70th birthday, but still Mr Celtic wanted bigger and better presents.

Celtic, Rangers, Aberdeen and Hearts were invited to take part in an end-of-season 'British Cup' to mark the Glasgow Empire Exhibition. None of the teams who finished in the top four places in England could make it, but the English opposition was still formidable: Sunderland, Everton, Chelsea and Brentford, the latter club then enjoying its greatest era.

All the matches were played at Ibrox, as the exhibition was just up the road at Bellahouston Park. That did not in any way deter the Celtic fans turning out to support their Bhoys, who needed a replay to beat Sunderland before they scraped home against Hearts in the semi-final by a single Johnny Crum goal.

The final was against Everton and proved an exciting match in front of 82,000 fans, most of them Scottish. It lacked only one quality: goals. Extra time was required, and Johnny Crum yet again proved the match winner, the striker doing a jig behind the goal after netting in the fifth minute of extra time. The magnificent trophy was presented by the Earl of Elgin and can still be seen at Celtic Park.

It was a perfect way to mark the club's Golden Jubilee, and the following week, at an anniversary dinner, Willie Maley was presented with a cheque for 2,500 guineas: 50 guineas for every year of his service to the club. It was presumed by many that Maley would then retire, as he was, after all, now 70, but Mr Celtic had other ideas.

Another man who had bewitched a nation put a stop to any hopes that Maley could build yet another long-running successful team. Adolf Hitler's Germany invaded Poland the following year, and football was just about the last thing anybody worried about for the next six years.

7

In Seventh Heaven

19 OCTOBER 1957

SCOTTISH LEAGUE CUP FINAL

CELTIC 7, RANGERS 1

There are some matches that are remembered simply for the scoreline, so that if you say the words 'seven one' to any Celtic fan they will know exactly which match you are talking about: the Scottish League Cup final of season 1957–58.

It is a match that has long since passed into legend as Celtic's biggest victory over the other half of the Old Firm in the history of the derby. That it took place in a cup final at Hampden only adds to the lustre of the victory, all the more so because such a demolition was totally unexpected.

It is often thought that no one outside of the Celtic community really gave the men in the hoops much of a chance that October Saturday. That is just not true, because, though Celtic's main problem in that era was a maddening inconsistency, on their day they were capable of beating all and sundry, and just a few weeks previously they had gone to Ibrox and won a handsome 3–2 victory. Despite that loss, Rangers remained favourites for the League Cup, but only because of their better consistency over the previous two seasons.

The Celts went into the final as League Cup holders, defending the trophy they had won the previous year when they beat Partick Thistle 3–0 in a replay after an initial goalless draw. That had been Celtic's first final in what was the youngest of Scotland's three major domestic trophies, first competed for in season 1946–47.

Almost remarkably, given their domination of the main Scottish Cup, neither half of the Old Firm had really made the League Cup their own, and if Celtic could beat Rangers in 1957 it would only bring them level, in terms of trophy wins, with Rangers and Dundee. They would still be one behind the 'winning-most' club in League Cup terms: East Fife.

Hearts had beaten Celtic in the Scottish Cup final of 1956, adding to the loss to Clyde the previous year, and Celtic then lost to Kilmarnock in the semi-finals of the 1956–57 Scottish Cup. More worryingly for the fans, Celtic's league form was merely respectable, and in the preceding two seasons Celtic had twice managed to finish only fifth in the First Division.

The club had very good players, as we shall see, but the management by Jimmy McGrory was less than inspiring. In 1957, when close analysis by a manager of players' training, fitness and lifestyle was still in the future, McGrory had little to do other than to decide on some simple tactics and the team selection and to try to gee up the players before each game. He also collected the wages in cash from the bank each week: Celtic did not live out of a biscuit tin, as is often maintained, but out of the manager's two leather satchels.

McGrory was no 'tracksuit man', and the physical training – sprints, laps around Celtic Park and running up and down the terraces, mostly – was left to Willie Johnstone, who had replaced Alex Dowdalls, one of the club's best-ever 'physios', as they were then called.

Club chairman Robert Kelly had idolised McGrory as a player, but he and the rest of the directors would regularly query McGrory's team selections. This should not be seen as something unique to Celtic and Kelly, however. The boards of most clubs allowed managers or coaches to pick the team and then had their say. It was a practice that continued into the 1960s – some say it has never died at certain clubs.

Kelly had achieved this almost dictatorial status a few years earlier when he had vehemently campaigned against the SFA's demands that Celtic remove the Irish Tricolour from their flagpoles. Kelly's strong stance and ultimate victory – in which he was aided by Rangers, it should be said – made him undisputed ruler of Parkhead. 'He was a very strong man,' said his long-time friend Sean Fallon, 'but he needed to be for Celtic.'

Certainly, when Jock Stein eventually replaced McGrory eight years later, he made it a condition of his employment that all managerial decisions would be his and his alone, and he let that stipulation be known to the press and Celtic fans, indicating that it had definitely not always been the case for McGrory.

Stein had retired from playing in 1956, after his dodgy ankle finally gave out, and moved smoothly into the Celtic backroom, as chairman Kelly intended. He was initially given the job of coaching the youths and later the reserve team – Celtic played in the Scottish (Reserve) League, the brackets used to distinguish this league from former versions, and would go on to win it three times in succession from 1958–59 to 1960–61, the club's only triumphs of note in that era.

Rangers, by contrast, had won the championship proper in both seasons 1955–56 and 1956–57, in the latter year beating Celtic by a massive seventeen points – and those were the days of two points for a win. In the European Cup, they were looking forward to a glamour tie against AC Milan in the November.

Scottish football was entirely different back then: the Old Firm did not win almost every trophy, as they do now. McGrory arrived as Celtic's manager after the war, during which Jimmy McStay had finally replaced Willie Maley. The 1940s were completed as a blank for Celtic in terms of major trophies, the Scottish League and Cup being suspended during wartime. At one time, in 1948, Celtic even flirted with relegation but eventually avoided the drop, though the scare made the directors do something to improve matters and bring in Bobby Collins and Charlie Tully.

Hibs, with their 'Famous Five' forward line, and Rangers, with their 'Iron Curtain' defence – why did the Scottish selectors never play the two together? – dominated the league from 1946–47 for six seasons. Only Dundee, second in 1948–49, had intervened in a run in which Hibs and Rangers finished in the top two places in the league each season, the Easter Road men winning three of their total of four championships at that time.

Celtic's Double under new captain Jock Stein in 1953–54 had been as welcome as it was unexpected, but the club had not been able to maintain the momentum, despite having some great players. By the time season 1957–58 came around, the Hibs Famous Five of Gordon Smith, Bobby Johnstone, Lawrie Reilly, Eddie Turnbull and Willie Ormond had split, but another threat from the east, in the shape of Hearts, with their 'Terrible Trio' of Alfie Conn senior,

Willie Bauld and Jimmy Wardhaugh, was proving powerful. For the uninitiated, the trio were not terrible – they were terrifying and splintered opposition defences as Hearts enjoyed a magnificent spell under manager Tommy Walker that would bring them the league championship of 1957–58, with a goal tally of 132, still the highest for the top league in Scotland.

Other clubs were doing well at the time. Aberdeen had won their first championship in season 1954–55 and finished second in 1955–56. Kilmarnock had begun what would turn out to be the best-sustained period in their history by finishing third in 1956–57, and Raith Rovers, Partick Thistle and Motherwell all also enjoyed spells of good form, with Ian St John about to make a big impact at Fir Park.

Falkirk and Clyde were forces to be reckoned with in cup tournaments, the former winning the Scottish Cup in 1957 and the latter picking up that trophy a year later. In short, there really were no easy games in the top flight of Scottish football, but the Celts contrived to do themselves damage on several occasions against lesser sides, and that glaring tendency to have a bad day at the office was the main reason they were not fancied to beat Rangers.

Celtic's progress to the League Cup final had been slightly erratic. The team was little changed from that which had won the trophy the previous year. It contained eight players who are rightly classed as Celtic legends – more about them later – while a certain Bertie Auld was a regular squad member.

As always at Parkhead, the start of a new season was greeted with optimism, even if the players were perhaps growing old together. 'We were an ageing team at that time,' admitted Sean Fallon. 'One or two of us were in the veteran stage of our careers, but the fans were very good to us and were right behind us. They appreciated what we had given to the club and also appreciated that there was only so much we could give at that stage.'

As was usually the case at the time, the season began with the sectional matches in the League Cup, with Celtic drawn against Airdrieonians, East Fife and Hibs and all teams playing each other at home and away, the sectional winner progressing to the quarter-finals.

The season opener was against Airdrie, who took a shock 2–1 lead at Parkhead before a fightback saw club legend Bertie Peacock grab the winner for Celtic, the scoreline being 3–2. With Sammy Wilson making his debut the following Wednesday, Celtic thrashed East Fife at Methil, Billy McPhail scoring a hat-trick in a 4–1 win.

Hibs had lost to Airdrie midweek, so on the second Saturday of the season Celtic travelled to Easter Road with some confidence. Match reports indicate that they performed well, but right-back Frank Meechan was at fault for two goals as Hibs ran out 3–1 winners. That meant Celtic, Hibs and Airdrie all had four points after the first three matches, so the section was nicely poised.

With Meechan replaced by John Donnelly, it was Celtic who drew first blood in the second set of matches, beating Airdrie 2–1 at Broomfield while Hibs could only draw 2–2 with East Fife. Celtic duly hammered East Fife 6–1 in the second midweek match of the season, but Hibs also beat Airdrie 5–1 to set up a decider at Parkhead on the first day of September.

Hibs knew they needed victory, while Celtic would qualify even if they only drew. Gordon Smith, Eddie Turnbull and Willie Ormond still remained of the Famous Five, and Hibs had reached the semi-final of the first European Cup the previous season, so were always going to be a threat. When half-time was reached with a 0–0 scoreline, there were plenty of Celtic fans in Parkhead who were just a tad nervous.

They need not have worried. Sammy Wilson's and Billy McPhail's new partnership proved profitable, both scoring in a half dominated by Celtic and in which Tully performed to his best. Celtic rarely lost when that happened, and the 2–0 scoreline put the Bhoys into the quarter-finals.

These were played over two legs in the second week of September, and Celtic's opponents were fellow Glaswegians Third Lanark. Celtic had the tie sewn up after the first leg at Parkhead, with a 6–1 victory achieved in some style. The second leg was a formality, and Celtic cantered home 3–0 for a 9–1 aggregate.

With Rangers having scraped through against Kilmarnock 4–3 on aggregate, the Old Firm went into the hat with Brechin City and Clyde. Celtic got the tougher draw, against Clyde of the First Division – the conquerors of Aberdeen in the quarter-finals – while Rangers faced the Second Division Brechin City, who had beaten another side from the same division, Hamilton Academical, to reach the penultimate round.

The semi-finals had to be played on neutral territory, so while Rangers went to Hampden and disposed of Brechin by four goals to nil, Celtic played Clyde at Ibrox. The chief worry before the match was the Asian flu that had decimated the Clyde squad, but Celtic were also missing an injured Tully. In the end, it was Bobby Collins who inspired Celtic's victory, and despite Clyde's comeback from 2–0 down to 2–2 at half-time, Collins scored the third goal – a rocket from 30 yards – and a final counter from Willie Fernie made it 4–2 by full-time.

So to the final. The accounts of the press in the week before the match show none of the hyperbole we see today before every Old Firm game. The significance of the event was not lost on the Scottish sporting public, however. It was the first Old Firm final in the League Cup and the first in either of the two major domestic trophies since 1928. With both halves of the Old Firm having lost league games and Hearts going so well – they were unbeaten and would trounce Aberdeen 4–0 that day – this final might well be the only chance other than the Scottish Cup for Celtic or Rangers to gain the domestic honour their fans craved.

In the press and inside Celtic, there was little dispute about the team, the only real decision being where a recalled Neil Mochan would play. He was favoured over Bertie Auld, a decision that robbed the player of a unique distinction, as he would have been the only man to feature in the 7–1 match *and* the Lisbon Lions.

In retrospect, the prediction by some correspondents of a comfortable Rangers victory seems hopelessly misplaced. Any team with names like Fallon, Fernie, Evans, Peacock, Collins, Tully, McPhail and Mochan in it was never going to be a pushover. These men are rightly considered Parkhead legends, not least because of what they did that day.

At 35, Sean Fallon was nearing the end of his playing days and had suffered several serious injuries, but he was back to full fitness as the season began. He had played in all positions on the left and up front but was settled at left-back. The versatile Willie Fernie could also play in almost any role, except goalkeeper. The Fifer had played in Scotland's disastrous foray into the 1954 World Cup, but in his tenth season with Celtic he was playing as well as ever, and though his preferred position was on the right wing in attack, he had taken up McGrory's challenge to play at half-back with relish. 'It was very hard to get the ball off Willie,' recalled Sean Fallon.

Bobby Evans was the backbone of the team and had become the first Celtic skipper to lift the League Cup the previous season.

Always easily spotted on the field with his shock of reddish hair, Evans had turned 30 during the summer, but his energy showed no decline. During the close season, however, Bertie Peacock had been told he would captain the side. Evans was not told until the announcement was made, the decision having been taken by chairman Kelly, who had an eye to the future for several of his stars, as they would later discover.

Peacock was the first Protestant from Northern Ireland to captain Celtic. It caused little adverse comment at the time, but, as the man who has written the foreword to this book, Neil Lennon, would find to his cost almost 50 years later, Ulster politics subsequently regressed.

Always popular with the fans, Peacock was not large in stature but was huge in commitment. A skilful sort who could also tackle, he had begun as an inside-forward, the foil to Charlie Tully's rapier, but had settled into the left-half position, which he made his own in a long career at Parkhead, during which he played 453 times for the club and scored 50 goals. His standing in the game was shown by the fact that in 1955 he was selected to play for Great Britain versus the Rest of Europe.

Behind the half-back line of Fernie, Evans and Peacock was goalkeeper Dick Beattie, who was solid if a little suspect at cross balls, while full-backs John Donnelly, just 20, and the veteran Fallon were both men who loved to attack. Indeed, Donnelly had been converted from inside-right to right-back only two months prior to the League Cup final, while Fallon had played at centre-forward on many occasions. With such attacking instincts behind them, it fell to Fernie, Evans and Peacock to drop back and help out, a trend McGrory encouraged.

Up front were two players who were happy to do their share of trawling back to help out the half-backs. Bobby Collins was a true Celtic legend, 'the Wee Barra' – small barrow for those unacquainted with the Glaswegian dialect – who had started his Celtic career in 1949 as an 18-year-old right-winger in the Jimmy Johnstone mould: brave, pacey, skilful and of the same size as 'Jinky' at 5 ft 4 in. and 9 st. 3 lb. By 1957 he had moved to inside-right, which meant he had to score goals, act as link to the main strikers and carry out his fair share of defensive duties. It was just as well that Collins was such a fit man, despite several injuries in his career.

Another prepared to track back was Neil Mochan, who had been brought back to Scottish football from Middlesbrough by Celtic in 1953. It was a wonderfully timed move: Mochan scored the first goal in Celtic's famous Coronation Cup victory at Hampden before he had even played at Parkhead. Though of average height, he had made his name as a centre-forward, but his strong left foot saw him play at outside-left and left-back on occasion. He had performed well in the League Cup final replay of 1956 but was still not an automatic first-team pick, though his ability to move up and down the entire length of the left wing, albeit at his own pace, was to prove vital in the League Cup final.

The other link man, who also liked to score a fair number of goals, was Sammy Wilson, signed on a free transfer from St Mirren during the summer. He was initially seen as cover for the regulars but, with Bertie Auld out of favour, had formed an excellent partnership with Billy McPhail, which produced plenty of goals for both men. McPhail, of course, was the younger brother of John, goalscoring hero in the Double-winning side of 1954, and had signed for Celtic from Clyde the previous year. He would play just fifty-seven times in two seasons for Celtic, but for reasons that will become obvious he is still fondly remembered as a legend at Parkhead, and some will still recall him as 'Teazy Weazy', the nickname he was given because of his apparent resemblance to then celebrity hairdresser Teazy Weazy Raymond, a gentleman who was luckier than most: he later owned two winners of the Grand National.

The mobility of players like Collins and Mochan meant Charlie Tully could play out on the right wing and strut his stuff, which could be mesmerising. It would take a separate chapter to tell the story of Charles Patrick Tully. Suffice to say that even a modicum of research will show you why he is such a legend for Celtic. Signed from Belfast Celtic in 1948, he was a colourful, cheeky, combative character, a true celebrity who was more famous for the tales told about him than for the trophies he won. Tully really did score direct from a corner kick and, when ordered to retake it, put the ball directly into the net again – 21 February 1953, a Scottish Cup match at Falkirk, the home side leading 2–0 when Tully did his stunt after 53 minutes: final score 3–2 to Celtic. He really did sing a duet with Bing Crosby during a trip to Rome, and when playing for Northern Ireland he really did tell Alf Ramsey of England that his international playing career would be over when he had finished with him. And so many more tales – there was no point making up stories about a guy like Tully because the true ones were entertaining enough.

Tully was not just a trickster. He almost single-handedly destroyed the opposition at times, such as during his Old Firm debut against Rangers in 1948, when he personally annihilated them in a 3–1 win. And, yes, he often drove his colleagues insane with his antics and failure sometimes to do his bit for the team. But what an entertainer: it was said of him that he could dribble his way in and out of hell before the devil would know he was there. And, for that 1957 final, just for once, Charlie Tully was determined not to mess about.

The sun shone on Glasgow on that October Saturday. Just as well, for in the days before the match a deluge had hit the city and Hampden was supposedly going to be a mudbath. The *Scotsman* headline on the morning of Saturday, 19 October said it all: 'Heavy ground conditions favour Rangers.' The paper went on to praise the Rangers trio of Billy Simpson, Max Murray and Sammy Baird, who 'will not be dismayed at the miry prospects. Previous matches this season indicated that they took to it like buffaloes.'

The rain had not even been a consideration for McGrory, who had finalised his team after Neil Mochan scored in the 1–1 draw with Raith Rovers in the last match before the final. As was the case for cup finals in those days, both teams were announced the day before the match. When doing this, the Celtic manager had been calmness personified, saying that his side needed only to produce their current form to beat Rangers. He named the team as Beattie; Donnelly and Fallon; Fernie, Evans and Peacock; Tully, Collins, McPhail, Wilson and Mochan. Rangers went with Niven; Shearer and Caldow; McColl, Valentine and Davis; Scott, Simpson, Murray, Baird and Hubbard.

Just as for Bertie Auld, there was no place in Celtic's XI for Eric Smith, who had played in the previous match against Raith. It is often stated that Robert Kelly intervened to put Mochan in the team instead of Auld or Smith, but several players have been adamant over the years that McGrory picked the team, and if Kelly had influence or not he certainly did not change it after it was picked.

Sean Fallon said, 'Mr McGrory was a very quiet man, but he could get his point over when he needed to, in a nice way. He insisted on wingers in that team, and as a very experienced team we knew how to play that way.

'They've been saying for years that Bob Kelly picked the team, but while he had a say in things, as did the committee – and we don't know what went on with them because we were never invited to their meetings – it was Mr McGrory who picked the team. The directors always had their say, but it doesn't mean they were going to get it, and it has been said so many times that Bob Kelly picked the team that people just believe it, but it was Mr McGrory's selection, take it from me.'

The evidence favours that version, because McGrory was adamant that Celtic needed to play with out-and-out wingers to beat Rangers. His tactic was to stretch them wide at the back and allow Collins, McPhail and Wilson to work into the middle of their defence. His idea of Fernie at wing-half was inspired, as he also wanted to see Fernie, Evans and Peacock dropping deep to help young Donnelly and Fallon. They worked on this idea in training, pitching the forwards against a flexible defence, and it certainly upset at least one Celt, who found the system gave him less room: Charlie Tully had been switched to outside-right, having played at inside-left in the previous year's final.

Always a fiery personality, Tully had 'issues' with Bobby Evans, having hinted in a newspaper column at the time of Scotland's recent 1–1 draw with Northern Ireland that most of the Scots lacked 'class', perhaps forgetting that Evans was one of those he had summarily dismissed. Never the best of friends, as they practised the new tactics during training the two men began to brawl. Ever the diplomat, Peacock played his captain's role and made the peace, and it appears that chairman Kelly was none the wiser, as the strict disciplinarian would probably have suspended both men with goodness knows what consequences for Celtic's greatest Old Firm showing.

On the morning of the game, the crowd of 82,000 making their way to Hampden most probably had health matters uppermost in their minds, as Asian flu was taking its toll – some 33,000 people died from it in Britain, and fear of it probably kept the Hampden crowd's numbers down. Rather less fear was caused by the recent fire at the Windscale nuclear reactor in Cumbria, which made the material for Britain's atomic bombs. Had the public known the full extent of that disaster, rather more might have been said.

The main topic of conversation worldwide in October 1957 was high overhead, however. On 4 October the USSR had successfully launched into space the world's first satellite, Sputnik. America was in a panic, but the British reaction was cooler. Prime Minister

Harold Macmillan had assured the British people in a summertime speech that they had 'never had it so good', although that did not mean the country could afford to join the space race, and 'Supermac' reassured the public that they had nothing to worry about.

For Celtic fans at least, there has never been less to worry about at the Old Lady of Mount Florida than the events after 2.45 p.m. that Saturday, the unusual kick-off time being brought in because of the possibility of extra time at a stadium that would not acquire floodlights for another four years. The referee was Scotland's best, Jack Mowat of Rutherglen, renowned for fairness and for controlling matches.

The mood in the Celtic camp was one of anticipation rather than fear. Sean Fallon said, 'All of us, the older players and the young guys, all of us were determined to put up a performance for our fans. We felt we owed them for their support.' Rangers had some intimidating players, but Celtic were up for any physical challenges, too. 'As I say, we were experienced,' said Sean Fallon, 'and that meant we could look after ourselves, too. You had to be able to do that to be successful, and all the best Celtic teams have had that quality.'

Reading newspaper accounts of the final and listening to spectators telling their tales of the great day, it is impossible to avoid the conclusion that Celtic were quite unlucky – the scoreline really might have ended up in double figures.

Starting towards the traditional Celtic end of the ground, the men in hoops simply raged into attack after attack from the first whistle. On damp but springy turf, the ball sped over the pitch as Fernie, Tully and Collins orchestrated an unstoppable onslaught.

Rangers tried to stick to their defensive formation, even after it was clear that Celtic were being much more fluid, but they were soon being dragged this way and that by superb passing and dribbling play from the Celts. The untested Rangers centre-half John Valentine had a personal disaster as Fernie, Wilson and Collins directed play through the middle to McPhail, who was simply immense and destroyed Valentine in every facet of play. Rangers captain and right-half Ian McColl had a rare off-day, as did Korean War veteran Harold Davis on the other side of Valentine, while behind them those fine full-backs Bobby Shearer and Eric Caldow seemed unsure as to what to do – normally they would have man-marked Mochan and Tully, but now they had to contend with those two wingers while watching the Celtic inside trio advance incessantly. Such fluidity had them in palsies of uncertainty, but mostly they stuck to marking the wingers and left gaps for the Celts to pour through.

Any threat from Rangers' forwards, and there was precious little of that, was comfortably dealt with by Peacock and particularly by the imperious Evans, allowing Fernie to roam the field at will. His machinations enabled Collins and Wilson to play further up the field. In no time at all, it was clear that Celtic were on their very top form, while Rangers were desperately poor.

John Rafferty, writing in the *Scotsman*, was withering about Rangers: 'Their defence was incredibly feeble, and they were dinned down to ignominy under the impact of a green-and-white blitzkrieg ... McPhail and company exposed their defence as being as limp as a dish of spaghetti ... the entire rearguard was affected with indecision to a paralytic degree.'

Rex, in the *Daily Record*, wrote that Rangers' defence 'had a gaping hole down the middle wide enough to have taken the Guards Massed Bands ... I don't know when I have seen a more disgraceful exhibition by a Rangers team.'

Celtic's seasoned professionals sensed the problems with Rangers and took full advantage. Writing in the *Weekly News*, Bobby Collins later explained what happened: 'I don't know if Valentine had no faith in Niven or Niven had no faith in Valentine, but ultimately they had no faith in themselves, something you can sense very quickly on a football field. Valentine was covering Billy McPhail, and McColl and Davis were covering Valentine, which left three of our men with the freedom of Hampden.'

In contrast with the travails of the Rangers defence, almost everything Celtic tried came off. Their confidence was sky-high from the outset, and early in the match Collins hit the crossbar with a ferocious free kick before Tully hit the post with a shot – both efforts were of such ferocity that the woodwork continued to shudder for several seconds. Collins hit wood again later with another thunderbolt free kick, and in all Celtic hit those old Hampden surrounds at least four times during the match – now you know why it really could have been double figures.

It took 23 minutes for Celtic to open the scoring, McPhail winning an aerial duel with the defence and his header looping to strike partner Wilson, who hammered the ball home from 12 yards with the outside of his right boot.

After ceaseless waves of Celtic attacks, the second goal was a peach, Mochan cutting in off his wing and leaving Shearer and Valentine for dead before smashing his left-foot shot past goalkeeper George Niven, who was stranded and bewildered at the near post. Niven, it should be said, also made some fine saves but could be faulted for that Mochan counter – though he was possibly unsighted – and a couple of the later scores. That second goal also came just before half-time, always a good time to notch one, though as Jock Stein once asked, 'Is there a bad time to score a goal?'

The psychological damage was complete, however, and there was also some physical pain, too. Rangers centre-forward Max Murray was soon limping and pretty much out of the game, confined to the left wing, from where Johnny Hubbard moved infield to no avail. He was probably happy to get away from Donnelly, who had outplayed him, as Sean Fallon had done on the other wing to Alex Scott. Though Billy Simpson moved to centre-forward and at least competed against Evans, the only Ranger really to acquit himself well was Sammy Baird, but in later life he was never happy to be reminded of that fact. His frustration showed when he was booked for a rash challenge on Wilson.

The entire crowd expected Rangers to fight back in the second half, but rally came there none. Instead, Celtic poured it on, effectively securing the Cup with the third goal, scored by McPhail with a header from a pinpoint cross by Collins just a few minutes into the half. The centre-forward simply soared above Valentine and Niven, who had come off his line, the header swooping down into an empty net.

With 57 minutes on the clock, Rangers finally came to life, skipper McColl crossing for Simpson to score with a fine diving header. Surely Rangers still had a chance? Alas, alack, no, for Celtic just took up where they had left off, and for once they hammered home their superiority.

Ten minutes later, with the shadows lengthening as the sun dipped, McPhail restored the three-goal advantage with a classic poacher's goal. Niven failed to grasp Wilson's strong header off a Mochan corner, and McPhail pounced to score from point-blank range. The fifth came after 75 minutes, Mochan gaining his second of the final. Standing unmarked in space on the left, he volleyed home a deep Wilson cross with a shot that he hit into the ground but that bounced up and still beat Niven.

By now the Rangers fans were leaving in droves, those who remained mostly doing so to give their team some abuse, which, frankly, they deserved. With ten minutes to play, the sixth goal was arguably the best, McPhail collecting a long ball then turning and leaving the unfortunate Valentine in his wake as he strode away to lash the ball home with his right foot. Not a single Rangers player got within five yards of him – they had capitulated, and at one point captain McColl could be seen with arms outstretched, as if seeking the reinforcement of a higher power.

Not even divine intervention could have helped Rangers then, much less a helping hand from the man in black. For referee Jack Mowat really was a principled umpire of unimpeachable reputation who would earn a modicum of football fame three years after this final by taking charge of arguably the greatest club match ever played, the 1960 European Cup final at Hampden that ended with Real Madrid beating Eintracht Frankfurt 7–3.

For Celtic fans, however, Mowat has an undying place in the 1957 legend, as he scrupulously refereed the final, and in the last minute of the 90 he awarded a penalty when Shearer felled McPhail in the box. Up stepped Celtic's best player on the day, Willie Fernie – 'Yesterday I thought him the complete wing-half,' said former Rangers player Tom Muirhead in his newspaper column – to lash the ball low and fast into the net. Niven barely moved, and the slaughter, the devastation, the massacre, the carnage and the humiliation were complete. Mowat blew his whistle, and the greatest of all Old Firm routs was over.

Celtic had achieved the highest-ever score in a British senior cup final, a record they retain to this day. They had done so, in the words of Rex of the *Daily Record*, by playing 'pure unadulterated football', a phrase that Jock Stein would echo ten years later in Lisbon, where Celtic won the European Cup by playing 'pure, beautiful, inventive football', as the great man put it.

The reality of what had been achieved that Saturday would take some time to sink in, but for the Celtic fans the immediate reaction was one of utter joy. The bedlam that had invaded the Celtic half of Hampden grew to epic proportions, especially when Peacock lifted the trophy. At the other end, some Rangers fans disgraced themselves by hurling bottles and fighting the Glasgow police, a contest in which there has usually only ever been one winner.

The club and players held a celebratory dinner that night in a

Glasgow restaurant, with Jock Stein joining them. 'It was a great night,' said Sean Fallon diplomatically.

The judgement of the media on the beaten league champions was savage, none more so than the columns of the *Daily Record* and *Scotsman*. In the latter, Rafferty wrote that 'Rangers are at present fielding several players who are not fitted for the famous blue jersey,' while Rex of the *Record* stated, 'I don't know when I have seen a more disgraceful exhibition from any Rangers team.' For good measure he added, 'It's as difficult to pick out a star Celt as a star Ranger. Celts had 11. Rangers none.' The headline in the *Record* said it all: 'Gers were lucky not to lose ten'.

Celtic had rewritten the record books in style, and the only problem was that the match was never fully captured on film. The BBC had an arrangement to screen the match, but a technician in London who was supposed to film the transmission coming from Glasgow left the lens cap on the camera at half-time, and we can only now view what happened thanks to some cine footage taken by an amateur enthusiast. There's not a lot of film, but there's enough to give a flavour of that momentous match.

Sadly, it was the last high point for that fine Celtic team. They achieved nothing else of note that season, and though they improved to third position in the league behind Hearts and Rangers, they were fully 16 points behind the runaway champions from Edinburgh. On their way to winning the Scottish Cup, Clyde took a measure of revenge for their League Cup semi-final defeat by beating Celtic 2–0 in what we would now call 'the round of 16'.

The 7–1 side broke up quite quickly. Jimmy McGrory, who, lest it be forgotten, had signed every one of the Hampden 11, was powerless as chairman Robert Kelly caused apoplexies by selling Willie Fernie and Bobby Collins to Middlesbrough and Everton respectively, the transfer income going towards the cost of stadium improvements such as floodlights. Bobby Evans lasted until 1960, when he moved to Chelsea before returning to Scotland to play and then coach at Morton, Third Lanark and Raith Rovers until he retired at the age of 39. Evans died of pneumonia in 2001. Seven years after his death, he was inducted into the Scottish Football Hall of Fame.

Collins, 'the Wee Barra', played into his 40s and in 1965 became the first Scot to win the English Player of the Year award. By that time he was captain of Leeds United, where he was acknowledged as one of Don Revie's best signings, if not the best. After Leeds, he had a number of playing, managerial and coaching jobs, including a spell at Morton – where he discovered a certain Joe Jordan – that saw him return to play at Celtic Park and also score against Rangers. Living in Yorkshire, he is not in good health these days.

Dick Beattie was transferred to Portsmouth in 1959 and subsequently jailed for his part in the match-fixing scandal that rocked English football in the mid 1960s. He died in 1990. John Donnelly emigrated to South Africa, where he lived for 40 years before returning to live in Broxburn. He died in 2009.

Bertie Peacock, who won 31 caps for Northern Ireland, captained and played for Celtic until 1961, when he returned to his native country to play for Coleraine FC. Peacock became a huge figure in Northern Irish football, notably as co-founder of the famous Milk Cup youth tournament. In 1986, he was awarded the MBE for his services to football and the community. Peacock died in 2004.

Billy McPhail ended his career in 1958 after a serious knee injury. Having developed premature dementia, he fought a long and fruitless battle to have his illness officially classed as an industrial injury caused by heading the old heavy leather ball too often. He died in 2003.

Without his big mate, Sammy Wilson faded out of the scene, and not long afterwards Charlie Tully also ended his playing days, his love of the good life meaning no prolongation to his career. Neil Mochan left Celtic in 1960 to play for Dundee United and Raith Rovers before returning to find lasting fame as trainer of the Lisbon Lions under manager Stein. He died in 1994.

Sean Fallon retired from playing in 1958, gaining greater fame when he served under Jock Stein as assistant manager and taking over for several months when Stein was injured in a car crash. He lives on the south side of Glasgow and is an honoured guest at Celtic functions. Willie Fernie came back to Celtic briefly before moving to St Mirren. He was reserve coach under Stein and then managed Kilmarnock in the 1970s. Not in the best of health, he lives quietly in Glasgow and is looked after by his charming wife, Audrey, who had been Jimmy McGrory's secretary. The four boys in the Fernie family – Billy, Alex, Andrew and Donald – all made practical use of a souvenir of the final, namely their father's jersey. In what amounted to a revolutionary 'bonus', the Celtic board had decreed that the players could keep their shirts from the final.

Generous to a fault, you might say, and don't mention biscuit tins.

Less than six months after the final, Willie Maley died in a Glasgow nursing home. The League Cup was thus the last trophy won by the club in the lifetime of Mr Celtic. That it was won in such fashion against the club he had often outwitted would no doubt have pleased him immensely in his last days.

It would be a long time after that 1957 final before Celtic won a major honour again: almost eight years, to be precise. In the lean years, the Parkhead fans could always content themselves with the knowledge that, on one bright autumn day in Glasgow, football was played the Celtic way to perfection.

They could even sing a song to help them recall the event. Harry Belafonte's calypso-style hit 'Island in the Sun', from the film of the same name, was a chart-topper in 1957, and that Glasgow poet Mick McLaughlin, or Mick Garngad as he was known, who wrote 'The Celtic Song' and 'The John Thomson Song', is credited with the words of the version that soon became very popular with Celtic fans. *Oh, Hampden in the Sun . . .* is also the title of a fine book about the match written by Peter Burns and Pat Woods and published by Mainstream in 1997.

The chapter on John Thomson's tragedy ended with the sad song about him. It seems only appropriate to end this joyous chapter with the words that have gladdened many a Celtic heart since 19 October 1957.

> Oh Hampden in the sun,
> Celtic seven, Rangers one,
> That was the score when it came time up,
> The Timalloys had won the cup.
>
> I see Tully running down the line,
> He slips the ball past Valentine,
> It's nodded down by 'Teazy Weazy',
> And Sammy Wilson makes it look so easy.
>
> I see Mochan beating Shearer,
> The League Cup is coming nearer,
> He slams in an impossible shot,
> The Rangers team has had their lot.

Over comes a very high ball,
Up goes McPhail above them all,
The ball and Billy's head have met,
A lovely sight, the ball is in the net.

Young Sam Wilson has them rocked,
But unluckily his shot was blocked,
Then big Bill with a lovely lob,
Makes it look such an easy job.

Now here is Mochan on the ball,
He runs around poor Ian McColl,
Wee George Niven takes a daring dive,
But Smiler Mochan makes it number five.

Down the middle runs Billy McPhail,
With John Valentine on his tail,
With a shot along the ground,
The cup's at Parkhead safe and sound.

Here comes Fernie, cool and slick,
He ambles up to take the kick,
He hits it hard and low past Niven,
The Tims are in their Seventh Heaven.

8

ENTER THE GENIUS

23 OCTOBER 1965
SCOTTISH LEAGUE CUP FINAL
CELTIC 2, RANGERS 1

Without the arrival at Parkhead in early 1965 of John Stein, known to all except his wife and Bill Shankly as Jock, Celtic just simply would not be the club it is today. There is not enough space in a dozen volumes to describe Jock Stein and the supremacy of his achievements. Suffice to say that Celtic's history without him is unthinkable and that he changed not only the club but also football.

When he eventually made his move from Hibs in March 1965, there was an immediate buzz about Parkhead, matched in recent times only by the advent of Kenny Dalglish and John Barnes – the outcome was rather different with Stein, however. At Dunfermline and Hibs, Stein had proved that he could vastly improve teams. With all due respect to those clubs, there he had been working with crayons on a jotter. Now he had the chance to paint a luscious canvas with the finest oil colours.

'Big Jock was a huge personality,' said John Clark, who is still at the club as kitman and sage. 'If he walked into a room, you would see every eye turn to him. He was just that kind of man.

'We could see he was a very, very clever tactician. I saw in a newspaper recently that someone – not a Celtic player – who played under him was not too impressed by Jock's grasp of tactics. It must have been a different Jock Stein from the one we knew.

'He was also a great motivator and could really get us up for a match. Honestly, we won a lot of big games when we lined up in the tunnel beside the other team.'

The fag end of Jimmy McGrory's career as a manager had been depressing for Celtic fans. The club had not won a major senior trophy since that historic 7–1 thrashing of Rangers in the League Cup final in 1957. It had been a glorious day on Hampden in the sun, but the memory was distinctly cold comfort by 1965. The transfer of Pat Crerand to Manchester United for a record £56,000 in February 1963 was seen as highlighting the lack of ambition at Celtic, though in reality Robert Kelly and the board had had to balance the books because crowds had dwindled badly due to a lack of success. The club hit a new low the following month when only 8,000 paid to watch Celtic beat Raith Rovers 4–0 at Parkhead in the league.

However, the fans still came out for the big matches, especially the Old Firm games. The Scottish Cup final replay of 1963 drew 120,000 people to Hampden, just 11 days after 130,000 had watched the first match. Goalkeeper Frank Haffey had saved Celtic in the first encounter but could do nothing about Rangers' superiority in the replay, when, inspired by Jim Baxter and especially Willie Henderson, they ran out comfortable 3–0 winners.

The following season was also a blank in terms of trophies, with Celtic taking third place behind Rangers and Kilmarnock in the league and losing to Rangers in the fourth round of the Scottish Cup. Yet considerable consolation came from a fabulous run in the European Cup-Winners' Cup all the way to the semi-finals, where sheer inexperience in the international arena told against the young Celtic side. Celtic having beaten MTK Budapest 3–0 at Parkhead, it all went wrong in Hungary, and, inspired by the legendary outside-right Károly Sándor, MTK got the four goals they needed to progress to the final, where they lost to Sporting Lisbon after a replay.

By the start of season 1964–65, coach Sean Fallon was taking charge of the team on a regular basis, as McGrory was increasingly sidelined by illness. Chairman Robert Kelly's interference now even extended to trying to sign Alfredo Di Stéfano, then nearing the end of his time at Real Madrid. McGrory was sent with an offer of £200 per game, but the great Argentine, sadly, and probably wisely, said no.

Pragmatist that he was, Kelly realised that Celtic had to move with the times if they were to retain support, and he now put into place a long-term plan of his. Kelly's reputation has suffered in recent years, in tandem with the diminished stature of the dynasties who had run Celtic for so long – the Kellys, Whites and Grants, who took the club to the brink of bankruptcy – but that was not entirely fair on Sir Robert, as he became. Capricious and dictatorial he may have been, but he also made sure Celtic invested money in young players in the late 1950s and throughout the 1960s – they would be called Kelly's Kids. Above all, he brought back Jock Stein, the man he had always wanted to succeed McGrory but whom he felt should learn the managerial trade elsewhere.

Stein's transformation of Celtic was instant. The League Cup final had been lost to Rangers, and the league looked a lost cause – Kilmarnock would eventually win it – but even the news in January that Stein would soon be returning inspired the Celts to one of their greatest performances in the McGrory era, an 8–0 thrashing of Aberdeen. It was a late joy for McGrory, who became the club's public relations officer – Stein still called him 'Boss'. When the new manager did take over, in March 1965, Celtic went to Broomfield and hammered Airdrie 6–0 as a welcoming present. The following week they lost 0–1 to St Johnstone at Parkhead, showing the real problem in McGrory's nearly 20-year reign: inconsistency.

The core of the Lisbon Lions was already in place when Stein arrived. Veteran goalkeeper Ronnie Simpson had been transferred to Celtic from Hibs by Stein, but having been signed as backup to regular goalkeeper John Fallon, Simpson was now playing better than ever and had supplanted Fallon in the team.

Jim Craig was training to be a dentist and found it hard to break into the team, as usual right-back Ian Young was a solid defender.

Tommy Gemmell was arguably the most consistent player in the side, a left-back with a thunderbolt shot that he was too rarely allowed to use. 'Jock told me to get forward and have a go more often,' said Gemmell, 'and I never looked back from then.'

John Clark, dependable and versatile, could play anywhere in defence. Bertie Auld was in his second spell at Celtic, and midfield generals did not come any better. Jimmy Johnstone? Read the next chapter . . .

John Hughes, Lisbon's 12th man who never was – contrary to a myth in some quarters, no outfield substitutes were allowed in 1967 – was a magnificent sight when flying at defences; Bobby Murdoch . . . they said that if Murdoch played well, so did Celtic, and he became Stein's favourite all-round Celt.

Bobby Lennox was both a winger and a deadly striker and so fast he was known as 'the Buzz Bomb'.

Stevie Chalmers was similarly versatile in attack, and seemingly guaranteed to score goals, but was not above being the victim of Stein's psychological tricks.

'He used to con me rotten,' said Chalmers. 'He would leave you out of the team and then take you aside and say, "Look, I know you should be playing; you're a better player than so-and-so, but I've got to play him. You should be keeping him out of the side, but he's in and you're not, and it's up to you to do something about it. Force me to play you."

'So, even when you were dropped, your spirits were kept up because the boss thought you were better than the player in your position, and you just had to work that wee bit harder to get your place back.'

At the heart of the team was the towering figure of captain and stonewall centre-half Billy McNeill, who also had the happy knack of scoring important goals with his terrific heading ability.

Stein took the players he knew from his days in charge of the reserves, principally McNeill, Clark and Auld, added Kelly's Kids – Craig, Gemmell, Johnstone, Hughes, Lennox and Chalmers – and trained and coached them incessantly. What Stein did above all was to improve individuals as players and make them work as a team. With long punishing sessions at the Barrowfield training ground, the players' fitness levels increased massively, and all the time they were working with the ball, a revelation to the Celts of the day.

Jimmy Johnstone told the author in 2002, 'We were the fittest team in Europe, and people never saw the hard work we put in. A few of us enjoyed a drink, but when you are young you can train hard and play hard, and Jock made us train very hard. We always worked with a ball, though, and that's why I used to enjoy those training sessions – honestly, I did!'

A football autodidact, Stein's keen intelligence had seen him learn from all the greats, particularly the Hungarian masters of the 1950s and the Real Madrid team that ruled football into the early 1960s. He even went to Italy to study the methods of a man called Helenio Herrera, who had invented 'catenaccio' defence. Stein did not like it, and in common with a band of tracksuited Scottish football coaches of the 1960s – Tommy Docherty, Bill Shankly, Eddie Turnbull

– who had been inspired by Matt Busby's achievements, Jock Stein brought new attacking tactics and methods to football.

Earlier in the 1964–65 season, Celtic had lost the first domestic final of the season, Rangers winning the League Cup 2–1, thanks largely to a display of genius by Jim Baxter. But reigning champions Rangers had faltered in the league – Kilmarnock would take the title on goal average from Hearts on the last day of the season – and had lost to Hibs in the quarter-finals, Stein's last match in charge of the Leith club. Celtic were made Cup favourites before the semi-finals but needed a replay to oust Motherwell, while Stein's two previous clubs, Dunfermline Athletic and Hibs, fought out the other semi, the former winning 2–0.

It was Celtic against Dunfermline in the Scottish Cup final on 24 April 1965, and all Celtic fans will be aware of this pivotal moment in the club's history. Twice the Celts came from behind, Bertie Auld scoring both goals just a few months after his return from Birmingham City and cancelling out the strikes of Harry Melrose and John McLaughlin. Nine minutes from time, Celtic won a corner. Playing at inside-right that day and always a clever striker of a dead ball, Charlie Gallacher sent in a beauty, and there, soaring like a wingless hooped archangel, was Billy McNeill to power home a magnificent header. It was Celtic's first Scottish Cup win for 11 years, their first major trophy since 1957, and the Stein era was well and truly under way. He was about to fashion a Scottish football team like no other and in doing so make flesh of that deep urge of the Celts – with a 'K' – to create something beautiful, even on a football pitch. At the start of the 1965–66 season, with the Scottish Cup in the trophy room, Jock Stein set about building his perfect team, and he brought in former colleague Neil Mochan as trainer alongside himself and assistant manager Sean Fallon.

Fallon remembers how his appointment was a kind of payback for an earlier favour: 'I had been appointed captain in 1952, and I was allowed to select my vice captain. Bertie Peacock was my great pal, but I was friendly with Jock and I felt he had a bit more experience, so I asked him to be vice captain. I broke my arm and my collarbone, and Jock took over and then kept the captaincy. When he came back as manager, he returned the compliment and made me his assistant.'

The predominance of the Lisbon Lions in Celtic's collective

memory hides the fact that Stein's first great side of the mid to late 1960s was a squad of 14 or 15, with such fine players as Willie O'Neill and Charlie Gallacher always able to play their part whenever any of the Lions were not available. In defensive reserve were the likes of Ian Young, Jim Brogan, John Cushley, Davie Cattanach and goalkeeper John Fallon. That was no mean backup.

In season 1965–66, for instance, Cushley had an extended run at centre-half owing to an injury that kept Billy McNeill out for three months, and Ian Young actually played one game more than Jim Craig that season. Young was also instrumental in winning a game that proved the previous season's Scottish Cup win had been no flash in the pan and that Stein's team were going places fast.

The Scottish League Cup final of season 1965–66 was the match that, for many supporters, proved that Celtic were going to be challenging for top honours for some time to come. Celtic had not exactly strolled through the Cup until then, losing to both Dundee clubs in the opening section and needing a replay to get through the semi-final against Hibs, though the team's 12–1 aggregate destruction of Second Division Raith Rovers in the quarter-finals showed a welcome touch of ruthlessness.

Rangers were league champions and favourites for the final, yet there was no fear factor at Celtic. Bobby Lennox said, 'The fact is that for a long time they had had better players than us. They had the likes of Jim Baxter, wee Willie Henderson, Ralph Brand and Davie Wilson, though Jim and Ralph had moved south that summer. They were still quite a settled and very experienced team of good players, while we were just a bunch of young guys starting to get our act together.'

Stein set out the following team to try to capture the club's second major trophy inside six months: Simpson; Young and Gemmell; Murdoch, McNeill and Clark; Johnstone, Gallacher, McBride, Lennox and Hughes. Of that 11, only Joe McBride had not been at Parkhead before Stein's arrival. Celtic fan McBride was Stein's first signing in the summer, the player joining from Motherwell for £22,000, and was already banging in the goals regularly, including a hat-trick against Raith.

Rangers manager Scot Symon was in charge of the following team: Ritchie; Johansen and Provan; Wood, McKinnon and Greig; Henderson, Willoughby, Forrest, Wilson and Johnston. Whether that was Symon's original selection is a moot point, because the

Rangers' board had the last word on the team, unlike Celtic, where Stein had total control of playing matters.

The Ibrox side also no longer had 'Slim' Jim Baxter. In a decision that baffled Stein, but for which he was grateful, Baxter had been sold to Sunderland. Stein showed what he thought of that decision by promptly picking Baxter for Scotland during his brief spell as temporary manager of the national team in 1965.

Out of tradition, teams were still named in a 2–3–5 formation, but observers of Celtic realised that Stein was experimenting with 4–4–2 or even 4–2–4, with Murdoch and Auld in midfield and Johnstone and Hughes acting as midfielders-wingers. Full-backs Young and Gemmell were encouraged to go forward, and the latter revelled in his role.

The willingness to attack depended greatly on the skills of John Clark in particular. So often when Young, Craig, Gemmell and the other defenders went forward, it was left to Clark to 'sweep' in behind them, the man known as 'Luggy' never really gaining the recognition he deserved from the public, though he was held in high esteem by his peers. He also had a real appetite for big games, especially Old Firm matches. 'I could have played in them every day,' Clark said. 'I loved them. You had to be at your maximum in those games, just as you were for European Cup games. You had to be focused; you had to be strong and have total commitment.'

Another break with tradition was that this Celtic team would not come second in a kicking war. Stein was determined that his men would not be intimidated, and, if any Celtic player got 'the treatment', revenge was to be taken.

Ian Young's defensive qualities included the ability to crunch a player – fairly, of course. In front of a record League Cup-final crowd of 107,600, the Celtic right-back gave Willie Johnston a tremendous thump less than five minutes into the game. It was the kind of smash that would get the perpetrator an instant red card these days, but referee Hugh Phillips merely put Young's name in his book. The clash set the tone for what became a hard man's game, with five bookings in all. As a result of this introduction to the new Celtic approach, Willie Johnston was not the force he might have been – which is what Stein, who greatly admired the winger and once asked about signing him, had intended.

In the 18th minute, an amazing incident led to Celtic's first goal. Bobby Murdoch sent into the Rangers area a free kick that was going nowhere until Ronnie McKinnon, fearing he had been caught out of position, jumped up and palmed the ball. The referee had blown for the penalty even before the Celtic half of the crowd had roared the word. Up stepped John Hughes, and with a right-footed shot almost like a firm pass he sent Rangers goalkeeper Billy Ritchie the wrong way. Celtic were one up.

For those who have long held that Celtic never get penalties from the SFA's finest, what happened next was startling. Just ten minutes later, Charlie Gallacher sent a lovely chipped pass out to Jimmy 'Jinky' Johnstone on the right wing. With a typical flick past his man, Jinky hared away towards the box, pursued by Dave Provan. The Rangers left-back was not a dirty player, contrary to Celtic myth, but was tall and awkward and made to look even more so when confronted by Jinky. Provan's tackle-cum-lunge made contact with man and ball about a foot inside the box, Johnstone going down flat in front of the Celtic end, which erupted with a single shout: 'Penalty!' And for once, though dubious, a penalty it was.

Provan and the rest of the Rangers defence were incensed, but referee Phillips waved them away. Hughes sent his shot to the other side from his first penalty, and Ritchie got a hand to it but could not stop the ball going into the net. Celtic two up·with two penalties in the first half hour: who would credit it?

The rest of the match was 'X-certificate stuff', as one newspaper called it. Another memorably noted that it was 'a hard, grim game, and it could be that some like their football that way: people who chew tobacco, bite their nails, eat razor blades'.

Sean Fallon commented, 'As I said about the 1957 team, the best Celtic sides were those that could look after themselves on the pitch. That 1965 team could do so as well.'

Just before half-time, John Greig brought out the best in Ronnie Simpson. Earlier persuaded by Stein to stay at Celtic and not take an offer to move to Ayr United, Simpson, a two-time FA Cup winner, would gain his first major medal in Scottish football that afternoon, having turned 35 just 12 days previously.

The second half saw a lot of excitement, most of it generated by the kind of rough play that nowadays would see wholesale departures for an early bath. Hugh Phillips managed to keep control of the match, however, and occasionally some good football broke out. Most of it was provided by Celtic, though Willie Henderson enjoyed some good runs on Rangers' right, mostly because Tommy

Gemmell would never do to Henderson what Rangers had done to Jinky – well, not quite as much.

Six minutes from time, Rangers were awarded a free kick 35 yards out on the right. Henderson floated in a high one, and Simpson came to meet the ball, losing track of it under a challenge from John Greig. Behind them, Ian Young could do nothing as the ball smacked off his face and into the net.

Those final few minutes seemed to last an age, but Ronnie Simpson was calmness personified and the defence held out under a furious onslaught from Rangers. Mr Phillips eventually blew his whistle, and Celtic had won their third Scottish League Cup. When Billy McNeill went up to collect the trophy, no one in the crowd, not even the most fanatical person in the Celtic end, would have believed that he would make that League Cup walk for the next four seasons running.

There was a sad postscript to the match. Celtic set off on their traditional lap of honour, but some Rangers fans came onto the pitch and attacked the Celts, with one even getting to McNeill and Hughes as they jointly carried the trophy. John 'Yogi' Hughes and Ian Young both went down under attack, and the Celtic players survived a few frightening moments as they made for the tunnel. The SFA promptly banned laps of honour.

The importance of that victory was not lost on the Celtic squad. Tommy Gemmell said, 'It was a marvellous win, and what made it even better for us was the fact we had turned the tables on Rangers. They had beaten us 2–1 in the League Cup final the previous year, and now we had won by the same score. Things were definitely changing.'

Bobby Lennox said, 'It was the first time we had beaten them in a big game for a while, and it showed that big Jock was getting us sorted out. It was a real turning point for us, and from then on we always thought we could beat Rangers.'

Not much later, Celtic would prove conclusively that the balance of power in Glasgow had changed by crushing Rangers 5–1 in the Ne'erday Derby – it actually took place on 3 January 1966 because of police concerns over post-Hogmanay drink-induced violence. This is perhaps the forgotten Old Firm spectacular from Celtic. For instance, it doesn't feature in David Potter's fine account of Celtic's 50 greatest games, and it is given perfunctory treatment in several players' memoirs – Tommy Gemmell doesn't mention it all, and he was playing at left-back.

Yet it was considered for inclusion in this book because it too, in many ways, was a key moment in the Stein revolution. Had Rangers won at Parkhead that day, the outcome of the league championship might well have been totally different. Indeed, it probably would have been, because at the end of the season there were just two points between Celtic at the top and Rangers in second, although the Bhoys had a superior goal difference. And fans from that era will remember that it took until the last minute of the last match of the season against Motherwell for Bobby Lennox to score the goal that gave Celtic those two clinching points.

More significantly, perhaps, the match contained 45 minutes that might well have been the best half ever played by Celtic against Rangers in the Stein era. Everything just seemed to click in the second half, and by the end of a sumptuous feast of goals the fans, who had seen Celtic hammer a poor Hamilton Academical team 8–0 on Christmas Day, began to believe that Stein's team could destroy any opposition if the mood took them.

Down 0–1 after 90 seconds to a goal by Davie Wilson, Celtic came back but could not gain the equaliser in the first half. A few interval words from Stein and Celtic ran riot. Chalmers scored a hat-trick – all of them 'poached' in the six-yard box – to add to fine strikes from Gallacher and Murdoch as the Celtic forwards destroyed their opponents. John Hughes was magnificent on the left wing, and the only real worry was the fog that swirled around the ground.

Celtic were on their way to the league title, though the Cup final was lost to Rangers after a replay. A blind or biased referee kept them out of the European Cup-Winners' Cup final, when a perfectly good goal in the semi-final second leg against Liverpool was disallowed and saw them eliminated 1–2 on aggregate.

These were the blots on a fine starting season for Stein, but the Scottish League Cup and the all-important Scottish Football League Championship had been won. Yet no one, not all the prophets in the Bible, the Oracle of Delphi nor Gypsy Petulengro herself could possibly have foreseen what was going to happen in season 1966–67. Stein's time – Celtic's time – had come, and not even the finest Rangers side for decades could stop them.

9

JINKY'S FLAG DAY

6 MAY 1967
SCOTTISH LEAGUE DIVISION ONE
RANGERS 2, CELTIC 2

When Celtic's fans chose Jimmy Johnstone as the club's greatest-ever player in 2002, in a sense they were choosing to honour the Celtic way of playing football. The man himself often spoke of being an entertainer on a stage, and surely there was no finer entertainment than to watch Jinky run at a defence and leave his opponents bamboozled in his wake.

Sean Fallon recalled, 'Jock knew how to get the best out of Jimmy. He was a lovely player with great balance and was a very strong little man, too. And, of course, he had all the skill in the world.'

In a long two-part interview with the author in December 2002, Johnstone said, 'I always wanted the ball, to show what I could do. I always wanted to take on opponents, to beat them and go forward and make the cross or get in the shot. And sometimes, when they kicked me, I would just go back and beat them again.'

So many times he did it, and almost as often he was clugged down by inferior beings who were not fit to share the turf with this magical performer. His manifest skills, indomitable courage, endless will to win, aye, and even his fiery temper, combined to make him utterly captivating. As the late great sportswriter John Rafferty said of another legendary Celt, John Thomson, Jimmy Johnstone had no predecessor and no successor: he was unique.

Was Johnstone's finest hour against Inter Milan in the European Cup final? Or was it the time he held onto the ball for eight minutes out of the last fifteen to see out time when Celtic were beating Aberdeen at Parkhead and needed a rest before a European midweek game? Or was it his solo turn against Red Star Belgrade at Parkhead in 1968? Or that night at Elland Road when he roasted the great Terry Cooper of Leeds United? Or maybe it was when he defied the scythes of Atlético Madrid? Or the time he turned poor Emlyn Hughes inside out and inspired Scotland to beat England 2–0?

His own choice was Alfredo Di Stéfano's testimonial against Real Madrid in the Bernabéu Stadium, a week after the Lisbon triumph, in which Johnstone was simply magnificent as Celtic won a competitive match 1–0 thanks to a Bobby Lennox goal.

'They couldn't get near me that night,' said Johnstone. 'I was loving it, playing in front of 130,000 fans. Then, afterwards, Alfredo invited me to get my picture taken along with the great Real Madrid players. I think that was the greatest compliment I ever got while playing.'

Whether it is that game or any other match that you believe to be Johnstone's finest, be assured of one thing: there will be many thousands who will agree with you and many more who will choose another game as Jinky's best. For a lot will depend on whether you enjoyed his teasing of the opposition, his creation of goals or his scoring of them: 130 in more than 500 matches for Celtic, including the Glasgow Cup and friendlies. Those younger people who have seen him only on TV get merely a whiff of the flavour of just how brilliant he was 'live on stage', and his election as the greatest-ever Celtic player was a foregone conclusion, notwithstanding the presence of Jimmy McGrory, Kenny Dalglish, Billy McNeill and Henrik Larsson in the poll.

Johnstone's best league season for goals was Celtic's greatest season, 1966–67, when he scored 13. In case any reader is unaware, that was the season Celtic won every tournament they entered: the European Cup, Scottish League, Scottish Cup, Scottish League Cup and Glasgow Cup, with three of the five tournaments won before the end of April 1967.

The Scottish League Cup final on 29 October 1966 was an Old Firm encounter for the third year running, with the score in this 'rubber' at 1–1 and Rangers determined to get revenge for the loss featured in the previous chapter. A crowd of 94,532 were inside Hampden for a match that was no classic. If anything, Rangers were the better side over 90 minutes. Celtic's 20th-minute goal was a result of swift interplay between Bertie Auld and Joe McBride, whose header went directly into Bobby Lennox's path – 'the Buzz Bomb' did not miss those. Rangers tried hard, and Bobby Watson had the ball in the net, but referee Tiny Wharton correctly chopped it off for a previous infringement.

The first trophy was in the bag, followed nine days later by the second, the Glasgow Cup, won in a swift autumnal canter by Celtic, who beat Rangers, Queen's Park and Partick Thistle in that order and all by the same score of 4–0. The Scottish Cup was also something of a stroll, frankly, with Clyde providing the only real problem, at the semi-final stage. Celtic edged them 2–0 in the replay after a 0–0 draw in which the Celts very nearly blew their chances of the Quintuple.

The final was one of Willie Wallace's finest hours, but he may not have made it into that team or the Lisbon Lions but for an injury to a brilliant goalscorer. It is astonishing to think that the top scorer in Celtic's greatest season was Joe McBride, who did not feature in the side after Christmas. He had played well and scored plenty in season 1965–66 but moved onto a different level in 1966–67 and by 24 December had accumulated thirty-six goals, including two four-timers and a host of penalties. But a knee injury sustained against Aberdeen on Christmas Eve put him out of football for a year, and he then moved to Hibs, where he was that club's top scorer for two seasons running.

It is often thought that Stein went out and bought Wallace from Hearts to replace McBride. Not true: with uncanny shrewdness, Stein had brought in the versatile Wallace as cover for the entire forward line, and he actually played alongside McBride twice before the latter was injured. Nor was Wallace an unknown: he had already been capped for Scotland, and it was thought to be just a matter of time before Rangers would sign him. Jock Stein beat them to it, signing Wallace for a club-record fee of £30,000, and the manager's prescience meant Wallace was on hand to step into the breach when McBride's injury occurred.

The man known as 'Wispy' because he spoke so quietly off the pitch, promptly did his talking with his boots, never more so than in the Scottish Cup final against Aberdeen on 29 April, when he scored both goals in Celtic's win. Earlier that month, it should be added, Wallace joined Bobby Lennox, Tommy Gemmell and the country's oldest international debutant Ronnie Simpson in Scotland's historic 3–2 victory over England at Wembley – and yes, it was historic, because they were the first team to beat the reigning world champions, and in their own midden, too.

Wallace also scored two crucial goals against Dukla Prague in the European Cup semi-final first leg at Parkhead, which was won 3–1. Untypically, Stein ordered his men to defend at all costs in the away leg, and the 0–0 draw meant that, as they entered the month of May, Celtic were a maximum of four matches short of a clean sweep. Inter Milan would await them on 25 May in Lisbon, but first there was a long-term job that needed finishing.

There is a common misconception that, because Celtic lost only three out of sixty-five matches in that glorious season, they must have run away with the league title. Nothing could be further from the truth, because those pesky chaps at Ibrox just simply refused to lie down and die and were making European progress of their own into the bargain.

Dundee United proved to be the bogey team, however. Celtic had been unbeaten all season when they went to Tannadice on Hogmanay and lost 3–2 to a team who were at one point 1–2 down and looking beaten. But by the time Celtic fans rolled up to Parkhead on 3 May 1967 for the return match against United, they knew that two points would make the league all but mathematically secure. The Taysiders did it again, however, winning 3–2 with the same sequence of scoring.

Celtic thus travelled to Ibrox on 6 May for a match that was actually the postponed Ne'erday Derby. They needed just a single point to win the championship. Rangers had also slipped up, with draws against Clyde and Dundee robbing them of an outright title decider against Celtic. It was Rangers' final match of the league season, and, even if they won, Celtic would only have to draw their final match of the season at Kilmarnock to win the league just ten days before the European Cup final – they had a far superior goal difference.

Rangers, too, had made a European final and would play Bayern Munich for the Cup-Winners' Cup a week after Celtic played in Lisbon. It almost beggars belief to think of it in terms of modern Scottish football – Scotland's league champions and Cup holders in the final of Europe's two biggest tournaments. *Sic transit gloria mundi* . . .

As Bobby Lennox put it, 'At that point we were in the European Cup final, they were in the European Cup-Winners' Cup final and Kilmarnock had only just been beaten in the Fairs Cities Cup semi-final. There were also a lot of good players around Scotland. It wasn't a bad time for Scottish football, was it?'

The Celtic team consisted of the 11 men who would become Parkhead immortals 19 days later: Simpson; Craig and Gemmell; Murdoch, McNeill and Clark; Johnstone, Wallace, Chalmers, Auld and Lennox. The soon-to-be Lisbon Lions were lining up together for only the sixth time in all, and contrary to a popular myth that has grown up since their heyday, those 11 were not invincible. Over the course of two seasons, they won most of their games but drew three matches and lost to Dynamo Kiev in the first round of the European Cup of 1967–68.

Though they were not to win a trophy that season, Rangers had some terrific players, and their pursuit of Celtic in the league had been tenacious. Their half-back line of Sandy Jardine, Ronnie McKinnon and John Greig was powerful, and in Willie Henderson and Willie Johnston they had two wonderful wingers, with the Smiths, Dave and Alex – the latter being Rangers' record signing at that point – forming a fine inside partnership. One weakness was that main striker Roger Hynd was a converted defender, drafted in after Rangers mysteriously sold Jim Forrest and George McLean. Their departure, after the devastating loss to Berwick Rangers in the Scottish Cup, indicated that Rangers' main frailty was probably managerial – decent and honourable man though Scot Symon was, he was in the veteran stage as a manager and the sale of the club's top scorers was against his will. Chairman John Lawrence often did to Symon what Robert Kelly did to Jimmy McGrory, and Forrest and McLean were the board's scapegoats after Berwick. Symon would turn fifty-six three days after the Old Firm match and looked positively geriatric compared with Jock Stein, who was only twelve years younger but whose youthful ideas and tactics were beyond Symon's conceptual capabilities.

Symon sent out this team to try to force the issue to the wire: Martin; Johansen and Provan; Jardine, McKinnon and Greig; Henderson, A. Smith, Hynd, D. Smith and Johnston. The same team would contest the Cup-Winners' Cup final 26 days later, so the match can fairly be said to have been a battle of European giants.

An almighty downpour lashed Glasgow for hours that day, and the match was played in constant rain. 'It was an appalling day,' recalled Jim Craig, 'and the pitch was soaking wet. It was a terrible day to be playing football.

'There was a lot of apprehension before the game because we knew the pitch would cut up and that would bother us more because we could play the better football.'

Bobby Lennox concurred, 'It was really heavy and really muddy. Our sleeves were hanging down, and our socks were filling up with water. But we tried to play football. We always did.'

The conditions would perhaps have suited Gargantua or any other giant you care to name, but instead it was a diminutive winger who beat the weather in what Jinky's biographer Jim Black called 'one of his finest performances in the hoops'. Among the 78,000 crowd was Celtic fan Sean Connery – his later interest in Rangers, it should be said, has never overcome his initial footballing love – while another interested spectator in the stand was Helenio Herrera, manager of Inter Milan, who was spying on his future opponents. He was probably not impressed with the weather nor with the overall standard of play in a tough but hugely exciting match, though surely he could not have failed to notice Jimmy Johnstone, the red-topped winger who was involved in the action from start to finish.

Chances were few and far between as the game developed into a tense midfield battle, with no quarter given in the tackles. It was industrial stuff, almost devoid of artistry except when Johnstone and Henderson got the ball and both took their share of punishment. The best early chance fell to Willie Johnston of Rangers, but he fluffed his shot, sending it over the crossbar. A shot from Stevie Chalmers in the 18th minute was deflected clear, and Willie Wallace could not take advantage of an opening created by Bertie Auld.

After 40 minutes of this frankly grim stuff, interspersed with glimpses of Jinky at his best, there came the first moment of really lovely football – and it was from Rangers. Dave Smith managed to evade his markers on the left and passed inside to Sandy Jardine. The right-half was up in support and controlled the bouncing ball with one touch before slamming a magnificent shot from 25 yards into the top right-hand postage stamp of Ronnie Simpson's goal. The veteran goalkeeper could only watch as the ball thudded off the stanchion and nestled in his net. 'It was a terrific goal,' said Jim

Craig, 'but we knew we could come back. That was the way we felt in those days.'

The Rangers fans' hopes were lifted, but only for a minute. Celtic raced up to the other end and won a free kick. Bobby Murdoch took it quickly to Bobby Lennox, who got in a powerful shot from just inside the penalty box that goalkeeper Norrie Martin did well to parry onto his left-hand post. Lurking there was Johnstone, and he prodded home the equaliser. His big pal Tommy Gemmell seemed ready to carry Jinky round the park in celebration. Gemmell said, 'It was just fantastic to score a goal that quick, and I wanted to show Jinky off to the crowd, but eventually I put the wee fellow down.'

Crestfallen at this immediate reverse, Rangers tried to hit back before half-time, but Simpson defied them and Celtic went in at the interval knowing that one more goal would seal the Quadruple. But who could conjure up a goal on a pitch that was getting heavier by the minute as the rain sluiced down?

Facing a Copland Road end jam-packed with Rangers fans, plenty Celts had a go. Auld beat three men on a run and then crossed to Johnstone, whose header was well saved by Martin at the cost of a corner. Chalmers was foiled by a defensive body for the second time in the match before Auld somehow shot over when the target would have been easier to hit. The excitement among the Celtic fans in particular was at fever pitch, but the Rangers' support was no less vocal, and it all added to the atmosphere, which was heated despite the precipitation.

Tommy Gemmell came closest in the 53rd minute with a shot that Martin needed two attempts to hold. Celtic won a series of corners, but Billy McNeill came up against a determined McKinnon and Martin in the box. All the time Johnstone was making audacious runs against John Greig and Dave Provan, while, on the other wing, Bobby Lennox was getting little change out of the impressive Kai Johansen. It looked as though Jinky would have to be the one to break the deadlock, and when he did so it was in spectacular style.

With 15 minutes left to play, and the rain still sheeting down, Celtic got a throw-in on their right wing in front of the main stand. Stevie Chalmers made a mess of the first throw but got a second chance, and as he lined up a target, Bobby Lennox ran from left to right across the Rangers defence. Distracted, they seemed to hang off Johnstone, who was by now quite bedraggled and mud-spattered. From 35 yards out the wee man cut inside at speed and was still going fast when he reached a spot 20 yards from goal just outside the penalty box 'D'. Even as McKinnon lunged despairingly in, by the immutable laws of footballing physics Jinky's momentum converted to force as he gave the ball an almighty thump with his left foot. Norrie Martin tried to save it with a prodigious leap, but the ball was up, over and past him into the roof of the net high to his right. How the wee man summoned up the strength for such a Herculean effort remains a mystery, but it was a fabulous goal.

Sean Fallon said, 'Jinky destroyed them that day. They could hardly get the ball off him. To score that goal with his left foot, too. We didn't know he could hit them that hard with his left, but we were glad he did.'

Jim Craig remembered, 'It was a fantastic shot, especially considering how wet the pitch was. And with his left foot, too. But that was the wee man for you, always surprising you.'

Bobby Lennox said, 'Honestly, I can still see him going for the shot, and I'm thinking, "Don't hit it, wee man." That's what flashed through my mind: don't hit it. Then he did, and he just nailed it. That was us – I was sure then we had won the league.'

John Clark commented, 'There were two tremendous goals scored that day, and people tend to forget Sandy's goal because Jimmy's equalled it and was more important. It was not often you saw two such goals in an Old Firm game, as they tended to be tight matches.'

The Celtic end erupted as the players danced for joy. The heads of the Rangers players went down, and, typically, rather than sitting on their lead – which would have guaranteed them the title – Celtic went in search of another goal. After a brief stoppage while police arrested some fighters and bottle-throwers – Tommy Gemmell picked up one bottle that nearly hit him and calmly put it on the track – Rangers recovered their composure. With several Celtic players stranded upfield, Henderson broke away on the right and sclaffed in a low cross that Simpson could only palm away. The ball stopped in the mud, and Hynd crashed it home for the equaliser.

Jim Craig swears that, if Henderson had not mishit his cross, he would have stopped the goal, 'Willie took it towards the byline, and the only cross that was on was a cut back across the goal. I read it and went for the interception, but he miskicked it completely and the ball rolled across and got stuck, and Roger came rushing in and cracked it in. If Willie had done what he intended to do, I'd have got to the ball.'

A nervous nine minutes followed for the Celtic fans, but the team was in control and Rangers looked exhausted. 'The equaliser had come too late for them,' said Bobby Lennox. 'I thought we might actually get another, and I thought we deserved to win, but the point was enough.'

When the final whistle blew, Rangers had retained some honour by denying Celtic the 'greenwash' of four victories over them in a season, but Celtic had won the league at the ground of their old foes. There was dismay and joy at either end of Ibrox, but on the pitch there were remarkable displays of genuine sporting goodwill.

Jimmy Johnstone went to both John Greig and Dave Provan and was warmly embraced by both men, who recognised that it had been Jinky's day. In the context of an Old Firm league decider, those hugs were surely two of the finest pieces of sportsmanship ever displayed at Parkhead or Ibrox. Jinky returned the warmth of the two men he had tormented, and all over the pitch players shook hands and wished each other well in the higher missions awaiting them later in the month – life was different then, and anyway, Johnstone inspired affection and admiration wherever football was played.

Jim Craig said, 'It was one of those days when everything went right, apart from us not winning. Rangers were a really good side at that time, and the same two teams that played that day went on to play in that season's European finals.

'Rangers took the defeat really well. It was a big game for them to lose, and to show that they were good sports must have been hard for them to do.'

Bobby Lennox recalled, 'I have photos of us all coming off the park, and everyone is shaking hands and smiling. I remember having a bit of banter with Willie Johnston, and, of course, we all knew both teams were going into the European finals.'

Celtic went on to glorious victory on 25 May in Lisbon, about which there is surely nothing more to say. Jim Craig recalled that the first person to meet them off the plane home was Rangers chairman John Lawrence.

It should not be forgotten that Rangers came very close to emulating Celtic's European success just six days later in Nuremberg. It was practically a home tie for Bayern Munich, but Rangers fought hard against a team containing Sepp Maier in goal, Franz Beckenbauer at centre-half and Gerd Müller up front. It was only in extra time that Franz Roth got the winner for the Germans.

Celtic would march on into season 1967–68, though nothing could ever match their *annus mirabilis*. Scot Symon, these days correctly recognised as one of Rangers' greatest managers, paid the price for the failures against Berwick Rangers, Bayern and, above all, Celtic. Even though he was managing a team that was top of the league, Symon was sacked in the November and replaced by Davie White.

Jock Stein had taken the measure of Symon and bested him. He would do even more to White. The big man of Celtic and Scottish football now reigned supreme.

10

WHEN THE MATADORS WERE TOUGHER THAN THE BULLS

26 APRIL 1969
SCOTTISH CUP FINAL
CELTIC 4, RANGERS 0

The story of the 1969 Scottish Cup final is rather easy to tell. You could actually sum it up in one sentence. With skill and pace, backed by no little physical commitment, a tough and disciplined Celtic side overwhelmed a Rangers team whose main tactic seemed to be to try to bully their opponents to defeat.

There was so much more to it than that, of course. Within the Celtic ranks there was a feeling that the greatest side in the club's history was on the verge of breaking up. In 1968–69, however, the Celtic fans were constantly reassured by talk of the 'Quality Street Gang' in the reserve and youth teams, and the names of Danny McGrain, David Hay, Lou Macari and especially George Connelly were being bandied about as seriously good prospects. The latter three would all make their debuts that season, but the inside track from Parkhead was that a certain Kenny Dalglish, who, like McGrain, had been stolen from under the nose of Rangers, might turn out to be the best of them all.

With Ronnie Simpson and John Clark suffering recurring injury problems, those 'eternal reserves' John Fallon and Jim Brogan both got extended runs in the team, the former having been forgiven his horrendous blunder in the 1968 Ne'erday game in which he had gifted Rangers a late equaliser. Davie Cattanach and new signings

Tommy Callaghan and Harry Hood were both blooded in that season.

In March, AC Milan put paid to the dream of another European success for Celtic, winning 1–0 at Parkhead following a goalless draw in the San Siro. It was a sad way for the adventure to end, not least because of Jimmy Johnstone's extraordinary performance in the 5–1 defeat of Red Star Belgrade in the previous round. Still, the month of April 1969 could bring Celtic three domestic trophies, and Rangers barred the way to two of them. The treble had never been accomplished inside a calendar month before – could Celtic make yet more history?

The Scottish League Cup final had been postponed from earlier in the season because of a fire at Hampden Park. The semi-final had been played at Hampden as long ago as 9 October, when Harry Hood had played well for the Shawfield side – a sure way of getting yourself signed for Celtic was to shine against them – though George Connelly had struck the winner 15 minutes from time. Celtic had put Rangers out in the sectional ties in August, winning both matches, and after a good run Hibs were their opponents in the final.

Celtic poured it on from the start, and Bobby Lennox scored a hat-trick as Hibs were dismantled. They were six down by the seventy-fifth minute but struck back twice to make the scoreline a slightly more respectable 6–2. On the same day, Rangers went to Tannadice, and their bid for the league title crumbled as they unexpectedly lost 1–2 to Dundee United. The loss meant that Celtic required only a point from their three remaining matches to clinch the league. This was duly acquired in the 1–1 draw with Kilmarnock on the night of Monday, 21 April. Celtic now had two legs of the domestic treble, with the Cup final to look forward to, as they had easily disposed of Morton in the semi-final, winning 4–1. In the other semi, Rangers had destroyed Aberdeen 6–1, the Dons' goal being scored by former Rangers man Jim Forrest.

Jock Stein did not have his problems to seek, because on the day Celtic won the league Jimmy Johnstone was suspended by the SFA for accumulating three cautions, one of them for verbals to a referee – how many of the prima donnas in British football nowadays would complete a game if referees applied the laws on speech play as firmly as they did in 1969? Curiously, Rangers' new hope, and Scotland's most expensive player, £100,000-striker Colin Stein, was also suspended, and there was a move by some fans with typewriters to try and get Stein's suspension postponed. Rangers themselves scorned that one, and two potential match-winners, one for either side, were out. Two days before the final, John Hughes's ankle was finally declared not fit for purpose after Yogi had spent a month recuperating, and now Jock Stein had only one recognised winger, Bobby Lennox, though he had been playing a more central role all season.

'Not having wee Jimmy and big Yogi was a big blow to us,' said Bobby Lennox. 'I think that's why the bookies made Rangers the favourites on the day.'

Cometh the hour, cometh the man. When Jock Stein announced the team, there were metaphorical, and probably some actual, intakes of breath among the Celtic supporters. At number seven, indicating he would play outside-right, was George Connelly. What was Stein thinking? The boy had made a handful of appearances and seemed skilful and composed – but replacing Jinky? Yet those who had followed the club all season knew that Connelly had filled in at outside-right before, way back in October. Sean Fallon recalled, 'He was a big quiet lad from Fife, but you could see right away that he had great skill. He showed it that day, too.'

Bobby Lennox agreed: 'George was a big shy boy, but he had tons and tons of ability. His skill was obvious, but nobody really knew how shy he was.'

Celtic knew that history was against them. Rangers had not been beaten in a Scottish Cup final for 40 years, and Celtic had not defeated Rangers in a Scottish Cup final since 1904, Jimmy Quinn's Final, as we saw in Chapter Three. Rangers had won all three Old Firm finals since then, and many in the Celtic squad were still smarting from the defeat in 1966. But the lure of taking the domestic Treble for the second time in three years was very great, while Rangers still had a chance of a European trophy, as they were due to play Newcastle United in the Fairs Cities Cup semi-final in the May.

Stein was highly confident that Connelly would do the needful for him, and he used his psychology on the whole squad. Jim Craig said, 'We had been told by the newspapers that this was Rangers' chance to get back to being on top. Jock just said to us, "You've seen what the papers are saying; go and prove them wrong."'

Stein also began to play mind games with Davie White, the Rangers manager, emphasising how the younger man had yet to win a trophy. Stein also knew full well that Hughes had little chance of making the final and had made his plans many days before Yogi failed his fitness test. Everything Stein said indicated that he would make his men play through the centre with a packing defence in behind. The reaction from White was exactly what Stein wanted: the Rangers manager decided it was a bluff and that Celtic would go to the wings. White also decided on a course of the rough stuff to try and unsettle the Celts in midfield, to break up their passing play and to allow Willie Henderson and the impressive Swede Örjan Persson to penetrate down the right and left flanks respectively.

Scotland in 1969 was a place of some disquiet. Harold Wilson's Labour government had sent British troops into Ulster in support of the Royal Ulster Constabulary the weekend before the match. It was the biggest escalation of the Troubles to date and followed the raised feelings caused by the jailing of Rev. Ian Paisley earlier in the year for his part in a demonstration that had ended in violence. Many thought it was just a matter of time before serious sectarian fighting would erupt in Glasgow.

The previous month, the Longhope lifeboat had been lost at sea off Orkney, with her crew of eight all perishing. But there was also some good news for Britain: Lulu jointly won the Eurovision Song Contest with the highly forgettable 'Boom Bang-a-Bang', and solo sailor Robin Knox-Johnston had just completed his voyage round the world, for which he would be knighted. Abroad, Golda Meir had become Israel's first female prime minister, while former US president Dwight D. Eisenhower died at the end of March. The Beatles were still together and so were the Lisbon Lions, just.

Football could still pull in the crowds like no other sport in Scotland. Just under 133,000 came to Hampden for the final, and, perhaps as a result of concern over the Northern Irish situation, extra police were drafted in. They would be needed.

The Celtic team as printed on the team sheet was Fallon; Craig and Gemmell; Murdoch, McNeill and Brogan; Connelly, Chalmers, Wallace, Lennox and Auld. Rangers fielded Martin; Johansen and Mathieson; Greig, McKinnon and D. Smith; Henderson, Penman, Ferguson, Johnston and Persson. Refereeing this potential powder keg was James Callaghan of Glasgow.

The scoreline might suggest a walk in the park for Celtic. It was anything but. John Fallon made more saves than Norrie Martin, though he didn't have to pick the ball out of his net, and Celtic

The original Celtic team and officials from 1888. Back row: John Anderson, James Quillan, Daniel Malloy, John Glass, John McDonald. Middle row: Willie Groves, Tom Maley, Paddy Gallagher, John O'Hara, Willie Dunning, William McKillop, Willie Maley, Michael Dunbar. Front row: Johnny Coleman, James McLaren, James Kelly, Neil McCallum, Mick McKeown.

Mr Celtic – Willie Maley.
(Courtesy of Scottish Daily
Record and Sunday Mail Ltd)

The famous cartoon of
1905 that popularised
the 'Old Firm' name.

Jimmy McGrory, Celtic's greatest-ever goalscorer. (Courtesy of the McGrory family)

John Thomson in action against Rangers. (Courtesy of Scottish Daily Record and Sunday Mail Ltd)

'GERS WERE LUCKY
NOT TO LOSE TEN

What a
Celtic
joy day

The author pictured beside the memorial stone at John Thomson's grave in Bowhill Cemetery, Cardenden, Fife, in July 2010. (Picture by Frances Anderson)

How the *Sunday Mail* reported the 1957 Scottish League Cup final. Yes, it really could have been ten. (Courtesy of Scottish Daily Record and Sunday Mail Ltd)

In his early days at Celtic, Jock Stein revolutionised training methods with his hands-on approach – in this case literally so, as he takes a turn in goals in 1965. (Courtesy of The Scotsman Publications Ltd)

Jimmy Johnstone ready to pounce and score the first goal in the 2–2 draw that clinched the title in 1967. (Courtesy of Scottish Daily Record and Sunday Mail Ltd)

Bobby Lennox scoring in the 1969 Scottish Cup final.
(Courtesy of The Scotsman Publications Ltd)

It's not from the main match featured in Chapter 11, but this picture had to be included: King Kenny Dalglish scoring his first-ever goal for Celtic at Ibrox in the 2–0 Scottish League Cup victory in 1971. (Courtesy of The Scotsman Publications Ltd)

Roy Aitken turning away in jubilation after scoring Celtic's second equaliser in the titanic 1979 Premier Division decider. (Courtesy of The Scotsman Publications Ltd)

The aftermath of the 1980 Scottish Cup final. (Courtesy of The Scotsman Publications Ltd)

The evidence was captured on camera, m'lud. Chris Woods exchanges pleasantries with Frank McAvennie in the Battle of Ibrox, 1987. And not a handbag in sight. (Courtesy of Scottish Daily Record and Sunday Mail Ltd)

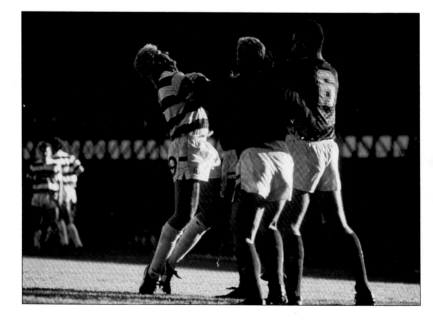

The moment that sealed a love affair between Celtic's fans
and Lubo Moravčik: the first goal in the 5–1 match in 1998.
(Courtesy of Scottish Daily Record and Sunday Mail Ltd)

Henrik Larsson turns away after scoring in the 6–2 match in 2000.
(Courtesy of Scottish Daily Record and Sunday Mail Ltd)

Chris Sutton celebrates his winner in the 'greenwash' match in 2004. (Courtesy of The Scotsman Publications Ltd)

Scott McDonald saluting fans after scoring in the 3–2 match at Celtic Park in 2008. (Courtesy of The Scotsman Publications Ltd)

The victorious Celts after the 2009 Cooperative Insurance League Cup final victory. Note the fellow in black waiting in the wings. Let us hope such scenes will soon be seen again. (Courtesy of Scottish Daily Record and Sunday Mail Ltd)

had to stand up and counter some tactics that John Rafferty in the *Scotsman* called 'deplorable'.

Davie White's master plan of intimidation would make itself known early in the match, but by that time Celtic were already one up. Stein's replacement was Alex Ferguson, then, as now, a combative type, though in 1969 he preferred elbows to verbals. He had been well warned beforehand that, if Celtic won a corner or free kick and Billy McNeill came forward, it was his task to mark the Celtic captain. Celtic duly won a corner on the left after only two minutes, and Bobby Lennox struck the perfect corner kick to just beyond the penalty spot. Ferguson was ball-watching, as were the rest of the defence, and McNeill soared above them all to head powerfully back across goal and in at the far post. The Rangers defence had been nowhere, and the recriminations began, with Ferguson taking the blame for missing his target – it would come back to haunt him later – and Kai Johansen being excoriated for not taking his usual place at the right post, where he would easily have intercepted the scoring header.

Tommy Gemmell said, 'We got a flier of a start, with Billy scoring that goal in only the second minute of the game. It was a costly goal in more ways than one for them. Alex Ferguson was supposed to pick up Billy, but he didn't, and that lapse cost him his first-team place at Ibrox, and he was eventually transferred.'

Now the strong-arm tactics began in earnest, and for once there was near universal condemnation of Rangers in the press afterwards for stooping to methods more associated with nasty foreigners.

The Celtic players decided to get their retaliation in first. Jim Craig said, 'They could hand it out, but so could we. And I have to say, when the rough stuff started, we kicked them off the pitch. They could hand it out, but we could look after ourselves.

'I remember one incident clearly. I chased Willie Mathieson and tackled him in the time-honoured fashion, coming in from the side and taking the ball first and then lifting my leg to make sure I got him as well. He limped back to his full-back position, and Davie Smith took the throw-in, sending it back to Willie. He couldn't control it, and the ball rolled forward a yard. I stepped forward, and, in Glasgow parlance, I wellied him. He went right up in the air and landed on all fours. It was absolutely disgraceful, I'll admit. It would be a straight red card nowadays, but I wasn't even booked.'

Stein's bluff on White had also worked, as the Rangers defence spread itself thin while Connelly and Auld dropped deeper than usual to be the wing partners for Lennox and Stevie Chalmers, who linked up behind Willie Wallace to create a solid phalanx in midfield in which Brogan was the fixer and Murdoch the man with the rapier thrust.

Rangers tried to come back, and Fallon had to look lively to cut out crosses and save some efforts, but all the time Celtic were probing the Rangers defence, even as the rough stuff got rougher. Ferguson, Greig and especially Willie Johnston – what a waste of a ball-player – dished out a lot of it, but this Celtic team had experienced Racing Club of Argentina in the Club World Championship, and Rangers were no Racing. Billy McNeill, Bobby Murdoch, Jim Brogan and Tommy Gemmell had proved for years that they could more than look after themselves, and Brogan in particular was soon involved in ferocious tackling contests.

Referee Callaghan waved play on more times than he should have done, and on several occasions a melee formed round him, not least when Ferguson attempted to go in hard on goalkeeper Fallon and was unceremoniously bundled to the ground by Murdoch. When Ferguson rose and tried to remonstrate, Brogan faced him nose-to-nose. Fergie would remember that and later in the game blatantly kicked Brogan in retaliation for the Celtic player's tackle. Brogan himself was booked before one tough tackle too many saw him injured and replaced by John Clark.

'I came on for the last half hour,' said Clark. 'I had only just got myself back from a knee injury, and just about the first thing I saw was Örjan Persson coming in to "do" me. But I saw him in time and said, "On you go," as his boot came right by me – it was a tough game, okay. But that was football in those days. If someone gave it you, you gave it right back.'

Ferguson was also accused of headbutting both Bobby Murdoch and Billy McNeill but claimed they were both accidents. Willie Johnston could have been sent off three times for very rough stuff, but the referee apparently saw nothing. It was that kind of day.

'I felt Fergie was under pressure to deliver something that day,' said Jim Craig more than 40 years later. 'Alex had done really well at Dunfermline and was a really good striker, but there was all sorts of talk around Ibrox that he wasn't Rangers class. On that day, I think he was determined to show what he could do, and he blew it right at the start and was chasing the game after it.'

Some players tried to get on with it, notably Murdoch, who rose above the intimidation he received to play some incisive passes, and the classy Dave Smith of Rangers, who created a real chance for a John Greig shot that was saved by Fallon at the second attempt. McNeill also had the ball in the net again but was correctly adjudged to have fouled Martin.

Towards the end of a half of visceral excitement and a modicum of quality, supplied mostly by Celtic, a moment of real class all but decided the destination of the old trophy. With just over a minute to the interval, Bobby Lennox, who was enjoying his liberated role in midfield, popped up on the right wing at the halfway line to collect a smart pass by Connelly. Like a flash, the Buzz Bomb took off, leaving Mathieson for dead and haring away into the penalty box, where he fired a shot low past the stranded Martin.

Lennox recalled, 'Rangers played it square, and Big George intercepted and put me away on the halfway line. It was a long, long way to their goal – I never knew Hampden was that long – but I got there anyway.' It was a fine goal, and Celtic were now two up at a crucial time, but better was still to come.

Lennox almost scored again seconds later when he hit a fierce shot over the bar. The goal kick went from Norrie Martin to John Greig, who did not see George Connelly coming up behind him. Connelly dispossessed the Rangers captain, skipped round the advancing Martin and placed the ball in the net for a goal of elegant composure. Referee Callaghan blew for the interval shortly afterwards, and at 3–0 the match was as good as over.

'Bobby's goal came at just the right time for us, as they were pressing up,' said Jim Craig. 'And then Big George's goal couldn't have come at a better time. We knew it was ours then.'

At half-time, Stein's main job was to try to keep his players' feet on the ground. 'It was the happiest dressing-room I was ever in during an Old Firm game,' said Jim Craig. 'Jock came in and said, "Careful, they might come back in the second half," and for once he was met with a gale of laughter. "Aye, right, Boss," we said. We knew we had them. We had started the first half kicking them, and we would do the same at the start of the second half.'

Up in the terraces, some folk even dared to mention the words 'seven' and 'one'.

The match continued in a towsy manner, but for all their brutal efforts Rangers just could not penetrate the Celtic midfield, in which Connelly and Murdoch were coping with everything that was being thrown at them. Fallon had a couple more saves to make, restoring his popularity with the fans, and George Connelly brought out the best in Martin with a low shot. After 75 minutes, with Rangers pressing, Stevie Chalmers broke away and raced towards goal before sending a fine shot past Martin with the outside of his right foot.

Chalmers said, 'The build-up came right from the back, and then Bertie Auld put me through with a great pass. The only thing I could hear was Bobby Lennox shouting for the ball, but I decided to go on my own instead and put it past Rangers keeper Norrie Martin.

'Bobby and I have played a lot of golf over the years, and he has always dug me up about the goal, claiming I should have passed. Needless to say, I'm glad I didn't.'

Jim Craig said, 'It was a typical Stevie goal, a wonderful effort. The television pictures show the goal from behind and show the skill he had in taking the ball with the outside of the right foot. Great stuff.'

The fourth goal was the cue for what at first looked to be a pitch invasion by the Rangers fans behind Martin's goal. Some were fleeing the bottles that were being hurled from behind and falling short. Glasgow's finest arrived en masse, contained the hundreds who had come onto the track and arrested several miscreants who would not go quietly. Then something quite bizarre happened. Appearances may have been deceptive, but it really did look as though most of the invading Rangers fans were actually trying not to stop the game but just to get out of the stadium. Certainly many hundreds took the opportunity to escape via the gate to the side of the terracing. John Rafferty in the *Scotsman* wrote, 'It seemed a bit sadistic on the part of the police when many were ushered back onto the terracing, as if they were being told, "Aye, ye'll watch."'

Play restarted shortly afterwards, and Celtic coasted home to the final whistle. Celtic had won their 20th Scottish Cup, and the Treble was theirs. The attempt to bully Celtic off the pitch had been met by matadors who not only could handle themselves as men but had the eye for a killing goal or four.

There were a range of postcripts. Jim Craig recalled, 'All 22 players were summoned by the SFA for a talking to. There were photographs in the papers of us coming out of the SFA's offices in Park Gardens after we were all warned as to our future conduct.'

Several men were made scapegoats for Rangers' defeat, most

notably Alex Ferguson, who was rightly blamed for failing to mark McNeill for the first goal but hardly deserved being left out of the side until he was transferred to Falkirk that autumn. Former Rangers hero Willie Waddell was now working as a sportswriter, and he led the chorus of bitter disapproval against manager Davie White. When White was sacked after Rangers were put out of Europe early the next season, Waddell got the job.

That greatest of all Celtic teams would have one last hurrah the following year, peaking on two wonderful nights against Leeds United in the European Cup semi-final and proving once and for all that Stein's Celtic were the best team in Britain. Given their excellence against Leeds, that Celtic did not go on to beat Feyenoord in the 1970 European Cup final remains somewhat of a mystery to this day.

As we shall see, the core of the Lisbon Lions would move on, though Lennox, Johnstone and McNeill stayed until the mid 1970s, helping the transition of the Quality Street Gang into the next great Stein creation.

Stein always said that his greatest achievement was keeping the mercurial Johnstone in the game for five years longer than he might have expected and that his greatest disappointment at Celtic was not managing to prolong the all-too-brief career of George Connelly, who seemed to have Einsteinian brains in his feet but scrambled ones in his head. Connelly nevertheless left many good memories behind when he finally left Celtic but perhaps none more memorable than his cool display as a 20 year old on an April afternoon in 1969 in a match in which brawn alone was never going to be allowed to triumph.

Which, if you love football, is how it should be.

II

CHANGE CAN BE A GOOD THING

11 SEPTEMBER 1971
SCOTTISH LEAGUE DIVISION ONE
RANGERS 2, CELTIC 3

The reverse against Feyenoord apart, the 1970s started well for Celtic as Jock Stein laboured to build a new side, knowing that the Lisbon Lions would retire or move away. Simpson had already effectively retired after one too many shoulder injuries. Sentimental at heart, Stein paraded the Lisbon Lions for one absolutely final match at the end of the 1970–71 season, the league having been won two days previously against Ayr United at Parkhead. There was not a dry eye in the house at Parkhead on 1 May 1971 when the Lions took to the field and received rapturous applause from everyone inside the stadium, including their opponents, Clyde. Ronnie Simpson was immediately replaced by Evan Williams, and 'the Faither' left to the sound of resounding cheers. And just to prove they could still muster the old fire, the Lions went on to win 6–1.

Most of the Lions then went their separate ways, with six of the side moving on over the following months. Bertie Auld went to Hibs, and John Clark to Morton, and by the end of the year Stevie Chalmers had joined Clark at Morton. John Hughes and Willie Wallace left for Crystal Palace, and Tommy Gemmell signed for Nottingham Forest.

Not the least of the miracles accomplished by Stein was how he handled the transition to a new side. Over time, and allowing players to mature at their own pace, Stein blended in members of the young group nicknamed the Quality Street Gang: Danny McGrain, David Hay, Kenny Dalglish, Lou Macari, Vic Davidson, Brian McLaughlin, Pat McCluskey, Paul Wilson and the enigmatic George Connelly.

Davie Hay remembered how the youngsters looked up to the Lions: 'When I first started as a fifteen year old, we were training two nights a week, and then when I signed, we were training full-time alongside that exceptional side. I have no doubt that helped us develop into the players we became.

'My great hero as a boy was actually Denis Law, but at Celtic it was big Billy McNeill – and then I got to play alongside him. But the best player was Jimmy Johnstone. In training you couldn't get the ball off him, and then to be playing alongside him – it was just an honour and a privilege.'

The feelings were mutual, as Jimmy Johnstone told the author in December 2002: 'There were all these great young guys coming through, the Kenny Dalglishes, the Davie Hays, the Lou Macaris and the rest. Big Jock knew when to start putting them in the team, and they were so good that even the Lions had to look over their shoulders.'

Stein made crucial signings, too, bringing in goalkeepers Evan Williams and Denis Connaghan to replace Simpson and Fallon, and a month after the match profiled in this chapter he would add John 'Dixie' Deans from Motherwell for a fee of around £18,000, which turned out to be a steal, given that the player went on to set several scoring records.

In that period of the early 1970s, Celtic would regularly beat Rangers, a club that had been devastated by, yet had recovered manfully from, the second Ibrox Disaster, in 1971. That catastrophic event overshadowed everything in season 1970–71, when Celtic won the Double, beating Rangers in the Scottish Cup final by edging them out 2–1 in a replay after a 1–1 draw in a final like no other Old Firm match: it was almost eerily quiet at times – not surprising, perhaps, as it was the two sides' first meeting since the deaths of 66 spectators on Stairway 13 at Ibrox after the derby on 2 January. The tragedy of those Rangers fans' deaths put football into its real context for a while, and there were pious hopes expressed that the genuine grieving across all religions and those of none in Scotland might bring an end to Old Firm bigotry. It is sad to report that did not happen – with the Troubles in Northern Ireland reaching their peak, the politico-religious nature of the conflict had already seeped into Scotland, and the banners and chants of both sides of the Old Firm soon carried a distinct Ulster accent, egged on by blinkered extremists on both sides.

It was not quite 'business as usual' when season 1971–72 arrived, and there was a sad note for Celtic even before a ball was kicked in anger, as Charlie Tully proved that legends do die by passing away in his sleep at his Belfast home on 27 July at the age of just 47.

Forget the Drybrough Cup, which took place before the season proper and was won by Aberdeen beating Celtic in the final. Designed for the four top-scoring teams, as opposed to the best sides, in Divisions One and Two, it was thought to be an ersatz tournament then, froth like the beer it was named after, and hindsight only serves to reinforce that opinion, even if Celtic made five of the six finals and won it in 1974.

The League Cup sections were once again the pipe-opener of the genuine season. Obviously someone forgot to tell the balls in the Scottish League's hat how to do their job, because Celtic and Rangers were drawn in the same group. Celtic were forced to play both ties at Ibrox, as the new main stand at Celtic Park was under reconstruction. Rangers did not want to concede the advantage to Celtic of playing at Hampden Park – well, it was Celtic's second home in those days – so Ibrox hosted the game.

Bobby Lennox recalled, 'Before the season started, Big Jock told us that, when we came to play the three games at Ibrox inside a month, if we were to win them it would be unbelievable and the Celtic supporters would never forget it. It was exactly the right thing to say.'

In the first match, on 14 August, Bobby Murdoch, whom many people had written off because of injury problems, was at his very best alongside Jimmy Johnstone. Jinky got the first after sixty-seven minutes with a shot from a Bobby Lennox corner, and three minutes later John Hughes was brought down in the box. Kenny Dalglish was given the ball and told to take it. Cooler than a cucumber that had been in an icebox for a month, the tyro Dalglish took the time to retie his bootlaces before slotting the ball past Peter McCloy. Celtic continued to pile on the pressure, and Hughes was robbed of a third when his shot almost broke the crossbar near the end.

There was an interesting postscript to that match for Evan Williams, the goalkeeper originally from the Vale of Leven who had taken over when Ronnie Simpson retired. Williams was living in Glasgow at that time, and his route home took him through hostile territory.

Williams said, 'Even though I lived in Glasgow, I never usually got any hassle. The only time I was ever frightened after an Old Firm game was after we beat Rangers 2–0 at Ibrox and I had to get the train to Bridgeton. I walked off with my collar up, hoping that nobody would recognise me.'

The second match at Ibrox a fortnight later was almost humiliating for Rangers. It was a tough decision to choose between that match and the one that features in this chapter, so exceptional were Celtic that day. Stein's mix of old and new had blended perfectly, and they simply tore Rangers apart, with McNeill at the heart of a defence that barely gave Rangers a kick of the ball in front of their own fans. Had it not been for the expertise of Peter McCloy in the Rangers goal, it might well have been a triumph of 1957 proportions, but as it was, Celtic still helped themselves to three goals against a Rangers side that didn't actually play that badly but was just no match for the Celts.

Tommy Callaghan had been in and around the squad since signing in November 1968, Stein often using him as a substitute or giving him a run when a player was injured or Bertie Auld needed a rest. That day at Ibrox, Callaghan's running power was seen at its best – it remains a shame that he never hit the heights more consistently – and he took Rangers apart. The only puzzle was why it took Celtic so long to score. McCloy defied the Celts until the 49th minute, when Dalglish grabbed the opener, his first competitive goal for Celtic. Rangers almost equalised shortly afterwards, but Jim Brogan cleared brilliantly off the line at Derek Johnstone's feet. Celtic then turned on the power, Callaghan firing in a cracker and Lennox completing the rout. When the third goal went in McCloy's net after 82 minutes, there was the rare sight of Ibrox emptying. Except for the Celtic end, of course.

There was to be no rest for Rangers. Two weeks later, Celtic were back at Ibrox on league duty, and even this early in the season it was clearly going to be an absolutely vital match. It may well have been just the second Saturday in the league, but if they could win it Celtic might just run away with the title.

They could not have started the league chase more strongly, hammering Clyde 9–1 on the first weekend, with Lennox scoring a hat-trick, Lou Macari notching a double, and Murdoch, McNeill,

Callaghan and Dalglish getting the others, as if to emphasise that the blend of older and younger players was working. Willie Waddell was a worried man ahead of the match on 11 September 1971.

Glasgow police were worried, too. They feared sectarian violence marring the match and perhaps sparking serious unrest in the city. Internment without trial had been introduced in Northern Ireland and was already causing mayhem, Edward Heath's government sending in more than 12,000 troops to the province. Heath had also started talks on joining the Common Market, yet still found time to be part of the British winning squad in the Admiral's Cup on his yacht *Morning Cloud*. Meanwhile, showjumper Harvey Smith was the national hero of the day for giving the V-sign to the judges at the Hickstead Derby.

There were plenty such two-fingered signs in evidence on the terraces at Ibrox that afternoon. Or maybe it was just the Rangers fans' way of showing that their heroes had scored two goals. For in a match that had everything – fine goals, controversy, a sending-off and excitement by the lorryload – Celtic had to come from 1–2 down to win.

The Celtic team that day was: Williams; Hay and Brogan; Murdoch, McNeill and Connelly; Johnstone, Lennox, Dalglish, Callaghan and Macari. Rangers fielded: McCloy; Jardine and Mathieson; Greig, Jackson and McDonald; McLean, Penman, Stein, Conn and Johnston. On the bench for Celtic was Tommy Gemmell, while Willie Henderson was substitute for Rangers. The only real surprise in either team was Colin Jackson replacing Ronnie McKinnon. The referee was the highly experienced Mr J.W. Paterson of Bothwell, and he showed a great deal of courage in front of 67,000 fans in a supercharged atmosphere.

The early exchanges were lively, Jimmy Johnstone drawing a good save from Peter McCloy in the first minute before Willie Johnston fired over the bar at the other end. Tommy McLean then tried a lob over Evan Williams but was well wide with his attempt.

After just nine minutes, Celtic took the lead. Bobby Murdoch swung in a free kick from the right wing, and Bobby Lennox glanced it on to Lou Macari, who made no mistake with his header from bang in front of goal. Rangers looked stunned, but, with Jinky Johnstone playing in a subdued midfield role, Celtic were not able to take advantage of their lead. Instead, Rangers came back into the match with some robust play and rather more direct tactics.

Scotland's most expensive player, Colin Stein, became the target man as Rangers charged forward. Williams saved well from Stein before the centre-forward robbed Jinky of possession and ran in on goal, only to shoot into the side net. The tackles had plenty bite, and Sandy Jardine was booked for a cruncher on Johnstone. When Jardine and Davie Hay clashed moments later, it was the Ranger who emerged limping – revenge had been taken, and Jardine now knew why Hay would earn the soubriquet 'the Quiet Assassin'.

Hay recalled those clashes with relish: 'We were a side that was full of skill, but we were also prepared to dig in when necessary. I loved playing against Rangers, and they were always great games, especially at Parkhead, where I was only once on the losing side as a player. But to go and win at Ibrox – that was something else.'

Tommy McLean was another who seemed to take a knock that the referee didn't spot. Mr Paterson did see Alfie Conn's clugging of Hay after 27 minutes, however, and booked him for the offence.

After Colin Stein missed another good chance, Rangers gained their equaliser in a dubious manner. Willie Johnston was heading goalwards when Jim Brogan appeared to slip and fall. The ball hit off his outstretched arm, and referee Paterson immediately blew the whistle for the penalty. It was certainly a soft award, but Johnston took no notice of the Celtic outrage and despatched the ball behind Williams.

The two most skilful players afield, Jinky and McLean, were unable to influence events, the former effectively being shackled by Alex MacDonald. The goal galvanised Rangers, who pinned the Celts in their own half. Celtic's frustration showed when Davie Hay was booked for a foul on Stein, and the big striker added to the Celts' misery right on half-time, Willie Johnston firing in a shot that Williams could only parry away and Stein pouncing to score and put Rangers 2–1 up. It was the first time Rangers had led Celtic in the three matches they had played that season.

It was the other Stein, Big Jock, who made the crucial alterations at half-time. Jinky Johnstone was sent to play on the right wing against Willie Mathieson, and that would soon become no contest, as the wee winger revelled in the new-found space. Bobby Murdoch and Tommy Callaghan became the attacking midfield behind the potent strike force of Johnstone, Lennox, Dalglish and Macari, while George Connelly was encouraged to go forward and play the long defence-splitting passes at which he excelled.

Now the true mettle of the younger members of the Celtic side would be discovered, and once again it was the manner of the performance in the face of adversity that makes this one of Celtic's greatest Old Firm matches. The earlier League Cup victory had been a triumph for superior skill, but this match showed that, like all the great Celtic teams, Stein's new blend not only had quality but could battle as well.

Rangers tried to continue where they had left off and had some success at first, largely due to Alex MacDonald no longer having to mark Jinky, allowing him to get forward himself. The introduction of Willie Henderson for the ineffective McLean also boosted Rangers. It looked to have been too much of a risk by Stein to alter the formation and tactics, but it paid off after 66 minutes when Tommy Callaghan won a corner after one of his increasingly effective runs.

There was a lot of controversy about what happened next. As the ball made its way into the penalty area, Kenny Dalglish found himself in plenty space and drilled home a left-foot shot. The Rangers' defence, probably aware they had all been caught napping, protested that Bobby Lennox had been in an offside position in front of Peter McCloy, but photographs showed that Lennox was in line with the last defender when the ball was hit.

'Never offside,' said Lennox. Who's arguing? In any case, referee Paterson ignored the protests and proved that he was no 'homer' a few minutes later when he sent off Alfie Conn for his second bookable foul, this time on Callaghan.

The anger of the home crowd at Conn's departure was nothing compared with their incandescent rage just two minutes later when Paterson chalked off what the Rangers contingent felt was a perfectly good goal. Evan Williams hesitated when a ball came through to the edge of the six-yard box, and Colin Stein got there ahead of him, jumping off the ground and with his left peg knocking the ball over the goalkeeper and into the net. The crucial aspects in the referee's decision to disallow the 'goal' were that Stein was off the ground, his boot being thus shoulder-high to Williams, and that the goalkeeper was injured on the arm by Stein's follow-through. Dangerous play, ruled Paterson, and Rangers were absolutely livid. 'Good decision,' said Evan Williams.

Down to ten men, Rangers nevertheless kept up the hunt for a winner, but, as the final whistle approached, Celtic looked dangerous on the break, and in the last minute of the ninety, Dalglish chased a ball deep into the Rangers penalty area. John Greig shepherded the ball towards the byline, and there appeared to be no danger, but Dalglish lobbed it into the middle of the box, and Jinky Johnstone soared above Willie Mathieson and powered a header behind Peter McCloy off the underside of the bar. Where Johnstone found the energy to outleap Mathieson is a mystery, but it was just one of a number of prodigious headed goals that Jinky accrued over the years.

'The wee man scored a lot of goals with his head,' said his great friend Bobby Lennox, 'and very often it was against guys that were much bigger than him, but that was typical of his bravery.'

There was no way back for Rangers, and for the third time in four weeks Celtic had won an Old Firm match. Evan Williams recalled the feeling of victory: 'I was proud of my record in games against Rangers. I very rarely lost a derby, and I had a good number of shutouts as well. I loved the Glasgow derbies. The feeling when you won is hard to explain. It was just brilliant. You walked about with a smile on your face for days.'

The victory was crucial to a massive season for Celtic, but the achievement of Stein's new side was not fully recognised at the time, largely because on the day after the match it was announced that Tommy Docherty would become the manager of Scotland, news that took precedence over all other football matters. It was only at the end of the season that the scale of Celtic's feat in beating Rangers three times in four weeks would become clear – and that was because of what happened to Rangers.

As Willie Waddell feared, this league setback meant a poor time ahead for his side but teed up Celtic for a good run, in which their main challengers were Aberdeen. After beating Rangers 2–1 with a last-minute goal by Jim Brogan in the Ne'erday Derby, Celtic coasted home to win the league by ten points. It was the club's seventh title in a row, a new Scottish record, beating that set by the Celts themselves from 1904–05 to 1909–10.

A stunning 6–1 defeat of Hibs in the Scottish Cup final, in which Dixie Deans scored a hat-trick, brought up the Double. Deans's feat at least made up for the European Cup semi-final in which his miss during a penalty shootout cost Celtic a place in the final. As for the other part of the domestic Treble, it must remain unmentioned, as the words 'Partick Thistle' and 'four' still cause nightmares for those of us who were at Hampden on that fateful October day.

In a fine game marred by post-match trouble, Rangers ended season 1971–72 by winning the European Cup-Winner's Cup final, beating Dynamo Moscow 3–2 in Barcelona in May to lift their first, and so far only, European trophy. It was a terrific achievement by Rangers less than seventeen months after the Ibrox Disaster, yet, while they could triumph in Europe, they had been 'greenwashed' by Celtic, losing all four matches to the Parkhead side.

Bobby Lennox said, 'It was very unusual to win four matches in a season against any team in those days because there were only two league games between teams. So to win all four against Rangers was really something, especially since three of the matches were at Ibrox.

'Because they play four times a season nowadays and can often meet in a cup match, the teams know each other pretty well, so while every Old Firm match will always be exciting and important, I don't think they are as good games of football as they were in our day.'

That record of four wins in a season against Rangers would stand for three decades, and when you consider that the Celts won the Double, reached the League Cup final and went out of the European Cup only on a penalty shoot-out in the semi-final, a fair case can be made that the blend created by Stein for that season was one of the all-time great Celtic sides.

As Jimmy Johnstone said in 2002, 'When you think that Rangers won the Cup-Winners' Cup but couldn't get a point off us, it makes you realise what a great team we had at that time.'

Yet, after a fantastic start, with a European Cup-final appearance and successive Doubles, the 1970s became an inconsistent time for Celtic. In terms of quality, probably the best performance by Celtic in an Old Firm match that decade came the following season on 16 September at Hampden Park – Parkhead was being renovated – when the Celts strolled to a 3–1 victory in the league, the scorers being Kenny Dalglish, Jimmy Johnstone and Lou Macari. Though Rangers would take revenge in that season's Scottish Cup final and Hibs would beat Celtic 2–1 in the League Cup final, by then Stein had established the basis of the side that would take Celtic into the mid 1970s, completing the world-record nine titles in a row in season 1973–74 and also winning the Double that year. There followed two seasons in which Celtic finished second and third in the ten-team Premier Division, which had been formed in

1975 after the rest of the old First Division got tired of the Bhoys winning it every year.

Celtic did win the Scottish Cup in 1975, and, inspired by Dalglish, and with Jock Stein back in charge after a near-fatal car accident, they won the Double in 1976–77, with the Cup gained by beating Rangers in the final, Andy Lynch scoring the only goal of that game from the penalty spot.

When Dalglish was sold to Liverpool in August 1977, for a British-record fee of £440,000, Celtic combusted. They slumped to fifth in the Premier Division, a full 19 points behind champions Rangers, who also won the Scottish Cup and the Scottish League Cup for Jock Wallace's second Treble, beating Celtic 2–1 after extra time in the final of the latter tournament.

Recognising that his time in charge was over, Stein temporarily agreed to be kicked 'upstairs' and run the Celtic Pools. He had no intention of quitting football management, however, and left soon afterwards for 44 days at Leeds United, which followed Brian Clough's bizarre spell there. Stein then succeeded Ally MacLeod as manager of Scotland.

Jock Stein had moved on because the board wanted to bring Billy McNeill back as manager. McNeill had cut his managerial teeth at Clyde and Aberdeen, whom he took to the Scottish Cup final in 1978, where they lost 1–2 to Rangers. The clamour for him to come to Parkhead was overwhelming, but he had mostly raw young talent to work with and the side looked potentially underpowered.

But on one glorious unforgettable night at the tail end of the 1970s, Celtic found the power and took the glory.

12

NIGHT OF NIGHTS

21 MAY 1979
SCOTTISH LEAGUE PREMIER DIVISION
CELTIC 4, RANGERS 2

There have been many fabulous nights at Celtic Park, and there have also been a few memorable days when Celtic have beaten Rangers to ensure that they won the league title. On only one occasion, however, has the Scottish League championship been won by Celtic beating the only other possible winners, Rangers, on a Monday evening in a match played at Parkhead.

The manner of the victory and the sheer drama of the occasion have ensured that this match has lived long in the memory of all of us who were there. It was simply the most exciting football match this author has ever attended and one of the most courageous victories in the long history of Celtic FC.

The reasons it was so sensational are numerous, but chief among them was the knowledge beforehand that Celtic required victory to win the Scottish League Premier Division. Any other result would allow Rangers to overtake Celtic and win the title themselves. A fixture backlog meant the Ibrox side still had two matches to play after the Old Firm derby, against Partick Thistle and Hibs. Their fans filled the Rangers end at Parkhead in anticipation of getting the result that would end Celtic's challenge and put them in pole position to surely win the title.

The decisive nature of the match had been caused by a dreadful winter. In those days, when compulsory undersoil heating was some distance in the future, frozen pitches meant that Celtic did not play a league fixture for ten weeks. They endured a dismal December in which they drew two league matches and lost to Rangers after extra time in the League Cup semi-final, a defeat that meant they would miss the final of that competition for the first time in fifteen years. After defeat by Morton at Cappielow two days before Christmas, Celtic did play a couple of Scottish Cup matches and flew to Estoril in Portugal to play a friendly against the local side, but there was no league action home or away until the Celts beat Aberdeen on 3 March at Parkhead.

The following week, Celtic promptly lost their Scottish Cup quarter-final to the same team after a replay, but the truth was that the winter-enforced break from the league had done Celtic some good, because they began to recover their form and reel in the league leaders, Dundee United.

For Rangers, the pile-up of fixtures was even worse. After missing much of January and February, in March they were still involved in the European Cup quarter-finals and League Cup, but the real damage to their schedule was caused by the Scottish Cup, where they needed a replay to beat Partick Thistle in the semi-final. By the time they came to Celtic Park on 21 May, they had already played the Scottish Cup final and a replay against Hibs, both of them goalless draws. Much controversy surrounded the fact that their second replay was put off until 28 May and their final two matches against Partick Thistle were scheduled for 23 and 31 May, well beyond the original completion date for the league. It all meant that, when they arrived at Parkhead on 21 May, Rangers could clinch the league and Cup in the space of a week.

Throw in the fact that the entire Home International Championship was being played from 19 to 26 May, ending at Wembley on the latter date, and you had fixture chaos that exasperated fans wanting to support both their team and Scotland. Not that the Old Firm players were involved: the records show that in season 1978–79 not a single player from Celtic or Rangers actually took the field for Scotland. The 'Anglo' regiment was just so much better, as Scotland manager Jock Stein had a squad that consisted of names like Kenny Dalglish, Graeme Souness, John Wark, Gordon McQueen, George Burley, Joe Jordan, Asa Hartford, Alan Hansen, Frank Gray, Andy Gray and John Robertson. Indeed, the only player from a Scottish club to feature regularly in that season's internationals was goalkeeper Alan Rough of Partick Thistle.

Danny McGrain, it should be said, was ruled out only by a long-term injury, or else he would have walked into the Scotland team – indeed, any team anywhere in the world, as he was recognised as the best right-back on the planet. He had missed out on the Scottish debacle in the 1978 World Cup in Argentina, events that cast a shadow over football in the country the following season, not least in the marked reduction in attendances – though this may also have had a lot to do with the deteriorating circumstances of the nation's economy.

Neither half of the Old Firm was anywhere near its best for most of that season. Rangers had won the domestic Treble in 1977–78 but had lost their manager, the late Jock Wallace, in circumstances that have never been explained. The new manager of Rangers was former club captain John Greig, and under him Rangers stuttered at first but later performed satisfactorily in the early part of his stewardship. Like Celtic, they were certainly not invincible and had already lost seven and drawn nine of the thirty-four league matches they had played before the crunch match, compared with Celtic's nine losses and six draws from thirty-five games. Nor was either side scoring freely, with Celtic notching 57 goals in those 35 games, while Rangers had scored just 48 in their 34 matches.

The Celtic fans' worries centred on the relative youth and inexperience of the Celts compared with the battle-hardened Rangers. In Billy McNeill, Celtic also had a relatively inexperienced manager in his first season in charge at Parkhead, though he was already a living legend of the club by then. The Fates had conspired to ensure that McNeill would face his old friend and footballing adversary Greig in their first season in charge of the Old Firm. It was just another intriguing aspect of that match in May 1979.

The league had been topsy-turvy even before the cold weather wrought its havoc. With players like Tom McAdam, Ronnie Glavin, Alfie Conn and George McCluskey in good form, Celtic had begun the season very well, and the first Old Firm match of the season saw the Celts triumph 3–1 at Parkhead. It looked a smooth run to the title.

Much was made in the press of the youngsters McNeill was bringing through, such as Roy Aitken and Tommy Burns. But the manager knew the team was not good enough, and he asked the board for money to strengthen the squad. The team promptly proved his fears by losing to Hibs, Aberdeen – a shocking 1–4 reverse – Dundee United, Hearts and Motherwell, with wins over only Partick Thistle and St Mirren and a draw with Morton to lighten the autumnal gloom. Rangers were just as bad, however, not winning a league match until the last Saturday in September. They improved steadily and produced excellent performances to despatch PSV Eindhoven and Juventus from the European Cup, but when the Old Firm met on 11 November, sharing the points in a 1–1 draw, both teams' claims to league supremacy looked fragile. Under manager Jim McLean, Dundee United had achieved their highest-ever league placing by coming third the previous season, and in December, with Celtic in poor form, United beat Rangers 3–0 and seemed a good bet to win their first league championship.

Then came that harsh winter. By the time they played their final match of the league season, on 5 May, Dundee United sat proudly atop the Premier Division, with 44 points from their 36 matches. It had been an impressive performance by the Taysiders, who had David Narey, Paul Hegarty and Paul Sturrock all in terrific form. But, with so many postponed matches still to play, both Celtic and Rangers could still overhaul United, and for the Parkhead faithful it seemed that an impossible dream might yet be realised.

Back in the previous autumn, McNeill had signed two fine young players, Davie Provan from Kilmarnock and Murdo MacLeod from Dumbarton. Provan was a tricky outside-right, and MacLeod was a left-footed player with a thunderous shot and deceptive pace – he won the sprint race at Balloch Highland Games – who could play in a variety of positions.

MacLeod in particular was thrown in at the deep end. He recalled, 'I was signed on the Thursday, had my first training session on the Friday and played against Motherwell on the Saturday.

'My second game for Celtic was the Old Firm derby against Rangers. It was played at Hampden, as Ibrox was in the middle of being rebuilt. We drew 1–1, and I supplied the pass for Andy Lynch's goal.

'It's no wonder that playing against the other half of the Old Firm was the highlight of the season for me. It was always a massive game, and, unlike other matches, there was never a let-up on the noise in the stadium throughout the whole 90 minutes.'

The addition of two men who would become club legends meant that Celtic emerged from the deep freeze with a balanced look for the first time that season. East Glasgow's most popular Englishman,

Peter Latchford, was solid in goal, while Danny McGrain, who had missed the first half of the season, with Joe Filippi taking his place, had fully recovered from injury over the winter period and came back as captain.

McGrain was a diabetic who had suffered some serious injuries in his career. At various times he had sustained a fractured skull, a broken jaw, a leg fracture and an ankle injury that kept him out of the first team for more than a year. His return as captain was timely for both Celtic and Scotland – he won sixty-two caps and captained his country ten times.

McGrain and the cultured Andy Lynch were attacking from full-back, while Iceland's best export, Johannes Edvaldsson, kept things solid in defence and was also a useful threat at corners.

'Big Shuggie', as Edvaldsson was universally known, could be a bit slapdash, but he was a good header of the ball and had started out at the club as a striker. Shuggie later formed a partnership in central defence, firstly with Celtic's own Highlander, Roddie MacDonald, and then with Tom McAdam, who was similar to Edvaldsson in that he had started the season as a striker. McAdam had lost his place, and in a moment of managerial inspiration McNeill selected him at centre-half for the last few games of the season. He continued as a defender for the rest of his career.

Young, fit, determined and more skilful than he was often given credit for, Roy Aitken was the powerhouse in midfield, the only man to play all 36 league matches that season. Making his opponents seem like carthorses, Tommy Burns was a Rolls-Royce of a player on the left, where MacLeod fitted in either at half-back or in the old inside-left position. Up front, McNeill could use Provan, George McCluskey, Michael Conroy and Johnny Doyle, and the loss of Alfie Conn, injured against Aberdeen in March, was not felt too severely.

McCluskey was enigmatic, remembered perhaps more for the quality than for the quantity of his goals. The wholehearted Conroy was the son of Mike – who had played for Celtic in the 1950s – and was a versatile player who featured mostly in midfield but often played further forward and even filled in at centre-half.

Johnny Doyle was, well, Johnny Doyle, a complete one-off but probably the closest imitation of Jimmy Johnstone that you could imagine, even hailing from Viewpark, Uddingston, the home village of Jinky. Signed for a club-record £90,000 in 1976 by Jock Stein,

Doyle came to Parkhead from Ayr United, where he had won a Scotland cap. Doyle was also slight of frame and, though not red-haired like Johnstone, had the fiery temperament that Jinky had often displayed – Doyle, too, was a regular in front of the beaks at the SFA. Blessed with a burst of pace, Doyle could play on either wing or in the centre, and on his game he was inspirational, never giving less than 100 per cent for the club that he supported all his life.

Very much in the veteran stage, Bobby Lennox was brought back by McNeill to Parkhead from the US, where he had gone to play for the Houston Hurricanes side in the North American Soccer League. Used sparingly, Lennox made a total of 14 appearances that season and scored some vital goals, none more so than the double he notched against Motherwell on St Patrick's Day, a match in which it was crucial for Celtic to perform, as they had just been eliminated from the Scottish Cup by Aberdeen after a midweek replay. It still looked like an impossible task to win the title, but at least Celtic were in with a chance and the victories began to roll in, albeit most of them narrow.

Celtic's problem was that none of the strikers was in scintillating form, but that drawback was solved by goals being scored by a variety of players: joint top-scorers for the season with just seven goals each were Tom McAdam, who scored all of his before the end of November and then became a defender, and penalty-taker Andy Lynch. No fewer than sixteen players scored for Celtic that season, and even Danny McGrain made a vital contribution, with three goals.

By the time it came to the third Old Firm match of the league season, on Saturday, 5 May, Celtic knew that a win at Ibrox would give them what might be a decisive advantage over their rivals.

Rangers were also going well and had won the Scottish League Cup in March, beating Aberdeen 2–1. Some of their more excitable fans, including those with typewriters, had mentioned a Quadruple earlier in the year, but FC Cologne ended that hope in the European Cup quarter-finals.

That third Old Firm match was played at Hampden because Rangers were building the Copland Road Stand and needed the extra capacity in Mount Florida for Celtic matches. Rangers knew the domestic Treble was well within their grasp, having already qualified for the Scottish Cup final against Hibs, who were enjoying a good season under manager Eddie Turnbull.

The game was as tense as any Old Firm match, and only Davie Cooper really stood out individually. A single goal scored after 57 minutes by Alex MacDonald decided the issue. Try as they might, the Celts could not gain the equaliser, though Johnny Doyle came very close with an effort that hit the post. At 4.50 p.m., it was very much advantage Rangers, because each of the two sides now had four matches left to play. Rangers had 41 points, while Celtic had just 40, with Dundee United having finished on 44. At least McNeill now knew the totality of the task they faced: if they won all four matches, including the remaining fixture against Rangers, Celtic would win the championship. Slip up anywhere and the title would almost certainly be heading for Ibrox.

Two days later, both halves of the Old Firm were in action again, Rangers comfortably beating Aberdeen 2–0. At Firhill, Partick Thistle gave Celtic an early fright, Doug Somner scoring in the third minute. Now McNeill's youngsters had to show real character, coming from behind to win 2–1, with goals from Provan and McCluskey.

The dream was still alive, and on Friday, 11 May, Ibrox Stadium – Love Street was also being redeveloped – was packed with Celtic fans who had to endure a barren first half against St Mirren before McCluskey put them ahead after 68 minutes. It was still a nervous Celtic contingent until Bobby Lennox popped up to score the second ten minutes from time.

Rangers were now having problems of their own. The Scottish Cup final was a drab 0–0 affair, and in those days there were no penalty deciders. The two sides would have to meet again, and the date for that replay had already been marked down as Wednesday, 16 May. Had they not drawn, Rangers could have squeezed in one of their remaining three fixtures, but in the meantime Celtic had to face Hearts.

On the night of Monday, 14 May, at Parkhead, Celtic were strong favourites to beat Hearts, who were about to be relegated, having failed to gain a single point since the first weekend in April. The men from Edinburgh were never going to lie down to Celtic, however, and packed their defence. With Davie Provan running amok on the right, it was a tale of missed chances until the 55th minute, when Provan laid one on the head of Doyle to knock it on to Mike Conroy, who evaded his markers to head home.

The final whistle came with no further score, and scenes of unconfined joy broke out in the stand and on the terraces. The single-goal victory made the arithmetic clear: gain both points against Rangers the following Monday and the league flag would be back at Parkhead. The once impossible was now possible.

There was a lot happening that May. Britain had a new prime minister, Mrs Margaret Thatcher, the first, and so far only, woman to hold the office, and already she and her team of ministers were cracking their whips. Even in her earliest pronouncements, Mrs Thatcher was saying things that grated with many Scots, who, as no one needed reminding, had not voted Tory. This was also a Britain in which the Austin Allegro was the best-selling car, which just proves that in the late 1970s there was no accounting for popular taste.

Celtic had gained their pole position in the league by winning 13 of their previous 17 matches, but all of that tremendous effort would count for nothing if they could not beat Rangers. It was no wonder that the Celtic majority in the 52,000-strong crowd felt a mixture of anticipation and worry as they approached Parkhead that balmy May evening.

Almost all of them had purchased tickets for the match that had originally been scheduled for the beginning of January and were now taking up their right to attend. But there was also a national drivers' strike, which affected public and private buses, and that definitely hindered access to Parkhead. For whatever reason, some unlucky people were unable to make it, more than five months after the scheduled date, and had to return their tickets. Those of us with good friends able to lay their hands on returned tickets will be forever grateful they could not turn up.

Those who were inside Celtic Park would be the only ones to see the match, as a technicians' strike at Scottish Television, who had the rights to show the highlights, meant that the cameras stayed switched off. There was no radio commentary either, so we must rely on memory and the highly accurate reporting of the match by the Scottish press, who, of course, went completely over the top in their accounts. For once, however, they were fully entitled to do so, as this really was one of the all-time great Old Firm matches – especially if you were a Celtic fan.

For Rangers, there was a familiar line-up: McCloy; Jardine and Dawson; Johnstone, Jackson and MacDonald; McLean, Russell, Parlane, Smith and Cooper.

In the absence of Tommy Burns through injury, McNeill was sure about his best team and picked Peter Latchford in goal;

Danny McGrain and Andy Lynch as the attacking full-backs; Tom McAdam and Johannes Edvaldsson in the middle of defence; Roy Aitken in central midfield, with Mike Conroy and Murdo MacLeod on either side of him; and Davie Provan, George McCluskey and Johnny Doyle up front. On the bench were Vic Davidson and Bobby Lennox, the latter being not a bad impact substitute to bring on if needed.

Three youngsters would be asked to do the most vital jobs on the evening: Conroy, MacLeod and Aitken were to play linking roles in midfield, covering back when required yet also getting up in support of the strikers, with Conroy in particular asked to play a more defensive role. The key battle was in midfield, where Aitken in particular was asked to dominate. It was a good set of tactics but would last only 55 minutes, for reasons that will become obvious.

'We all knew before the match that we just had to win it,' said Bobby Lennox. 'There was nothing else in our minds.'

In bright daylight, the pre-match preliminaries passed in a blur, the two sets of spectators cheering and roaring off the end of the decibel scale. After referee Eddie Pringle of Edinburgh blew his whistle for the start, the game was also a blur – it wasn't hundred-miles-per-hour stuff; it seemed much faster than that.

It was the Rangers goal that came under pressure first, and big Peter McCloy, 'the Girvan Lighthouse', had to look lively to smack away a header from McCluskey with the spectators barely settled. Aitken was already on the charge, and his early shot was well seen by McCloy, who dealt with it comfortably. There were occasional signs of early nerves, but these were settled for both sides when Rangers went ahead after ten minutes.

Ask most Celtic fans which Rangers player they most disliked at that time and Alex MacDonald would probably have been the answer. The general feeling was that the short but tough midfielder kept his best performances for Celtic matches, and, though he was never of the highest class as a player, there was perhaps grudging admiration for a hard worker who gave his all for Rangers. That he should open the scoring was probably the Celtic crowd's worst nightmare.

It was a well-worked goal, too. Davie Cooper made it with one of those clever runs of his when he just glided by players before sending in a cross that MacDonald, in space, gleefully despatched behind Latchford. Ten minutes gone, one down and the dream dying

– but this is Celtic, don't forget, the club that, perhaps more than any other, is the expression of the collective will of a community, and on that night those Celtic people wanted victory or, at the very least, a response to make them proud of the team.

They got it. Curiously, Celtic's first goal seemed to lull Rangers momentarily, and they organised themselves defensively in traditional manner, but Celtic now realised that they had a massive job to do to score at least two goals, and it was time to get on with it. There was no allowance for nerves now – it was time for 'the Celtic way'.

With whirlwind movement, the ball pinged across the pitch to Aitken and MacLeod, to Provan and Doyle, and the midfield and the two wingers began to press insistently. Most noticeably, they were not giving the Rangers players any time on the ball, and less than five minutes after MacDonald's goal McCluskey broke down the right and sent in a shot that McCloy turned away.

By now the Celtic crowd were in one soaring voice in support of the team, and the players responded, chasing every ball, closing down every man, trying everything to get play into the danger area, where McCloy and Jackson were the main stalwarts for Rangers. With all the Celts now committed to attack, Andy Lynch came forward and sent in a header that looked to be floating into the top corner until McCloy just managed to touch it over the bar.

There was some respite for Rangers with corners that came to nothing, and the men in blue seemed content to block rather than probe, which they did well. Perhaps it was a sign of frustration at the failure to get level, but after 25 minutes Aitken tackled Derek Johnstone high and was booked by referee Pringle. The caution did not hinder Aitken, who thundered forward a few minutes later when Gordon Smith conceded a free kick by fouling Doyle. Provan's kick was met with full force by the head of Aitken, but the ball came back off the intersection of the post and bar, and, maddeningly for the Celtic fans, the ball broke to a blue shirt and was cleared.

With the pace having slackened not one jot, and with Celtic now pouring it on, it seemed as though a goal would inevitably come. It nearly did – for Rangers. A Derek Parlane shot deflected off Edvaldsson and hit Latchford, who knew little about what had happened but claimed credit for the save anyway. And when a Jackson header was cleared off the line as the half-time whistle approached, it seemed as though Celtic had expended all that effort and been in charge for much of the half, only for Rangers to take the spoils.

At half-time, the manager did not mention legends or past greats. According to Murdo MacLeod, the manager concentrated on the present. MacLeod said, 'In his half-time team talk he basically asked us what we wanted for ourselves out of the game.

'We had to win the match, or there would be no title for us, so it was time to look inside ourselves and see what we had to give for Celtic.'

It was effective psychology, and the Celtic team emerged from the tunnel looking very charged up. They were well aware that they needed to score at least twice and threw everything into attack. Ten minutes into the second half came the incident that changed the course of the match and Old Firm history and gave the Celtic fans a song they chanted for years afterwards. Conroy felled Alex MacDonald, and there were plenty in the crowd who felt the Rangers man was making a time-wasting meal of lying on the ground, seeking medical attention, as a melee of players crowded rounded Eddie Pringle. Behind them, the tempestuous Johnny Doyle went to MacDonald, leaned over him and uttered words that were certainly not a 'get well' message as the incensed Celt also directed his boot at the prone Ranger. Some blinkered Celtic fans have since claimed that Doyle made no contact – oh, yes, he did, as he quietly admitted later. MacDonald reacted with incredulity. So did the rest of the players and the crowd.

The incident was sensed rather than seen by the referee, but the linesman could not miss the sly kick, nor could anyone in the main stand. Pringle consulted his linesman briefly and had no option but to send off Doyle. There was almost a communal groan among the Celtic fans, a shaking of heads at a moment of madness that was surely going to cost Celtic the league title.

In that moment, Celtic's history of being triumphant underdogs seemed to imbue the whole team and the support. In what may well have been the finest moment of his managerial career, 'Caesar' McNeill reordered his legions so that McCluskey was left up front. Provan was told to switch inside from the right wing, while MacLeod began an exhausting shift to cover almost three positions on the left. All over the pitch his players could be seen taking McNeill's lead and exhorting each other, and ten Celtic men responded as never before.

They somehow found new reserves of energy and renewed the

onslaught, so much so that Rangers resorted to illegal tactics to stop them, the names of Jardine and Parlane going into the referee's book. Surely they would hold out against a diminished side, however. Just sixteen days previously, Celtic had not been able to force a draw with eleven men on the pitch – how would they come back from a goal down and win with ten?

All thought of holding back was gone. Aitken and MacLeod pushed forward and cut inside, which allowed McGrain and Lynch to join the attack down the wings. Provan was drifting from side to side and looked more and more likely to be the main danger to Rangers, and so it proved after 66 minutes when the winger picked up a through ball from McCluskey and cut in from the left. Roy Aitken came barrelling up from midfield screaming for the ball, and Provan got to the byline and cut the ball back into space, where Aitken showed mature composure to control the ball with his right peg and dink it behind McCloy with his left foot. The Celts were level, and two-thirds of Parkhead erupted.

Danny McGrain said, 'We had been thinking that with a goal down and only ten men we could be stuffed, but this was Parkhead, and, as usual, the supporters pulled us through, and the fact that we scored so quickly after Johnny was sent off was a big help, too.'

The cheers rang out for a Celtic hero as McNeill replaced the tiring Mike Conroy with none other than Bobby Lennox. The fans took it as an omen – the Buzz Bomb was coming on to blow away the Rangers.

'I can't remember anything other than the excitement of waiting to go on,' said Lennox. 'It was as excited as I have ever been. The noise was just unbelievable, and, to be honest, the memory of the rest of the game is a blur, and we can't even check the television pictures to see what happened because there weren't any.'

At the same time, John Greig replaced Tommy McLean with Alex Miller, and it was the Rangers man who almost made a dream start, picking up a Cooper pass and shooting just wide in his first involvement in the game.

With dusk falling, Celtic's pace did not let up, and in the 74th minute Aitken let fly from the edge of the box. It was a poor effort that fortunately fell to George McCluskey, who whirled and fired the ball high into the net from 12 yards out. Now there was just total euphoria for those in green and white. The title was coming to Parkhead, they were sure of it.

Rangers thought otherwise, and two minutes later they had drawn level, which meant the championship was once again theirs to win. From a Cooper corner on the Rangers left wing Edvaldsson rose to head clear, but the ball fell directly to Robert Russell, and from an acute angle on the right side of the box the youngster struck a low shot that somehow found its way through all the bodies in the area to nestle in the Celtic goal.

'That's my main memory of the game,' said Danny McGrain. 'I was covering the right-hand post, and after the corner came in I saw the ball going out to Bobby Russell. I really thought his shot was going to go by the post, and I left it, but the ball went in off the inside of the post. I was just stunned, couldn't believe it.'

Instead of a quietened crowd and heads going down, Celtic's passion rose again. The team, the management, the fans simply were not going to be beaten, yet it looked as though luck was not going to be with Celtic as Aitken flashed in a header that McCloy saved quite brilliantly.

There were just five minutes left to play when Aitken took the ball off Miller's feet, ran forward and drew the defence before slipping the ball to McCluskey on the right side of the box. His control did not let him down as he dashed outside two defenders and sent in a fierce shot across goal that McCloy yet again managed to parry. This time, for once, the luck was with Celtic as the ball flew from McCloy's right hand straight at the face of Colin Jackson, standing three or four yards out. 'The Bomber' instinctively tried to head the ball away but watched in disbelief as it fell limply into the net for an own goal. McCloy looked up at his big mate and shook his head while utter bedlam broke out among the Celtic contingent. As soon as a semblance of sanity was restored, there came the realisation that Rangers had come back to equalise before, hence the shouts of 'Blow your whistle referee!' even though there was still three or four minutes to play. Rangers indeed showed they were not finished by forcing a corner that was cleared with no little trouble.

In truth, it would have been unfair on Jackson and McCloy, arguably Rangers' two best players of the season, for them to have unwittingly concocted an own goal that would send the flag to Parkhead – not that the Celtic fans cared at that point. Yet, on a night of almost theatrical drama, it seemed less than appropriate that such a scrambled effort should decide the outcome, and Celtic then conjured up a sumptuous goal that proved an utterly fitting way to bring down the curtain on a match of incredible excitement.

Inside the final minute, with Rangers pressing, McAdam cleared to halfway, where McCluskey controlled the ball and set off for goal with MacLeod racing down the left and Danny McGrain showing incredible energy to get up in support from right-back. The exhausted Rangers defenders seemed to hang back, as McCluskey had plenty time to pick out his pass to Murdo MacLeod, who had come belting up on his left. The youngster had several choices – Provan had gone wide on the left, and McGrain was now in the clear on the right side of the box – but from around the stadium, and especially from the Celtic dugout, came the shouts of 'Hit it!' MacLeod was not always the most accurate of shooters in his early days, and the Celtic reasoning was simple: even if he missed by a mile, it would waste the necessary seconds as the ball was retrieved.

The 20 year old, who was still in only his first season with the club, promptly gained a measure of Celtic immortality by controlling the ball and letting fly with his left foot from 23 yards out on the left side of the pitch. It was a howitzer, a peach, a belter, a cracker, a cannonball and every other word you can think of to describe the perfect rocket shot. McCloy, for all his height and skill, had no chance as the ball flew straight and true into the top-right hand corner. Goal! Game over! Champions!

'I distinctly remember yelling at him, "Hit it, just hit it,"' recalled Bobby Lennox. 'He didn't half hit it, did he? What a goal.'

Danny McGrain said, 'I have no memory at all of getting up on the right when George got the ball, and I've never seen any film of it, but I'm told I was there. George made the right decision to pass to Murdo because, let's face it, I wasn't the biggest goalscorer, though I had scored three that season – a real purple patch for me.

'Murdo could really hit them, and all I can remember is seeing the ball in the back of the net and thinking, "That's it."'

In its context, MacLeod's thunderbolt might well have been one of the finest goals ever scored at Celtic Park, for, while other goals have secured league titles, surely none has ever been taken with such aplomb. His detractors might say MacLeod could have hit it anywhere, but the man himself knew what he was doing, and he got it right.

MacLeod said, 'After Colin Jackson's own goal, it was all about running down time, and we were all back in defence, but then we managed to break away.

'At the moment I gathered the ball 20-odd yards from goal, I could actually hear the guys in the dugout telling me to boot it anywhere just to eat up time.

'I had time to look, and I could see Davie Provan to my left and Danny McGrain to the right, but I just looked up and aimed to put it into the top right-hand corner. Honestly, that was where I was aiming, but I knew that if I hit it with power it might end up over the bar. It just flew straight where I wanted it, and then the celebrations began.

'In the circumstances it was the most important goal of my career, and I was really honoured a few years ago when the goal was voted Celtic's best-ever goal in an Old Firm derby.'

There was barely time to restart, and when referee Pringle blew the whistle, Celtic were Scottish League champions for the 31st time. Billy McNeill had emulated his mentor Jock Stein by winning the title in his first full season in charge of Celtic, and it says much for his fellow debutant manager John Greig that he was the first to shake McNeill's hand and congratulate him.

For Danny McGrain, the comeback from a career-threatening injury was complete, 'Before the start of the season, I was told I might not play again. Now I was the captain of the champions. That was really something.'

In the Jungle and the Celtic end, the fans could barely contain their joy, while in the main stand there could be heard the popping of champagne corks – at least one party had smuggled in a bottle or two. Can't remember who ...

The Rangers fans roared their defiance and then seemed to take a communal decision to leave. On the pitch, the Celtic players and staff defied exhaustion to dance merrily while scarves cascaded onto the old blaes track around the pitch. Johnny Doyle, convinced he had cost his team the league title, had to be summoned from the dressing-room to join in. Tommy Burns, Roddie MacDonald, Joe Filippi, Vic Davidson and all the other players who had made a contribution came out also, and Billy McNeill and his men took the long and richly deserved applause.

'In the dressing-room afterwards everyone was piling in,' said Bobby Lennox. 'It was great to see all the guys like Jimmy Johnstone and the others from Lisbon and afterwards coming in to congratulate Billy and the boys. It showed how much the club still meant to them.'

Danny McGrain has only one regret about that evening: 'It

would have been nice to have been presented with a trophy to show our fans and thank them for their support. But there wasn't one that night, and because it was the last game of the season we never really got the chance to say thanks to all our fans.'

A couple of familiar Celtic chants arose from that evening. To the tune of Boney M's then recent hit 'Brown Girl in the Ring' were sung the words 'Ten Men Won the League', and the British Airways advertising slogan 'We'll take more care of you' was hijacked to become 'We've won the league again, fly the flag, fly the flag'. The latter has been used many times since, thankfully.

There was consolation to come for Rangers. The second Cup-final replay against Hibs went to extra time before Rangers finally prevailed 3–2, with the medals going to the same dozen men who had lost to Celtic.

The nature of Celtic's victory brought huge compliments from the press. Writing in the *Evening Times*, Hugh Taylor opined that Celtic had put on 'a display of fantastic football unsurpassed by any of the heroes of Parkhead past – a torrid, heart-stopping, courageous display that had everything that is superb in Scottish football'. His colleague Alan Davidson wrote, 'Celtic didn't just win the 1979 championship deservedly, they won it magnificently.'

In the *Daily Record* the day after the match, Alex Cameron summed up the events succinctly: 'There has never been a championship decider quite like this one.' That is surely true, and some of us who were there consider it to be the greatest Old Firm match of all time from a Celtic point of view, though of course we can really only judge what we see in our own lifetime. As Mike Aitken, who covered the match for the *Scotsman*, wrote 20 years after the event, 'The greatest Old Firm game of all time? Well, it was the best one I've ever seen.' The memories of it do not dim. Nearly 30 years on from that night, Roger Baillie, doyen of Scottish football writers, wrote, 'In a half-century of reporting Old Firm matches, I thought I had seen everything, but this game was simply incredible.'

There would be other games with superior scorelines in Celtic's favour, and other Old Firm matches with a better quality of football, but, on that night of nights at Parkhead, Celtic's indomitability shone forth. Ten men won the league, and yet another Celtic legend was created.

13

JUST A BOYS' GAME?

10 MAY 1980
SCOTTISH CUP FINAL
CELTIC 1, RANGERS 0

In all the tens of thousands of words that have been written about this match, it is often forgotten that it was one of the most exciting of all Old Firm games. It lacked goals, certainly, but for 120 minutes this match provided enthralling entertainment. What happened on the pitch afterwards is most remembered, of course, as events came to greatly overshadow the match and, indeed, caused Scots Law to be altered.

A lot was at stake in football terms, because for the first time in 15 years the Scottish Cup was very much a consolation to be fought over by the Old Firm, the Scottish League Championship having gone elsewhere – to Aberdeen, in fact. A great many people contend that Alex Ferguson's Aberdeen did not win the Scottish League Premier Division in 1979–80. No, they say, Celtic lost it. Poppycock and balderdash – the fact is that the league was played over 36 games, and at the end Aberdeen won by a point. Just as happened with Celtic the previous year, a long winter-enforced break allowed Aberdeen to recharge their batteries, and with Celtic faltering against north-east sides – they also lost to Dundee United and, embarrassingly, 1–5 to Dundee – the dandy Dons slowly but surely made their way to the top.

Ferguson's Aberdeen were tough, durable and skilful, containing men of the quality of Jim Leighton, Alex McLeish, Willie Miller, Stuart Kennedy, Gordon Strachan, Steve Archibald, Drew Jarvie and Mark McGhee – a wonderful collection of players by any standard. They had put Celtic out of the Scottish League Cup at the quarter-final stage, and in the closing stages of the league they won it the hard way. The Dons came to Parkhead twice in the month of April and won 2–1 and 3–1 against a Celtic side whose defence was perhaps less than solid.

Celtic's seasonal highlight had been a European Cup quarter-final against Real Madrid. The first leg was one of the greatest of all European nights at Parkhead, when Real turned out in all blue – always calculated to endear you to Celtic fans – and strutted about the pitch at first. It was a night that the 67,000 fans in Parkhead would never forget. Real had Camacho, Benito, Del Bosque, Juanito and Santillana, and that fine German player Uli Stielike. At outside-left was their first English recruit, the mercurial Laurie Cunningham, England's first black internationalist, who was to die at the tragically young age of 33 in a car crash in 1989.

Not only did he shackle Cunningham, but Celtic's young right-back, Alan Sneddon, was quite brilliant in attack on the night. He fired in a shot that Madrid goalkeeper García Remón could not hold, allowing George McCluskey to score the first, and later Sneddon sent in the cross that saw Johnny Doyle leap like a gazelle to score the second. The second leg in Madrid, however, took so much out of the Celts – not least because they went down 0–3 – that it seemed likely they would suffer in the season's climactic weeks, which they did.

Yet on the last day of the league season Celtic could still win the championship as long as they beat St Mirren at Love Street. If Celtic won, Aberdeen were required to beat Hibs at Easter Road to win the league on goal difference. If Aberdeen lost and Celtic won, the league flag would stay at Parkhead. An Aberdeen draw and Celtic would need to win by ten clear goals, such was the Dons' superior goal difference. Hibs were already doomed to relegation and were a poor lot. St Mirren were third in the league, two places ahead of Rangers, and had already beaten Celtic at home.

Celtic had a late penalty claim turned down, but otherwise the tension got to all concerned and it ended 0–0. It mattered not a whit, as Aberdeen had won convincingly, Steve Archibald and Andy Watson scoring the goals that took the title to Pittodrie for the first time since 1955, their only previous championship. Celtic dwindled badly, yes, but Aberdeen won it.

So a week later Celtic had two options: they could either let the league failure get to them or go out and stuff Rangers and win the Scottish Cup. The team had moved on from McNeill's heroic first season in charge. He had bought in Dom Sullivan early in the season, and in March Celtic signed Frank McGarvey from Liverpool for a club-record fee of £250,000.

McGarvey was an instant hit, netting the only goal of the game against Rangers shortly after arriving. Though he didn't score, he did show his ability with 'assists' in the Cup semi-final against Hibs on 12 April, when five different players scored in a 5–0 romp.

Now the vast experience of Billy McNeill came into play. Celtic having had a 4–3–3 formation for most of the season, McNeill knew he could not play the same tactics, as the Celtic manager had to cope with the loss of his entire central defence. Roddie MacDonald failed to recover from injury in time, Tom McAdam got himself suspended and the backup man for both of them, Jim Casey, suffered an ankle injury in training. So McNeill switched to a fluid 4–4–2 formation and asked Mike Conroy and Roy Aitken to drop into defence. Young Jim Duffy, later to be manager of Dundee, Hibs and other clubs, was the only other defender available but lacked the necessary experience.

With Johnny Doyle, Davie Provan and Murdo MacLeod playing much deeper in midfield, the flame-haired Tommy Burns had a more liberated role. McGarvey and George McCluskey were left up front. Captain Danny McGrain, who had been playing at left-back for a while to accommodate Alan Sneddon, did the same again – both men would play a crucial part, especially in attack.

The team as listed was Latchford; Sneddon and McGrain; Aitken, Conroy and MacLeod; Provan, Doyle, McCluskey, Burns and McGarvey. The substitutes were Bobby Lennox and Vic Davidson, just as they had been a year previously on the momentous night when Celtic beat Rangers to win the title.

'It was a good team,' said McGrain, 'that was unlucky not to win the title again, but the Cup made up for a lot.'

Alan Sneddon recalled, 'Aberdeen beat us by a point, but Rangers were well off the pace that season. We fancied our chances in the final.'

Yet the bookmakers were not convinced, as Frank McGarvey remembered: 'Rangers were the favourites because we had players like Tom McAdam and Roddie McDonald out, and then we lost

Jim Casey, but Mike Conroy came in and we practised high balls to him in training. He went on to have a fine game.'

For Rangers the team was: McCloy; Jardine and Dawson; Forsyth, Jackson and Stevens; Cooper, Russell, Johnstone, Smith and MacDonald. The latter MacDonald was young John, not Alex who had bothered Celtic so often and who had been sold to Hearts earlier in the season.

With the crowd limit reduced at the increasingly dilapidated Hampden Park, the attendance numbered just 70,000. It cost only £2 for a terracing ticket, and, as it was a very warm day, many thirsts were slaked before the start and kept on being satisfied during the match. Given what happened after the game, it is enlightening to consider the mood of Scotland at the time. The Conservative government was hugely unpopular and had just refused to stop the closure of Corpach Pulp Mill, a symbol of economic hope for the Highlands, while the TUC was planning a 'Day of Action' against all sorts of cuts. Even Britain's Olympic athletes had voted against the Tory whip, agreeing to go to the Moscow Olympics, much to Prime Minister Thatcher's fury. But Maggie herself was basking in the glory of the SAS ending the Iranian Embassy siege just five days previously, which contrasted strongly with the recent failure of the American bid to free their hostages in Iran. It was a time of conflict, so perhaps people thought 'battling' was in vogue. Or maybe they were just drunk.

There were plenty signs before and during the match of potential trouble. Outside Hampden, there were clashes at the demarcation lines, and inside the atmosphere was poisonous, pervaded with the litany of chants and songs imported from Ulster. The ending of Special Category Status for the paramilitary prisoners on 1 April had already led to protests, and Glasgow was awash with rumours of IRA and UDA activity in the city – fortunately, all massively exaggerated.

Ah, you may say, what about the football? Well, it was absolutely marvellous. Okay, neither team produced their highest quality for very long, but it was end-to-end stuff for most of the match and hugely exciting. For some reason, McNeill's tactics produced a reaction from Rangers that gave Celtic an open game, albeit with the usual tackles from hell – on both sides – and controversy galore.

Rangers almost took the lead after two minutes, Davie Cooper swirling and sending in a dipping angled shot that Latchford did well to save. At the other end, Murdo MacLeod picked up a deflection from a Sneddon shot and fired only just wide from 16 yards out.

MacLeod said, 'It was a frantic start as usual, and it could have been two or three each at half-time. I remember it was a hot day, and we were all sweltered quite quickly.'

Referee George Smith ensured the match did not descend into the sort of donnybrook that had bedevilled Old Firm matches in the previous decade. Early on, he booked Tom Forsyth for a typical cruncher, and that was the necessary warning sign that he would brook no nonsense.

George McCluskey ended a great solo run with a shot into the side netting before Frank McGarvey headed a McGrain cross just over the bar. At the other end, after 35 minutes, Derek Johnstone spurned the chance of the half, sending his shot from a deep Cooper cross skywards.

Cooper was doing much of the damage for Rangers, who perhaps relied too much on him, while Celtic had a handful of players taking responsibility, Mike Conroy coping superbly in his unexpected position, though Johnstone evaded him once before missing with a header from Sandy Jardine's cross.

Around Conroy were men intent on going forward. Burns and the impressive McCluskey set up a shooting chance for McGarvey, and, even though he struck it well, Peter McCloy got down brilliantly to parry the ball behind for a corner.

In the second half McGarvey tried an audacious chip, but McCloy pulled off a superb save, and that was largely the story of the match from then on – the two goalkeepers were kept busy but were more than equal to the tasks set them.

'Big Peter McCloy broke my heart that day,' said McGarvey. 'I could have had a couple at least, but he was in great form. So was Peter Latchford. I thought a single goal might just do the trick.'

John Greig sent on Tommy McLean for John MacDonald, and that move almost changed the outcome, McLean being much more direct, as he showed five minutes from time when sending Gordon Smith through, only for Latchford to yet again make the save. It was Davie Cooper who almost conjured a winner for Rangers, his cross being bulleted in by Colin Jackson, Roy Aitken managing to deflect the ball just wide of the post.

Despite all the great efforts of both sides and the undoubted drama they created, it was 0–0 after 90 minutes. McLeod said, 'At full-time we just tried to get as much water into us as possible because we knew another 30 minutes in that heat would be a struggle.'

No one really thought the extra half hour could possibly be as exciting as the previous hour and a half, but it was, and the end-to-end stuff just kept flowing. In the first half of extra time, Tommy McLean sent over a cross-cum-shot that deceived the Celtic defence but also seemed to con Derek Johnstone into thinking it was goalbound, as the striker left the ball alone only to see it drift harmlessly by the post. Not even the addition of Bobby Lennox for Johnny Doyle could break the deadlock.

'It was my last final for Celtic as a player,' said Lennox. 'I didn't manage to score, but I was grateful to get on and collect my last winner's medal.'

Two minutes into the second half of extra time, Frank McGarvey won a corner on Celtic's right. Davie Provan sent over a kick that Ally Dawson headed out as far as Sneddon, who returned the ball into the box on the volley. Forsyth headed the ball high and clear, and even as the ball fell to Danny McGrain, standing 25 yards from goal, the feeling among Celtic fans was 'What a pity. It's Danny, and he'll mess it up.' McGrain had not scored all season, and if his shot had carried on to its target it would have been at least a yard wide, but as it careered into the box George McCluskey instinctively stuck out his left leg. The ball veered off his shin and flew past McCloy, who had to change direction in mid-save yet still managed to get a left fingertip on it – not enough to stop the goal, however.

Danny McGrain is candid about his contribution: 'It shows how your memory plays tricks on you, because I thought I hit it on the volley from 30 yards out and it flew through the air to George. But I saw the tape recently, and I mishit the shot completely. It went down into the ground and was going well by the post – I thought it would end up a throw-in for Rangers, but thankfully George got to it.'

Frank McGarvey said, 'We saw the ball coming out from big Tam Forsyth straight to Danny, but we thought he would sclaff it because Danny always sclaffed it, and right enough he did, but George did what any good striker would do and put a leg on it.'

Despite late efforts by Rangers, it was Celtic who finished in the ascendancy and won the Scottish Cup for the 26th time. The Celts were all heroes, but Latchford, McGrain, Conroy, Provan, MacLeod and McCluskey were superhuman with their contributions, especially in extra time.

Let's now deal with the aftermath as briefly as possible, because even at the distance of 30 years it is still painful to consider.

Before receiving the trophy, the Celtic players went to salute their fans. Nothing wrong with that – it was only a lap of honour *after* the Cup had been presented that had been banned back in 1965 when Celtic players were attacked by Rangers fans. As McGrain and crew cavorted, some young Celtic fans came on to join in the fun and began taunting the Rangers fans. As Danny McGrain collected the Cup, there were still dozens of Celtic fans on the pitch.

'We didn't actually see the real trouble starting,' said McGrain, 'because we were taken into the dressing-room with the idea being that we would come out on a lap of honour for our own fans once the Rangers fans were away.'

They had not gone, however. Emerging from the other end of the ground, hundreds of enraged Rangers supporters came charging up to the Celtic contingent. The majority were in their teens, but many of the rioters were grown men in their 20s and 30s, and, judging by the injuries sustained by both sides, it certainly was not just small boys handing out punishment.

Within a minute a full-scale riot was under way, during which, quite obviously, the police backed off at first, as there were so few inside the stadium, senior officers having anticipated that any trouble would happen outside. Across the Hampden turf raged the battle, with bottles and boots the main weapons. There were many injuries and frankly disgusting scenes of mob violence that the police could not handle. Eventually a contingent of mounted police arrived, including WPC Elaine Mudie on her grey-white horse, Ballantrae. With long batons drawn and used unsparingly, they charged about the pitch and eventually restored a semblance of order. The battles continued outside, and one witness in Battlefield Road likened it to civil war, saying the street name was appropriate.

McGrain said, 'We were still in the dressing-room all this time, and then we heard there was a riot going on, but we had no idea how bad it was. We got ready and got out onto the bus straight away. It was only when we got home that we learned how bad it had been.'

Bobby Lennox said, 'I honestly had no idea what had really happened until I got home and saw the telly. I'm just glad we were not involved.'

Frank McGarvey added, 'I didn't see it. We were just ushered into the changing-room, and we stayed there until it was over. Was I shocked to see the pictures later on the telly? Not really. Glasgow was a powder keg waiting to explode back then. Different now, thank God. I have lived in Glasgow all my life. Nothing in Glasgow takes me by surprise. The amount of hatred between these fans? It was always ready to ignite.'

Some estimates had up to 9,000 people on the turf at the peak of the riot. If so, it would have made it the biggest pitched battle in Scotland since Culloden. The whole riot had been shown live on both ITV and the BBC. Lord Provost Michael Kelly, member of the Celtic dynasty that had begun with James Kelly from Renton, saw all his work to improve the image of the city crumble before his eyes. Then the politicians weighed in at national level, condemning all involved.

The recriminations were long and loud. Celtic's fans, and even the players, were blamed by the police for starting trouble, causing chairman Desmond White to defend the club. Tam Dalyell MP rounded angrily on Scottish Secretary George Younger in Parliament for repeating that slander. Another Tory minister, Alex Fletcher, wanted both sides banned from the following season's Scottish Cup. The other clubs did their sums and rejected that idea.

For the first time, however, the Scottish press in general fixed on bigotry as the real reason for the debacle. Yet few had a clue how to solve that problem. The inquests and pronouncements went on for days and weeks, with very few people pointing out the simple truth that ageing Hampden itself was not fit for purpose and that there had been far too few police in the ground. That does not excuse the rioters, but proper stewarding and policing would have made a difference.

Perspicacious types who were around at the time will know that the title of this chapter is taken from a brilliant BBC *Play for Today* written by Peter McDougall and starring Frankie Miller. Earlier in the '70s, Greenock-born McDougall had penned the extraordinary *Just Another Saturday*, the first mainstream television film to examine the culture that produced sectarian violence in Glasgow. Nauseatingly, Glasgow's great and good had queued up to condemn McDougall and the BBC for showing the city in such a poor light. On 10 May 1980, the world saw in vibrant colour that, if anything, McDougall had downplayed the widespread bitterness of the sectarian divide. Ministers, MPs, councillors and church people alike fell over themselves to condemn Old Firm bigotry in the following months, and the seed was sown that, someday, something would have to be done to tackle it. It took a long time, but yes, eventually something was done.

The main immediate result was that the Glasgow Cup final between the two sides scheduled for the Monday evening was cancelled. The Conservative government was then able to push through Parliament some clauses in the Criminal Justice Bill to ban all alcohol, and even containers that might carry alcohol, from football stadiums across Scotland. It is a fallacy often repeated that Thatcher's government rushed through the Criminal Justice Act 1980 just to ban booze from football grounds. That is simply not the case, because the Bill, being piloted by then Scottish home affairs minister Malcolm Rifkind, contained these provisions *before* Hampden as a consequence of previous drink-related football violence. What did happen was that the considerable opposition to the ban on drink evaporated overnight, and the government was able to put through tougher restrictions.

Buses taking fans to matches and even public trains that could carry fans were also made 'dry'. Now part of the Criminal Law (Consolidation) (Scotland) Act 1995, that alcohol ban still applies, except for enclosed 'corporate' or executive boxes. Despite many pleas for even a partial lifting, 30 years on the ban is still in place.

The teenagers and men on both sides who fought at Hampden were not heroes. Rather, they besmirched the game, their clubs, a city and a country. What's more, they ruined the memory of a terrific Celtic performance in an Old Firm Scottish Cup final.

There would not be another one of those until the end of the decade. A former Rangers player who lost his position at Ibrox because he couldn't do a simple marking job would help see to that.

14

THE BEAUTIFUL GAME

22 MARCH 1986
SCOTTISH LEAGUE PREMIER DIVISION
RANGERS 4, CELTIC 4

He may not have been able to stop Billy McNeill scoring in the 1969 Scottish Cup final, but Alex Ferguson proved that, in managerial terms, he would curtail the Old Firm's dominance.

Ferguson's Aberdeen had broken the Old Firm's stranglehold on the Scottish League Championship in 1979–80, and deservedly so. Many people think that Fergie's Dons then dominated Scottish football for years, along with Dundee United, but the facts rather undo that thesis.

For it was Celtic, not Aberdeen, that won the Premier Division for the next two seasons, romping home by thirteen points in 1980–81 and winning a much narrower contest the following season by two points. Yes, Aberdeen may have been second in both seasons, with Rangers in third, but in no sense were Aberdeen then the dominant team in Scottish football. Indeed, in season 1981–82 Celtic won three of the four league encounters between the teams.

Sadly, Celtic flopped in Europe right through the early 1980s, and the only domestic cup they won in that period was the Scottish League Cup of 1982–83, in which they beat Rangers 2–1 in an excellent final courtesy of a Charlie Nicholas strike and a Murdo MacLeod thunderbolt – another match considered for this book.

With Rangers struggling to keep up – their final league positions from 1980–81 were third, third, fourth, fourth, fourth and fifth successively – the Old Firm matches did not decide the destination of the title as much as they used to. The 'New Firm' of Aberdeen and Dundee United were now the 'enemy', though, of course, the Old Firm matches were always contested as keenly as ever.

The final match of season 1982–83 was a case in point. Dundee United were across the road at Dundee and knew that victory would guarantee them the title. A draw for United would mean Celtic needing to beat Rangers by three clear goals, and if United lost to their city rivals, Celtic just needed to win to take the title. In an astonishing match at Ibrox, Celtic were two down at half-time, but two penalties from Nicholas and superb goals by Frank McGarvey and Tom McAdam gave the Celts a 4–2 win. But the news was already through that Dundee United had won 2–0 and the championship was theirs by a single point.

The following month saw Billy McNeill leave to take over the managership of Manchester City, a week after Charlie Nicholas signed for Arsenal. Nicholas had become a huge hero to the Celtic fans, not least because he had a habit of scoring against Rangers, and his departure saw many condemn the board. Davie Hay and Frank Connor were the new managerial team, and they were unlucky in their first season because they came up against an Aberdeen side that was the best ever produced in that city. The Dons won the title in 1983–84 by seven points from Celtic, whom they also beat 2–1 in an epic Scottish Cup final. Roy Aitken made unwanted history as the first man ever to be sent off in a Scottish Cup final, before ten-man Celtic fought back to force extra time, losing to a Mark McGhee goal. Celtic also lost in the final of the League Cup, beaten by Rangers via a penalty in extra time.

With the likes of Paul McStay, Peter Grant, Brian McClair, Maurice Johnston and John Colquhoun now regularly in the team, and Pat Bonner finally solving the long-term problem of the goalkeeping position, the side had changed considerably from 1980 but still featured McGrain, Aitken, McAdam, Provan and MacLeod. No league title for them, though, as Aberdeen again won the league in season 1984–85 by seven points. Dundee United put Celtic out of the League Cup at the quarter-final stage, but the Celts more than got revenge with a stirring victory over United in the 100th Scottish Cup final, on 18 May 1985. Thanks to a Stuart Beedie goal, United were ahead 1–0 until the 76th minute, when Davie Provan equalised with a terrific free kick. Then Frank McGarvey scored the winner five minutes from time with a fabulous diving header.

It was regaining the championship that Celtic wanted above all, and season 1985–86 started brightly when Hearts were leading 1–0 in the first league match of the season at Tynecastle, only for Paul McStay to equalise with seconds left. It was a sign of things to come, because Hearts would be the surprise package in the league and Celtic would have to chase them all the way.

There were not too many other distractions for Celtic. Hibs put them out of the League Cup and Scottish Cup at the quarter-final stage, and in the Cup-Winners' Cup, with the Parkhead leg played behind closed doors because of the trouble during the previous season's clashes with Rapid Vienna, Celtic lost 1–3 on aggregate to their old enemies from the Stein era, Atlético Madrid.

The first leg of that tie came eight days after the death of Jock Stein, who suffered a heart attack during Scotland's World Cup qualifying match against Wales in Cardiff. The sense of loss across Scotland was palpable. The country's greatest-ever manager was mourned far and wide, and the minute's silence held for him at the following Saturday's matches at every ground in Scotland was impeccably observed. At Celtic Park, grown men could not hold back their tears and the players were visibly affected. As if in tribute, Celtic showed all their innate fighting qualities to overcome a stuffy Aberdeen, winning 2–1 with McClair's second goal two minutes from time.

The gloom over Stein's death did not disperse lightly, however, and Celtic's form slumped, with defeats in successive weeks by Dundee United, Aberdeen and Rangers. The signing of Mark McGhee from Hamburg had been a boost, but, when they came to face Rangers again in the Ne'erday Derby, Celtic had slipped to fourth in the table behind Hearts, Dundee United and Aberdeen, with Rangers in fifth. Perhaps it was the sight of blue shirts, but Celtic revived and ran out comfortable 2–0 winners, thanks to a McClair goal that followed an early strike by the underrated and highly unlucky Paul McGugan. His career was savaged by injuries, and indeed he broke a bone in his foot during that match but insisted on playing the 90 minutes.

All that good work was undone the following week when Dundee United beat Celtic 4–2 at Tannadice. On the same day, Hearts consolidated their lead by beating Motherwell away, adding to their victories over Rangers and Hibs in their previous two matches. Though they had games in hand on Hearts at the top,

Celtic's chances of winning the league looked very slim indeed. But after Hibs put them out of the Scottish Cup on 8 March, it was all they had left to go for, and Davie Hay was insistent that Celtic would fight until the arithmetic beat them.

That month saw the return to television of Scottish League football, the television companies and the league having been at loggerheads over broadcasting rights since the previous September. The cameras were switched back on in time to capture an utterly sensational end to the season. The television news earlier that year had covered the Space Shuttle Challenger disaster and the Westland Affair, which so nearly brought down Margaret Thatcher's government and certainly initiated the beginning of the long end to her premiership. The deal to build the Channel Tunnel was signed, and in Edinburgh municipal collywobbles were beginning to develop over the cost of the forthcoming summer's Commonwealth Games.

By the time Celtic came to the last Old Firm match of the season, Hearts were still six points ahead of them but had played two games more. Dundee United, in second, were much better placed to overhaul Hearts, and Aberdeen, in third, conceivably had more of an opportunity than Celtic. At that point, it was all-square between the Old Firm sides – won one, lost one, drawn one – and both were out of the Scottish Cup. The *Scotsman* was surprisingly dismissive of Celtic's chances of catching the Tynecastle side. 'Civic supremacy all that is left' said the snooty headline above Hugh Keevins's piece that stated, 'All that stops today's match resembling a contest between two extinct species is Celtic's slender hope of the championship and Rangers' need to obtain the points which will get them into next season's UEFA Cup on the strength, if that is the correct word, of finishing fifth in the Premier Division.'

It was 'red rag to a bull' stuff. Both managers, Davie Hay and Jock Wallace, were sick to the back teeth of hearing the words 'Hearts' and 'New Firm' flung at them, and Wallace was almost weirdly prophetic when he defended the match as meaningful and stated, 'People come because they know it will be a great game with chances at either end.' Little did he know how accurate his forecast would be.

By contrast, Davie Hay thought it would be a typically tight Old Firm game: 'They were nearly always close games at that time, and I didn't think this one would be any different. I certainly didn't foresee what happened.

'We were going for the title even though our chances didn't look good. We knew that we had to win, and I'm sure Rangers were motivated by the fact that they could really damage our chances, if not end them.'

Celtic's team was Bonner in goal, with Willie McStay, the brother of Paul, and 17-year-old Derek Whyte as the full-backs; Roy Aitken and Pierce O'Leary were the central defenders; Paul McStay, Murdo MacLeod and Tommy Burns were in midfield, with Brian McClair just behind Mo Johnston and young Owen Archdeacon up front, the latter charged with making the runs down the left wing that were his trademark. Rangers fielded Walker, Burns, Munro, McPherson, McKinnon, Durrant, McMinn, Russell, Fleck, Fraser and McCoist. Only Dave McPherson, Bobby Russell and Ally McCoist survived from the team that had beaten Celtic in the League Cup final less than two years previously. That there was no room in the starting XI for Davie Cooper, so often their tormentor, delighted Celtic's fans, who thought little of Rangers winger Ted McMinn.

For young Derek Whyte, the match was to become something he would never forget: 'That game was unbelievable. I'd never played in a game like it, and I doubted afterwards if I ever would again.'

To try and describe this match without using superlatives is impossible. Suffice to say it is the most entertaining 90 minutes of domestic football this author has seen in more than 45 years of watching and writing about the sport. From start to finish, the ball scooted about a soggy Ibrox pitch with some abandon, as the two teams all but tore up their defensive strategies and went hell for leather for goals.

On a cold, wet and windy day, Rangers started the match very well, with McMinn in uproarious form on the left wing and confounding the Celtic support. 'The Tin Man' on his game could open up any defence, and he gave poor Willie McStay a torrid time as Rangers had the best of the early chances. With almost his first contribution to the match, McMinn cut in from the left and fed Ian Durrant, and his clever chip set Ally McCoist free to hammer in a left-foot volley from 12 yards that Packie Bonner held at the second attempt.

McMinn was hauled down by McStay, and then two minutes later the Celtic full-back went clean through the Rangers winger with a late tackle that earned a booking from referee Davie Syme.

Rangers were on top, if not creating too many clear-cut chances, but it seemed only a matter of time before they would go ahead.

Yet, as so often happens in football, a goal came against the run of play. With 20 minutes gone and Celtic having weathered the opening storm, Paul McStay broke from midfield, evaded three challenges and fed Owen Archdeacon in space on the left wing. His cross was met on the drop by Murdo MacLeod, who uncharacteristically mishit his shot completely. It bobbled into the ground and sat up very nicely for Mo Johnston to divert the ball past Nicky Walker from ten yards out.

The mini-saga between Ted McMinn and Willie McStay now took a twist. This time it was the Rangers player who did a judo throw on McStay after he was dispossessed by the full-back. Referee Syme, even-handed as always, showed the yellow card to McMinn. McStay himself took the free kick, and it was cleared by Dave McKinnon only as far as Archdeacon, who skipped round Hugh Burns and sent in another dangerous cross. MacLeod again did not connect properly, and this time it was Brian McClair waiting to pounce. With half an hour gone, Celtic were two up, a little luckily it must be said, having scored with their first two decent chances.

It all went belly up, or rather backside down, for Willie McStay. He chased Ted McMinn into the corner, and the winger's clever flick invited McStay to do exactly what he should not have done: slide in full tilt. The Celtic player ended up flat on his back, McMinn made a meal of it and the referee had no choice but to order off McStay for a second bookable offence.

Celtic quickly reorganised, with Murdo MacLeod going to full-back at first. There was still confusion in the defence when, less than two minutes after McStay's departure, Durrant sent McCoist clear on the Rangers left and the ace poacher turned provider with a sweet cross that Cammy Fraser headed home powerfully.

Now the play went from end to end, like an 11-a-side tennis match, and at half-time it was a case of everyone in the stadium catching their breath. Davie Hay decided to try to strengthen the midfield and withdrew Owen Archdeacon and put Peter Grant on, for his battling qualities. And there was much more extraordinary drama to come, as well as a lot of quality football: neat passes, flicks and mazy dribbles were the order of the day, even on a rain-soaked pitch.

Celtic were now attacking the Broomloan Road end, where their fans were congregated. They had to wait just two minutes to see a goal right in front of them, and it was a thing of simple beauty. Mo Johnston collected the ball just inside the Rangers half and strode forward before sending a well-weighted pass straight through the somnambulant defence to Tommy Burns on the run. The midfielder almost dug his shot out of the glaur past Walker, and Celtic were two in front again.

The Celtic fans were delirious but knew that, on their own territory, Rangers would never accept defeat. They could not have anticipated such a barnstorming comeback, however. In a route-one effort after 52 minutes, Nicky Walker's wind-assisted clearance bounced over Peter Grant and into Ally McCoist's path. He needed no second invitation to turn inside past two defenders and bury his shot in the corner of Bonner's goal from 20 yards.

Rangers were now rampant, and as the ten Celts drifted suicidally upfield, Durrant almost put Rangers level with a fierce shot that Bonner brilliantly tipped past the post – so brilliantly that the referee didn't see the touch and gave a goal kick. The equaliser was delayed only a couple of minutes, however. With the rain having made the pitch very soft as the hour-mark approached, Peter Grant failed to connect properly to clear a McPherson cross. The ball almost trickled out only as far as Robert Fleck, whose quick shot deflected past Bonner. The Rangers supporters were incredulously happy, while the worried looks on the Celtic fans' faces told their own story.

Still both sets of supporters kept up their din; still the football was good and exciting, and, with Davie Cooper on for the battered and exhausted McMinn, Rangers went in search of what would surely be the winner. Though Celtic tried to attack, they were wary of pushing too far forward, and Rangers' extra-man advantage told as Fleck attacked down the right in space and Aitken was forced to thump it clear. From the throw-in, Hugh Burns forced a corner off McClair, and when the kick from Cooper arrived in the box there seemed no danger, as Bonner rose to fist the ball clear. Lurking just inside the box, however, was Dave McKinnon, who cleverly returned the clearance with a long looping header that dropped in under the crossbar, where Cammy Fraser headed it home to 'mak siccar'.

'Sick' wasn't even close to describing how the Celtic fans felt. In the space of twelve minutes, Rangers had gone from two down to leading by a goal, and surely now Celtic's slim title hopes had been banished by their old enemies.

But, like all the best Celtic teams, this XI was not for folding. A couple of half chances from Rangers came to nothing, and the best opportunity fell to Johnston, who was robbed in the act of shooting by goalscorer Fraser. That was before the 70th minute saw a denouement only a diehard Celtic fan could dream of. Mo Johnston collected the ball 35 yards out on the left wing and cut in, running diagonally across the pitch. The Rangers defence hung back as if expecting Johnston to shoot, but instead he slipped the ball to Murdo MacLeod. The midfielder controlled the ball with one touch before letting fly from fully 30 yards, the ball bending and dipping beyond Walker at his left post.

MacLeod said, 'They had scored three times in eleven minutes, and we just couldn't believe it, so to get back level was fantastic.

'But one statistic which stands out from that afternoon for me is that the first goal in the game was scored in the twentieth minute and the last of the eight came when there were still twenty minutes left, which meant that all eight goals were scored in just fifty minutes. No wonder the fans went crazy. The rain was tipping it down, but the fans were soaking up the excitement.'

It was a magnificent goal, worthy of winning the match instead of just making things equal. Both sides then had their chances to win the match, the best of which fell to McCoist. Fleck turned O'Leary and, chased by MacLeod on the Rangers' right, fired in a low cross that McCoist took first time just eight yards from goal. Packie Bonner had instantly spread himself wide, and he made a fantastic stop at point-blank range.

It would have been a travesty if Rangers had scored at that point, because the ten men of Celtic had matched them for an hour. And when the final whistle blew, something rather wonderful took place. For the first time that anyone could remember, both sets of fans stood and cheered their heroes. It was an awe-inspiring sight, as if the Old Firm was saying to the New Firm, Hearts and any other pretenders to the throne that they might take the titles, but they could never take the history.

The standing ovation went right round the ground, and even the match officials were seen to join in. The players were equally warm to their opponents in their congratulations, while Davie Hay and Jock Wallace grinned at each other because they knew they had concocted something really special.

Hay said, 'It was just a marvellous game to be involved in, both for the players and the managers. We knew during the game that it was turning into something special, and though we were disappointed not to win, obviously, the way the game had gone, with first us being in front then Rangers going ahead and then us coming back to equalise – well it was just terrific stuff, and we were happy to still be in the hunt for the title.'

MacLeod said, 'Out on the pitch we could see that, when the final whistle blew, the crowd in all four corners of the stadium just rose to the players.

'I can see it in my mind's eye now. It is a moment that still lives in my memory because it was so unique in the rivalry between the two clubs. I don't know if there has ever been anything similar in a history that stretches back over a century.'

Of course, the fans were cheering for their own team, but, for once, maybe for once, there was a realisation that the other mob had contributed to the sensational spectacle we had seen. Just for a few seconds, there was a glimpse of what it must have been like back at the beginning of the clubs' relationship, before bigotry soured everything and when the rivalry was purely sporting between the blue and the green. In the rain at Ibrox we saw the beautiful game – why couldn't it always be like this?

Derek Whyte recalled the extraordinary atmosphere among the players: 'I remember that there was a strange sort of feeling in the dressing-room afterwards. Usually after an Old Firm game like that, especially one played in that sort of weather, we'd all be knackered and dying to get into the hot bath, get changed and head home. But the adrenalin was pumping, and if the ref had come in and asked us to go out and play for a deciding goal, none of us would have refused. We could have gone another 90 minutes like that, no problem.'

Yet, even as they made their way home, the 'high' of seeing such a great match was brought down for the Celtic fans, as Hearts had beaten Hibs and moved a point further clear. That was that, everyone thought, but not Davie Hay and his men, not even when Hearts played a postponed fixture on the Tuesday against St Mirren and gained another two points.

Celtic could afford no slip-ups, and victories over Clydebank, Dundee, St Mirren, Aberdeen and Hibs followed, before Hearts dropped against Aberdeen at home. Two more victories against Dundee and Motherwell, both by 2–0 scorelines, meant that on

Saturday, 3 May Celtic would travel to St Mirren requiring an unlikely miracle. Hearts were away to Dundee but needed only a point to clinch the title. They were also four goals better off on goal difference, which meant that Hearts had to lose and Celtic had to win by four clear goals or more to win the championship of Scotland. Who cared that Rangers had signed some fancy player-manager called Graeme Souness? Celtic could still win the league, even if most of their fans' prayers were being directed to St Jude, patron saint of hopeless causes.

All Celtic fans worthy of that description know what happened that day. Celtic tore into St Mirren from the off, and two goals from Mo Johnston and one each from Brian McClair and Paul McStay meant that at half-time the requisite four goals had been achieved. Meanwhile, at Dens Park there was still no score. Nor was there any by the time Brian McClair notched his second and Celtic's fifth. There was nothing more to do than see out the 90 minutes and hope for a miracle.

It is often forgotten that Dundee had something to play for that day – if they won and Rangers did not, Dundee would make the UEFA Cup, with the cash boost that would bring their club. Manager Archie Knox, who would be Walter Smith's assistant at Rangers within a few years, badly wanted that win and sent on local boy Albert Kidd, a Celtic fan, in place of future Celtic and Hearts player Tosh McKinlay. Kidd had not scored all season, but with seven minutes left on the clock he banged in one from close range after Hearts failed to clear a corner. As their shell-shocked fans gaped in utter disbelief, the Hearts defence went to sleep as Kidd played a neat one-two through their middle and shot home to send the Tynecastle club into despair and Celtic fans everywhere into utter ecstasy.

It was a cruel way for Hearts' season to end, and the fact is that Dundee did not even make it into Europe, as Rangers beat Motherwell to earn the fifth place. But Celtic had suffered perhaps similar, though not quite as horrendous, late disappointments before that season and have certainly done so since. The league is always won and lost over the season, and Celtic's run of 16 matches unbeaten in the league from January is what gave them the title. That and some help from a man called Kidd.

15

See You in Court

This match was no classic of skill and grace. On the contrary, it was eye-wateringly tough stuff. Nor was it totally decisive in a tournament. It featured Rangers scraping a last-minute draw against the Celts, so why is it one of the 20 greatest Old Firm matches from a Celtic standpoint? The reason is that it was one of the most important matches in Scottish football history, and even though the points were shared, and indeed Celtic threw away victory, it was one of Celtic's most momentous draws, temporarily halting a developing juggernaut at Ibrox and sparking off a truly memorable season for the grand old team.

It has gone down in history as the Battle of Ibrox, though that is a gross exaggeration – more like Handbags in Govan, actually. Celtic did not perform at their best, yet, with hindsight, it can be seen as a crucial turning point following the arrival of Graeme Souness at the helm of Rangers. With chairman David Holmes supporting him, and owner Lawrence Marlborough prepared to spend, Souness had brought in a coterie of top English players almost as soon as he had arrived at Ibrox. It paid an immediate dividend, as Terry Butcher, Graham Roberts and Chris Woods played vital roles in Rangers winning the Premier Division and the Scottish League Cup in season 1986–87. Mark Falco, Jimmy Phillips and Trevor Francis, plus Souness's old Liverpool colleague Avi Cohen of Maccabi Tel Aviv in Israel, joined the band from furth of these borders at Ibrox in time for the following season. The usual mould of Scottish football – players from here going down there for more money – was broken, and for good or ill the game in Scotland would never be the same again.

The arrival of Souness and his English brigade meant the end of Davie Hay's managership of Celtic, which took place in ignominious circumstances at the end of season 1986–87. The board well appreciated the significance of the centenary season and were desperate for success. They turned to Billy McNeill to take the managerial reins again after his spell of mixed fortunes down south. Yet how could McNeill build a team to deal with Rangers when he had a fraction of their budget?

The club had also lost fine players, especially Davie Provan, who was forced into premature retirement after contracting myalgic encephalomyelitis (ME), and Murdo MacLeod, who signed for German club Borussia Dortmund. The best Celt of the era, Danny McGrain, was 37 when he left for Hamilton Accies, though he later returned to Celtic as assistant reserve-team coach.

The Ibrox side seemed to have all the aces. Roberts and Butcher were big men and tough as nails, somewhat in the mould of Souness himself, who was suffering more and more from injury as his stellar career was winding down. Yet as a manager he was proving competent, if a little headstrong and with no regard for the rules about not criticising referees. It was Souness's ability to bite in tackles and bark at referees that provided the controversial background to this explosive match in October 1987.

Two incidents involving Souness in the first Old Firm match of the season foreshadowed the second encounter. On 29 August Celtic had played magnificently for much of a game that they had led by a single goal from Billy Stark early in the match. As Rangers tried to gain an equaliser, Souness scythed down Stark, and, having been booked earlier, he did not even wait until referee Davie Syme produced the red card to stalk up the tunnel in a fury. It was his third sending off in a year.

At the final whistle the Celts had won by that single Stark goal, and Graham Roberts pointedly refused to shake hands with the Celtic players, while Souness and McNeill had what might diplomatically be called an exchange of views in the tunnel. His anger having increased while sitting in the dressing-room, Souness sought out Syme after the match and lambasted him in language that proved the player-manager had a good command of basic Anglo-Saxon. The SFA duly hauled in Souness, gave him two more red cards for his post-match behaviour and suspended him for five matches, during which time Souness had to be persuaded by his chairman, Holmes, not to walk out on the club – it is tempting to think what might have happened to the Old Firm had Holmes not succeeded in calming Souness down.

By mid October, Rangers had mostly recovered from a poor start to the league and were four points behind Celtic, who were second and two points behind leaders Hearts, with Aberdeen in third. When Celtic came to play their second league match against Rangers at Ibrox, they were already out of European competition and the Scottish League Cup, beaten 2–3 on aggregate by Borussia Dortmund – Murdo MacLeod was given a hero's welcome at Parkhead – in the UEFA Cup and 0–1 by Aberdeen in the Scottish League Cup quarter-final. That left just the league and Scottish Cup if Celtic were to mark their centenary with what the fans most desired: a trophy, and preferably two.

At Ibrox that October day, Celtic took a big step towards that Double by showing the new English tough guys at Ibrox that this Celtic team, like other great sides that had worn the hoops, was not prepared to succumb to physical stuff. The Celtic board had also shown some determination at last, and after sanctioning Hay's last signing – Mick McCarthy of Manchester City for £500,000 – they gave McNeill more cash to acquire Frank McAvennie, the Celtic-daft former St Mirren striker, who was signed for £800,000 from West Ham United just hours after Rangers paid £1.5 million for the classy Richard Gough, the former Dundee United player then with Spurs.

Signing two big names from England showed that Celtic were willing to compete financially if it became necessary, and in McCarthy they got the solid centre-half the team had lacked, while McAvennie brought with him a natural flair for goals and many other things besides: page-three girls, a playboy lifestyle and a reckless streak that would endear him to the fans if not to the Celtic board.

McAvennie and Gough would make their Old Firm debuts in a maelstrom of a game. The atmosphere inside Ibrox was even more feverish than usual, and there were open predictions that Souness's men would want revenge for the last Old Firm match and might not be too careful how they took it. McNeill, on the other hand, emphasised to his players that they were not to get caught up in any rough stuff or 'afters'.

The referee was Jim Duncan, in charge of his first Old Firm match. He was going to have a busy day, as were Strathclyde Police, who would make 62 arrests in total.

It took just a few minutes for McAvennie to make his mark on the game, or rather on Chris Woods. Tommy Burns sent in a high looping cross that almost sneaked in under the bar only for Woods to leap and tip the ball over. Even as he did so, McAvennie arrived on the scene and bundled the goalkeeper into the net. Referee Duncan was clearly unsighted and unaware of the force of the challenge and gave a corner rather than a free kick. McAvennie had got away with it but would not be so lucky next time.

After Allen McKnight had saved well from Trevor Francis, Celtic had a chance at the other end when McStay played a superb ball to Chris Morris on the right wing. The full-back's low cross was skilfully intercepted by Jimmy Phillips, who took the sting out of the ball and nudged it back to Woods. It was not a 50–50 ball, nor anything like it, but the prowling McAvennie made as if to go for it, as any striker would do. No doubt remembering his early clattering, Woods came up with the ball and got his retaliation in first with a forearm in McAvennie's throat. The striker responded by slapping Woods on the back of the head, to which the goalkeeper reacted by grabbing McAvennie by the throat, causing the Celtic man to lash out and smack Woods on the chin. From yards away, Terry Butcher ran over and pushed McAvennie violently, just as Graham Roberts made his way into the affray with arms swinging. Woods, too, came back for another bite at his target. McAvennie later happily admitted that the sight of Roberts joining his other two assailants made him think that discretion was the better part of valour, and he hit the deck quickly.

Referee Duncan arrived on the scene just as the three Rangers men towered over their fallen opponent, which possibly saved McAvennie from further 'treatment', all of the trio looking enraged and out of control. The rest of the Celts remembered their manager's warnings and stayed away. Duncan then used an old refereeing tactic to calm things down and walked ten yards away from the scene of the 'crime', making Woods and McAvennie come to him for their punishment. Even with the additional time to cool down, Duncan was still annoyed and gestured quite openly to McAvennie that he had seen the player punch Woods. Duncan waved the red card at the striker, who trotted off in a daze, his Old Firm debut over after just 17 minutes.

With just a hint of the mischief that made him such a character, McAvennie said, 'That wee scrap between the four of us was the kind of thing that happens in football games up and down the country every week. There was a lot of tension, and we were all maybe a bit hyped up, but it was nothing.

'Really, I only raised my hand to stop me falling over. Honest, it was the three big boys did the naughty bit. When he sent me off, I just could not believe it.'

Duncan was not finished. He then told Woods what he had seen the goalkeeper do and again made a punching gesture. Given that indication, he had no choice and produced the red card that appeared to strike Woods into a state of catatonia before he grudgingly slunk away. As he did so, an apoplectic Butcher confronted Duncan, and, being a head taller than the referee, he looked somewhat menacing. Duncan had not even put away his notebook, and this time he showed a yellow card for dissent to the big Englishman.

'The referee panicked, frankly,' said McAvennie, 'and I don't think he ever took charge of another major game. I'm sorry, but I have no sympathy for him.'

In those days, there were only two men on the bench, almost always outfield players, and for Rangers that day the substitutes were Davie Cooper and the Israeli defender Avi Cohen. Cooper lacked the inches, and even though Cohen was over 6 ft tall, goalkeeping was not his bag. Someone from the ten men remaining on the pitch would have to take over, and in a fateful decision Graham Roberts, who at least had some experience between the sticks, grabbed Woods's gloves and red jersey.

Celtic now had a serious advantage and went about exploiting it. With the Rangers defence in a muddle, Celtic began to pour forward. Leaving Butcher flailing in his wake, Peter Grant was clean through on Roberts, but the replacement goalkeeper stayed big and deflected Grant's shot wide. But in the 33rd minute, Mick McCarthy's long clearance found Andy Walker, who sprinted away from Butcher, drew Roberts out of his goal and then calmly slotted the ball low past him.

The next goal was a personal disaster for Butcher. A chip ahead from Walker saw Peter Grant racing in on goal. Butcher got there ahead of him, but his attempted pass back to Roberts only succeeded in floating over the head of the replacement goalkeeper. Grant claimed the goal then, and still does, but it has gone into the record books as an own goal by Butcher. Peter Grant caused huge controversy by making the sign of the cross in front of the Celtic end, though it was not noticed at that point and became an issue only when Rangers fans complained – despite not having seen it. With crosses and such gestures officially seen as inflammatory in Britain since 2010 – as decided by the employment-tribunal ruling in the case of nurse Shirley Chaplin against the NHS – one can only presume that the Rangers fans were simply ahead of their time in their complaints about Grant and others who have subsequently crossed themselves.

The second half was one that Celtic would prefer to forget. Already booked, Terry Butcher was ordered off for a combination of a brutal mid-air challenge on goalkeeper McKnight and a shove on the Celtic man as he tried to get off the ground.

New signing Richard Gough then inspired a dramatic fightback by Rangers, his pinpoint pass setting up Ally McCoist for the shot in off the post that reduced Celtic's advantage to a single goal. Seeming curiously reluctant to press upfield, Celtic's best effort was a shot from Walker that was well saved by Roberts before Billy Stark's header came back off the bar with the goalkeeper beaten. Tommy Burns tried to float one past Roberts, but the Englishman was no mug in the gloves and saved comfortably, and indeed he was not put under much threat until the game entered the 90th minute. Roberts struck a poor goal kick upfield, where Derek Ferguson managed to collect it and send Durrant away on the right wing. He skinned Anton Rogan and sent in a cross that was intercepted by Mick McCarthy as McCoist threatened. But Durrant had kept running and picked up McCarthy's clearance before sending in a high cross that deceived McKnight and fell to Richard Gough, who was alert enough to stick out a foot and score.

Even after this dramatic equaliser, there was still time for more controversy. Owen Archdeacon chased a through ball into the penalty area, but Roberts gathered it comfortably and then collided with the Celtic man. After hesitating for a second or two, Roberts went down as if he had been shot, and when he finally rose it was to conduct the Rangers fans in a chorus of that tuneful ditty 'The Billy Boys'. A final hoof up the park and referee Duncan blew the whistle.

The Rangers fans celebrated as if they had won, but the Celtic supporters could see that the spell woven by Souness since his arrival had been broken, at least temporarily. Butcher, Roberts and Co. had been shown that, for all Rangers' physical advantages, the Celtic players could give as good as they got and were superior in the skills department, too. Andy Walker later called it the best Old Firm match in which he ever played, but its importance lies in the fact that, at a crucial moment in the season, Celtic took a highly educational stop on the learning curve – the Bhoys now knew they could win the Double if they wanted it enough.

Not everything went to plan in the centenary season, owing to failures in the UEFA and League Cups, and indeed, in the very next game after the Ibrox battle, Dundee United came to Parkhead and won 3–2. But from that match onwards, Celtic slowly but surely made their league-winning intentions clear. They simply refused to be beaten, and the fighting spirit shown at Ibrox surfaced again and again as they won by a single goal on numerous occasions or scrapped for draws to retain an unbeaten record that lasted from 28 October to 16 April, a run of 31 matches in the league and Scottish Cup. In match after match, winning or equalising goals were scored in the dying minutes. It was an ulcer-inducing but incredibly exciting time to be a Celtic fan, played out against the backdrop of a four-month-long ordeal for the club's biggest goalscoring asset, Frank McAvennie.

'It is so crazy, so far-fetched, what followed that game,' said McAvennie. 'It was just my bloody luck that, the first time the police got stuck into a football game, it was me that was in the middle of it.'

In the immediate aftermath of the Battle of Ibrox, it appeared the scenes during the game had annoyed just about everybody. The SFA and the moralistic Scottish media all reacted as per the usual manner: with lots of hot air. Those who had seen it all before expected the whole matter to blow over as usual, until Glasgow's Procurator Fiscal, Alexander Jessop, made the most extraordinary legal intervention in Scottish football's history.

Jessop viewed tapes of the incidents, and, on learning of the crowd trouble apparently inspired by the various players' misdemeanours, he ordered Strathclyde Police to carry out an inquiry. Jessop was accused of being a publicity-seeker, which was nonsense, as Scotland's Fiscal Service is famed for a low-key approach that disdains celebrity prosecutors. He wanted to make a point on behalf of the Scottish legal system that excessive misconduct on the field of play was a matter for the courts when appropriate, especially when it led to crowd trouble. On the same day as the Old Firm derby, Hibs had beaten Hearts 2–1 at Easter Road, and that match, too, had been marred by crowd disturbances. Jessop came from Edinburgh, so he might well have decided that trouble in both cities meant that an example had to be made. He was also being consistent: he had prosecuted junior footballers and rugby players for onfield assaults.

It is also often forgotten that McAvennie, Roberts, Woods and Butcher – they were soon christened 'Goldilocks and the Three Bears' by the press – were not the first Scottish professional footballers to be prosecuted for a crime on the pitch. Less than a fortnight before the Battle of Ibrox, Arbroath FC's player Adrian Brannigan had been convicted after a two-day trial of assaulting Jim Deakin of Albion Rovers during a match. That had been the first prosecution by the Crown of a professional footballer in Scotland, and Brannigan was convicted and fined £150. So when the police reported back to Jessop that the trouble on the field had sparked the problems off it, the Fiscal – apparently after consulting the Lord Advocate and Solicitor-General for Scotland – decided that there was a precedent and genuine public interest in charging all four and bringing them to trial if the players pleaded not guilty.

The formal charging of the players did not take place until the November, with McAvennie's arrival at Govan Police Station on 1 November being mysteriously leaked to the press.

Frank McAvennie recalled, 'I got a call from Billy McNeill on a Sunday morning telling me I had to go the police station that day. I had been out the night before, and, funnily enough, I'd had a few drinks, so my head wasn't exactly right.

'I couldn't take in what was happening. As I headed into the station, there were so many photographers' flashbulbs going off I felt as if I was walking down a catwalk.'

Terry Butcher was actually in bed recovering from a broken leg when he was charged by a policeman who, as a Rangers supporter, was mortified at having to do the deed. It seemed ludicrous to almost the whole world of sport that the four players would face a court for actions that were hardly on a par with the kind of thuggery often seen in rugby, American football and other contact sports. Procurator Fiscal Jessop was determined on a trial, however, possibly because the media had made such a huge issue of the Battle of Ibrox, but, as he also said with some logic at the time, the public would find it difficult to understand or accept that, if illegal actions took place on a sports field, they were treated differently from similar actions elsewhere.

The wheels of justice turn slowly at times, and it took until 12 April 1988 for the trial to take place at Glasgow Sheriff Court. It began on a Tuesday, with the four accused the centre of attention as the witnesses gave accounts of what they had seen. Reports of the trial at the time conveyed the excitement that surrounded the case. Long and detailed accounts of the evidence were conveyed each night on the television news and reported in the following day's papers. The media really did get into a lather, not least in England, as three of that nation's internationalists were involved.

The case turned on whether the players' actions were likely to cause trouble among the spectators, and those sixty-two arrests among the crowd now came back to haunt the Ibrox Four. Both clubs had acted in concert, the Old Firm way, and appointed top lawyer Len Murray to fight the four players' cases.

On the very first day, Assistant Chief Constable John Dickson impressively testified that there had been 'a direct relationship' between the incidents on the pitch and the trouble off it. He went on to say, 'There was unbridled hatred on the faces of some of the fans when they were shouting obscenities and insults at each other.' All 100 police officers held in reserve had been deployed to prevent a pitch invasion. He also accurately described the main incident, noting that Woods had grabbed McAvennie by the throat before the Celtic player retaliated.

Referee Duncan, in his evidence, bemoaned the fact of police involvement, but ACC Dickson's testimony had won the case for the prosecution. Woods and Butcher were found guilty of that uniquely Scottish offence, conducting themselves in a disorderly manner and committing a breach of the peace. Woods was fined £500 and Butcher £250. The charge against Roberts was declared not proven, and McAvennie was found not guilty, much to the player's amusement and the chagrin of Rangers supporters everywhere.

Sheriff Archibald McKay singled out Woods, who had 'jabbed McAvennie on the chin with your left forearm. It was an assault which constituted breach of the peace.' All four got an earwigging from the sheriff: 'A large percentage of supporters are readily converted by breaches of the peace into two rival mobs. That they were not so transformed is no credit to you. You must have been aware of your wider responsibilities, and you failed to discharge them.'

The Rangers trio were so upset that the club offered to let them leave, but they stayed and made their contributions to the forthcoming nine-in-a-row era. McAvennie had played dreadfully against Hearts on the weekend before the trial, but Celtic had still managed to win the Scottish Cup semi-final 2–1 with a late surge that was so typical of the season.

The day after the trial ended, Celtic travelled to Tynecastle, where they could win the league by beating Hearts. The whole team seemed to have been affected by the court proceedings, and most of them had an off-day, a remarkable 31-match unbeaten run being brought to an end with the home side winning 2–1. The aftermath in court thus played its own incongruous part in one of the greatest seasons in Celtic's history.

Frank McAvennie is in no doubt as to what motivated the authorities: 'We were arrested and charged and put on trial, and Chris and Terry got criminal records. We were a test case, and funnily enough no criminal actions have been brought against senior players for similar breach of the peace offences since 1987 because the test case failed and only two of us were found guilty. They wanted to make an example of all of us, and they failed.'

The court-case headlines were a thing of the past when Celtic entertained Dundee in front of a massive crowd at Parkhead on 23 April 1988, an early goal from Chris Morris and two in two minutes by Andy Walker in the second half securing the title in the centenary season. Celtic had previously proved they could raise their game when an important anniversary in the club's history was being commemorated, as Chapter Six showed, with the fiftieth anniversary of Celtic's founding. Now they had gone one better than that season and won the Double in grand style, beating Dundee United 2–1 in the Scottish Cup final. The scorer of the two late goals was McAvennie.

Unfortunately for Celtic, this was to be the last hurrah, at least as far as the league championship went, for a very long time. No Celtic fan needs reminding that the following season saw the arrival of David Murray as owner of Rangers, and with his financial power the Ibrox club duly ran up their own nine-in-row sequence of league titles under Souness and then Walter Smith.

Celtic did manage to win the Scottish Cup in 1989, but that would be the club's only trophy until 1995, when the Cup was won again. Behind the scenes, Celtic Football Club was in deep trouble, and money that could have shored up the side was just not available. As crowds dwindled due to lack of success on the field, the club signed high-profile and expensive managers in a bid to stop the ship sinking but succeeded only in racking up bigger debts. Liam Brady won precisely nothing, and then Lou Macari arrived, pledging to turn things round. But both men were hamstrung by a board that had failed to inject new directorial blood, new ideas and new cash – millionaire Brian Dempsey came and went quickly after he had the temerity to suggest some fresh approaches.

Under chairman Kevin Kelly, who had replaced his uncle Sir Robert Kelly on the board, the full extent of Celtic's problems became public knowledge only in 1994, when what had once been the richest football club in the world – albeit in the 1890s – came within hours of going bankrupt.

At the 11th hour, the most unlikely saviour imaginable, a man with a mid-Atlantic accent and a bunnet, arrived to rebuild Celtic. His name was Fergus McCann, and though he could do little about Rangers' dominance, he could certainly do something about Celtic.

16

DR WHO? LUBO WHICH?

21 NOVEMBER 1998
SCOTTISH LEAGUE PREMIER DIVISION
CELTIC 5, RANGERS 1

In the many years that Celtic FC has been in existence, the club has never operated any bar on employing players or staff because of race, religion or nationality. Yet by the mid 1990s no one other than a Scot or Irishman had managed Celtic. Indeed, the club had had only four managers in its first ninety years: Willie Maley, Jimmy McStay, Jimmy McGrory and Jock Stein. It took just sixteen years for the next four managers to come and go, as Billy McNeill (twice), David Hay, Liam Brady and Lou Macari all took charge before Tommy Burns was handed the job in 1994 by Fergus McCann.

This latter gentleman, who had made millions in golf tourism, came home from Canada to perform miracles in saving the club from bankruptcy and then putting together the plan that saw Celtic Park rebuilt. At first, the team on the pitch could not match the efforts of McCann and all those who worked to rebuild the club off it, the sole trophy of the period being the Scottish Cup win of 1995. When Rangers achieved their ninth league title in a row, and looked certain to break Celtic's record and make it ten, McCann decided to act. He was not a very popular person anyway, so when he sacked the much-loved Tommy Burns in early May 1997, it was not as if he was risking his standing with the fans, who, if they respected him at all, did so grudgingly.

McCann's two signings in that summer of 1997 mystified the Celtic support. Firstly, he drafted in Jock Brown, a lawyer and former television commentator, as general manager responsible for every activity except the actual coaching of the players. The logic of appointing a general manager when the club did not have a manager seemed fuzzy to say the least, but at least Celtic now had a public face who was supposedly good with the media, unlike McCann.

Brown was then instrumental in persuading McCann to look outside Britain for a manager, and it was a huge shock to Scottish football when Wim Jansen was appointed. The Dutchman was best known to Scottish fans as the shaggy-haired left-back of the 1978 World Cup Holland side who was the first player beaten by Archie Gemmill on the Scotsman's road to scoring *that* goal. He had played for Feyenoord when they beat Celtic in the 1970 European Cup final and also for Holland when they reached the World Cup finals of 1974 and 1978, but it's fair to say that, outside of Brown's office, he was not on anybody's radar as a possible Celtic manager. Though he had been successful as coach of Feyenoord, he had been working in Saudi Arabia and Japan until Celtic swooped to sign him in what was a genuinely stunning moment in the club's history.

Jansen seemed a little nonplussed at the hoopla surrounding his appointment as the first person from outside Britain or Ireland to manage either half of the Old Firm. He was very shrewd, however, and knew he needed local help, soon enlisting fans' favourite Murdo MacLeod as his assistant. He also brought in a certain Henrik Larsson, a Swede he had signed at his old club Feyenoord. Costing just £600,000 and with a distinctive dreadlocked hairstyle, Henrik Larsson turned out to be not a bad signing, to put it mildly, and we will reflect more on him in the next chapter.

Jansen led Celtic to the Scottish League Cup, and then his team reached a high point with a superb 2–0 victory over Rangers in the Ne'erday Derby at Parkhead. The team, built around Henrik Larsson, Tom Boyd, Jackie McNamara, further Jansen signings Craig Burley and Paul Lambert, and with Jonathan Gould sound in goal, was gelling together well when they came up against the league leaders.

Paul Lambert in particular played a vital role in midfield. The former Motherwell player had won the European Cup with Borussia Dortmund before being persuaded to join Celtic. His performances against Rangers saw him score vital goals such as the 30-yard cracker in that 2–0 win, which was seriously considered for inclusion in this top 20.

'I still get reminded of it by Celtic fans,' said Lambert. 'Every Old Firm game is a must-win match, but that was one of those "must-must-win" games. We were ahead with a goal by Craig Burley when the ball broke to me from their defence. It was one of those ones that you see coming at you and you decide just to have a go. The bounce was right, it felt right to hit it and it went right into the top corner. It was my first goal for Celtic and probably my best.'

The stunning goal secured a victory that sparked a run that saw Celtic win the title on the last day of the season, beating St Johnstone 2–0 with goals from Larsson and his fellow Scandinavian, the oft-maligned but worshipped-for-one-day Harald Brattbakk. Lambert still cites stopping the ten-in-a-row by Rangers as a career highlight.

Jansen did not stay around for the celebrations. The Dutch manager's success in leading Celtic to a 'Double' of Premier League and Scottish League Cup in his first season in charge would usually have guaranteed him a long run in the job, but relationships had been strained, and if his arrival had been a shock, it was a mere stomach rumble compared with the earthquake caused by his departure. Two days after Celtic had beaten St Johnstone, and prevented Rangers winning that elusive ten-in-a-row, Jansen left Parkhead, MacLeod following shortly after. The Dutchman left a great many bewildered people behind him.

Celtic's next managerial signing was, if anything, even more of a shock than the recruitment of Jansen. Former Slovakian coach Josef Venglos̆ was a doctor of physical education whose specialism had been psychology. He had been forced to retire early from playing because of injury and had started a peripatetic career as a coach and manager in Australia before returning home to Czechoslovakia, where he managed his old team Slovan Bratislava, which he had captained in the 1960s, and then became assistant manager of his national team, which memorably won the European Championships in 1976.

He then became manager of Czechoslovakia and led them to third place in the European Championships of 1980. After spells in Portugal and Malaysia, where he coached the national team, he took over the reins of the Czechoslovakian national team again, guiding them to the quarter-finals of the 1990 World Cup in Italy. Venglos̆ came to England to manage Aston Villa – the first person born outside the British Isles to manage a top-flight English club –

but lasted just one season before two years at Fenerbahçe in Turkey. The ructions in Eastern Europe saw Czechoslovakia dissolve, and Vengloš came home to manage the new Slovakian national team. He left after two seasons for a spell as coach of Oman. In other words, he was in football's nowhere-land when Celtic came calling.

The headlines said it all: 'Dr Who?' This, of course, showed up the insularity of the Scottish press and footballing public, for, as Fergus McCann and Jock Brown plaintively stated, Vengloš was a hugely respected figure in international football. His arrival at Parkhead hardly set the heather alight in the Garngad and other Celtic enclaves, however, but the fact that he was a 'doctor' was certainly impressive. Not so impressive was Celtic's initial form under him – after a very satisfying 5–0 victory over Dunfermline Athletic to start the league campaign, the Bhoys had managed only 10 out of a possible 24 points by the end of September.

That 1998–99 season witnessed the introduction of the new Scottish Premier League (SPL), and though the ten-team format was retained, there was much talk of league expansion. Whether the SPL had ten, twelve or more teams, such a poor start was always going to be a massive handicap for Celtic, especially with Rangers recovering from an opening-day defeat by Hearts to go on a twenty-two-match unbeaten run in all competitions.

When Vengloš made Lubomir Moravčik his second signing after Norwegian defender Vidar Riseth, the head-scratching about 'Dr Jo', as he had become known, became dandruff-creating. According to some newspapers, Vengloš was simply handing out a career extension to an old pal at the age of 33, but shrewd pundits and former players realised that Vengloš had signed a cracker.

Moravčik had been out of favour at MSV Duisburg in Germany's Bundesliga, and for what was then a paltry £300,000, Celtic acquired a man with 73 international caps and a burning desire to repay the faith of Dr Jo, whom the player acknowledged as his mentor and who had made him captain of Slovakia. Lubo, as the fans came to know and love him, would start that repayment in spectacular fashion a month after his arrival at Parkhead.

What a month it was. As October became November, Celtic's fortunes dipped on the field and off it. Vengloš was trying to build a team without the proper resources, and there was much discussion about his failed attempts to sign Mark Viduka, the Australian of Croatian parentage who was then starring for Croatia Zagreb and had been a key player in that side's dismissal of Celtic from the European Cup in August.

That defeat had been the lowest point of a poor start to the season by Celtic, and clearly all was not well in the managerial team at Celtic Park. Having been recruited partly for his media skills, Jock Brown fell out with too many journalists and decided he would not speak to them. With a manager whose first tongue was not English, and an owner who garbled the language, communications should have been Brown's to handle, but instead, as the team's performances worsened, Brown became the focus of the fans' ire, not least because Rangers had spent money like water and were forging ahead in the league under their new manager, Dick Advocaat. With the best part of £25 million spent on just five players – Arthur Numan, Giovanni van Bronckhorst, Gabriel Amato, Andrei Kanchelskis and Colin Hendry – Rangers were totally dominant in the marketplace, and the Celtic fans could only hope that Fergus McCann would do what he promised and loosen the purse strings, especially when the first-team squad began to be depleted by injuries, the loss for the season of star Danish defender Marc Rieper being a particular blow.

As the second Old Firm match of the season approached, Celtic were convulsed. In the first week of November, just two hours before Celtic were due to play Dundee, Jock Brown fell on his sword and resigned, saying that it would be inappropriate for him not to acknowledge the difficulties that would be caused by his continued involvement with the club. That seemed to placate the fans for a while, not least because Celtic duly thrashed Dundee 6–1 with a hat-trick for Henrik Larsson, two for 18-year-old Mark Burchill on his first start for the club and the final counter for Simon Donnelly. It was the debut performance of Moravčik, however, that had the fans and pundits purring: his class was visible from the start.

When St Johnstone inflicted their second defeat of the season on Celtic a week later, Venglos̆ came under increasing media pressure, with one newspaper calling for him to resign and another predicting he would be gone after the Old Firm match, the subtext being that Rangers would win comfortably.

It all came to a head on the Thursday before the match, when Venglos̆ lost his famous cool at a press conference. Asked if the problems he was experiencing at Celtic would damage his reputation, the manager replied sharply that his reputation had been built over thirty years and would not be destroyed in three months.

The roller-coaster nature of Venglos̆'s time at Parkhead was never better exemplified than in the days before that Old Firm match. Injuries to goalkeepers Jonathan Gould and Stewart Kerr saw Venglos̆ call Liverpool, from whom he signed their fourth-choice goalkeeper Tony Warner. That was deemed almost a joke by the fans, who were further baffled by the signing of little-known Swedish international defender Johan Mjällby from AIK Stockholm. Yet Warner would prove perfectly sound when thrown into the cauldron of the Old Firm game, and Mjällby would become a crucial member of the side for years ahead. Venglos̆ could still not parade £4-million signing Mark Viduka, however, owing to a problem with a work permit, and though that was hardly the fault of the Celtic manager, the Parkhead faithful were losing patience with the Doctor.

On the morning of Saturday, 21 November, Celtic were in some disarray behind the scenes and were a full ten points behind Rangers – defeat would almost certainly mean that the league championship would not be heading for Parkhead. Not for the last time, both sides took to the field with a majority of their number born outside Scotland.

Celtic lined up with Warner in goal, a back four of Tom Boyd, Mjällby, Alan Stubbs and Stéphane Mahé, a four-strong midfield of Riseth, Lambert, Donnelly and Phil O'Donnell, with Larsson and Moravc̆ik up front. The Doctor's biggest gamble was to bench Mark Burchill to make way for Moravc̆ik in a forward position.

The Rangers team was Antti Niemi in goal, a back four of Sergio Porrini, Hendry, Scott Wilson and Numan, with Kanchelskis, Barry Ferguson, van Bronckhorst and Jörg Albertz in midfield and Stéphane Guivarc'h and Rod Wallace up front.

Despite the addition of Mjällby, Celtic still had a bargain-basement look compared with the many millions expended in creating the Rangers side. Even with Barry Ferguson as a no-fee home-grown player, the Rangers midfield had cost more than the entire Celtic team. Yet it was two men who cost just £900,000 in total who were to make all the difference that Saturday. For this was the first time that the devastating double act of Larsson and Moravc̆ik would really show what they could do together.

Paul Lambert had watched Moravc̆ik in training and knew Celtic had acquired a diamond: 'You could see right away that Lubo was a class act with great balance and control. But he was also a strong player, and he wasn't afraid to let people know what he was thinking, even if it mostly came out in French.'

Lambert by then knew what Old Firm matches were all about: 'They are great occasions, but you shouldn't let them overwhelm you. You musn't get caught up in that atmosphere and get yourself sent off. As long as you have 11 men on the park you have a chance of winning. A bit of luck helps, too.'

Celtic got some of that luck when a Rangers player self-imploded. Much was made in the press afterwards about the early red card for Scott Wilson, who was sent off by referee Willie Young for hacking down Moravčik from behind after 21 minutes. By that time, Wilson and his colleagues already knew that they were up against a Celtic team that was firing on all cylinders and led by a dreadlocked diamond and a diminutive genius. After just 11 minutes, Celtic survived a penalty scare when Alan Stubbs collided with Rod Wallace in the area. Moving swiftly upfield, Stubbs swung the ball out to Phil O'Donnell on the left wing. Simon Donnelly cleverly ran into space, where O'Donnell's pass landed at his feet, allowing the youngster time to move forward and strike a low teaser across the edge of the penalty area. Henrik Larsson might have taken the ball himself, but instead he sold Colin Hendry the mother of all dummies, which set up Moravčik in pole position front and centre, just 18 yards out. With sublime technique, the Slovakian did not even break his stride as he thumped the ball with his left foot, the shot curving low past the despairing dive of Antti Niemi.

Stand-in goalkeeper Warner then proved that he had been a good acquisition with solid saves from a typical thunderbolt by Jörg Albertz and a header from Andrei Kanchelskis before Wilson departed. The Rangers fans and some pundits felt it was very harsh, but referee Young had previously warned Wilson about his tackling. The only surprising thing about the rest of the first half was that Celtic did not score any more goals, such was their superiority.

The match was won in magnificent style with a devastating burst of three goals in eight minutes early in the second half. As happened for the first goal, again it was Alan Stubbs who started the move, sending an inch-perfect pass to the right wing, where Tom Boyd gathered it and floated in a lovely cross that begged to be headed home. Rising next to the penalty spot, with no defenders near him, Moravčik picked his target with a header that Niemi could only stand and watch as it fizzed into the net.

Next it was Henrik Larsson's turn. Donnelly picked up the ball in midfield and despatched a perfectly weighted pass into the path of Larsson. The striker sped past Hendry into the box and chipped the ball over the advancing goalkeeper with the outside of his right boot.

Giovanni van Bronckhorst pulled one back for Rangers with a fine free kick, but that seemed only to annoy the Celts, and in the 57th minute Phil O'Donnell looped over a smashing cross that Larsson leapt, spring-heeled, to head powerfully home. At 4–1 with less than an hour gone, Celtic understandably took their foot off the accelerator, though Moravčik continued to taunt Porrini in particular.

When the Slovakian made way for Mark Burchill after 82 minutes, the Parkhead crowd rose as one to acclaim their new hero. The show was not over, and in the final minute Larsson created a peach of a goal for Burchill, the youngster launching onto the Swede's delicious through ball and firing a low left-foot shot diagonally past the bedraggled Niemi.

'It was my first and only goal against Rangers,' said Burchill, who is now with Kilmarnock after an injury-strewn career north and south of the border. 'I remember it well, and, of course, I've watched it on tape a few times over the years.

'I had just come on for Lubo Moravčik, who, of course, got a massive ovation. I spotted Henrik cutting in from the right wing, and I moved to the left into space. His pass was spot on into my path, and I knew all I had to do was hit the ball hard and low back across goal. I can't tell you the feeling when it hit the net. I remember turning to the stand where the old Jungle used to be, and I could see the fans were so happy. It was one of the best moments of my whole career.'

Rangers had been outshone by a performance as brilliant as it had been unexpected. All of the Celtic players had risen to the occasion, perhaps to show that they still had faith in the manager, but Moravčik and Larsson had been the stars, and though the Slovakian was clearly in the veteran stage, the Celtic fans simply hoped and prayed that he would last a good deal longer.

The Scottish press were unanimous in their praise for Lubo. Here was a player with vision, touch, an eye for goal and an all-round quality of play that was out of the ordinary. Over the next few years he would prove to be a true Celtic great who is still fondly remembered by the fans. He was not the biggest player in the world, but on his game he was a giant among pygmies.

Neil Lennon came to appreciate Moravčik's talent very quickly after he joined the club the following year: 'Lubo was in the veteran stage of his career at that stage, but he was buzzing around the place, a brilliant footballer who lived for the game.

'His greatest attribute was that he was two-footed – the best two-footed player I ever played with. You could also give him the ball anywhere, and he would conjure up something.

'He had a great shot with either foot. I once saw him hit one from thirty yards against Hibs with his left, which was supposed to be his weaker foot. I don't think I've ever seen a ball hit so hard. He was also deadly from free kicks and corners.

'I only wish I had played with him when he was in his twenties instead of when he was in the final year or two of his career.'

If Moravčik was Dr Venglos's greatest signing, that famous 1998 victory over Rangers is remembered as the highlight of his year in charge of Celtic. Despite some impressive results in the second half of the season, including a 7–1 thrashing of Motherwell, Celtic suffered serious injury problems – Moravčik was out for months with hamstring problems – and Rangers had been given too much of a head start. Celtic fans had to suffer the pain of watching their old enemies win the title at Parkhead – the first time they had done so – on a day when football took a back seat. That 0–3 defeat saw referee Hugh Dallas struck with a coin in full view of the cameras, and the windows of his home were smashed later that night. Dozens of arrests were made inside and outside Celtic Park, with a pitched battle taking place in Duke Street. Much of the trouble was correctly blamed on the fact that the match had a 6.05 p.m. kick-off, which meant an afternoon's boozing for large numbers of fans and the inevitable consequences for law and order. Old Firm matches since then have had an earlier kick-off.

There was still a chance for some glory in the last match of the season, the Scottish Cup final at Hampden Park on 29 May, when the opponents were once again Rangers. There was to be no revenge for Celtic, however, as Advocaat's side lifted the Treble with a 1–0 win courtesy of a Rod Wallace goal after 48 minutes.

Dr Venglos duly moved on to be replaced by the 'Dream Team' of coach John Barnes and director of football Kenny Dalglish, Dr Jo becoming the club's European technical consultant, whatever that was.

Despite the efforts of players like Mark Viduka and Paul Lambert, and occasional brilliance from Eyal Berkovic, Barnes endured a nightmare, the low point of which was Henrik Larsson breaking his leg in the 0–1 defeat by Lyon in the UEFA Cup. Barnes was sacked after the infamous Scottish Cup defeat by Inverness Caledonian Thistle. At least King Kenny managed to win the League Cup before he, too, left in acrimonious circumstances.

The stage was set for a new king to take over Parkhead, though Celtic fans would eventually accord Martin O'Neill and his best player, Henrik Larsson, somewhat more exalted status than mere human royalty, not least because of the incredible start to the Blessed Martin's reign.

17

A BRILLIANT BRIGHT NEW DAWN

27 AUGUST 2000
SCOTTISH PREMIER LEAGUE
CELTIC 6, RANGERS 2

Celtic had ended season 1999–2000 a very poor second behind Rangers, who had romped away with the title, ending the season a full 21 points ahead of the Bhoys. If all was not well on the pitch, matters were not any better off it as the club floundered on for months without a permanent manager after the sacking of John Barnes, Kenny Dalglish making it clear he did not want the day-to-day responsibility of the job.

Dalglish and Barnes had been appointed by Kenny's golfing partner Allan MacDonald, who had taken over as chief executive in the spring of 1999 when Fergus McCann got ready to make his exit after the promised five years in charge. The sale of McCann's shares – he is arguably the only recent club owner to become much richer via Scottish football – and the restructuring of Celtic plc meant that Dermot Desmond, the multi-millionaire Irishman, had emerged as the club's biggest shareholder, and the board was soon dancing to his tune.

When the Barnes–Dalglish experiment failed, Desmond exercised his shareholding muscle to instigate the appointment of Martin O'Neill, then manager of Leicester City, as the next manager. MacDonald also favoured O'Neill, but with the expected 'yes' failing to materialise from the Northern Irishman as quickly as wanted, MacDonald also spoke to Guus Hiddink, the Dutch manager of Spanish side Real Betis and former coach of Holland and Real Madrid, while a certain Sven-Göran Eriksson made his interest known briefly.

When McCann placeman Frank O'Callaghan stepped down as Celtic plc chairman in the summer of 1999, Desmond made his move. Club director Brian Quinn, a former deputy governor of the Bank of England and a close ally of Desmond, was promoted from vice chairman to chairman at the same time that MacDonald hinted that he would like to step down. He had one more task to fulfil, however, and that was to secure a manager. With Desmond in particularly persuasive mood, Martin O'Neill was enticed to Parkhead.

Neil Lennon recalled, 'It was certain that Martin would go to Celtic if they came for him. He asked me for my opinion, and I told him that he would be daft not to. Celtic were so much bigger than Leicester and were known all round Europe.'

Signing a three-year contract in the June, after a period of wrangling, lifelong supporter O'Neill made all the right noises to the fans, and though most Celtic supporters were prepared for a long wait for improvement due to the poor form under Barnes and Dalglish, O'Neill was determined to start putting things right immediately, and he wanted men around him that he knew. After weeks of negotiations with his old club, he eventually brought with him from Leicester John Robertson as assistant manager and Steve Walford as first-team coach. The trio had enjoyed success beyond expectation at Leicester City, but could they now revitalise the ailing giant that was Celtic FC?

Kenny Dalglish was still technically director of football, but his departure had already been signalled, and he duly left. Also leaving was Mark Viduka, the previous season's top scorer and Scottish Player of the Year, who was desperate for life in the English Premiership and joined Leeds United for £6 million, roughly double the sum Celtic had paid for him. Having learned that Viduka could be a disruptive influence, O'Neill was perhaps not entirely unhappy to see him go, and the new manager showed iron will when dealing with dressing-room problems, as Eyal Berkovic found out to his cost – the Israeli international played little part in the revolution that was to come.

Part of O'Neill's understanding with Desmond was that the purse strings would be loosened, and the money for Viduka was promptly spent on Chris Sutton, the Chelsea striker who had been a hit at Blackburn Rovers but had not made quite such an impact in London. Failing in his first bid to lure his protégé Neil Lennon from Leicester, O'Neill then bought Joos Valgaeren, the Belgian international defender, and the two new signings made their debuts in the same match, the opening SPL game of the season against Dundee United at Tannadice.

In what would become something of a recurring theme over the next few years, Celtic won when not playing particularly well. O'Neill's winning mentality was obvious from the outset in the squad, however, and goals from Sutton and Larsson in a 2–1 victory suggested that the pair might well form a profitable partnership in the season ahead.

The duo was temporarily sundered the following weekend when Sutton was sent off along with Jackie McNamara in the 1–0 home victory over Motherwell. Further victories over Kilmarnock and Hearts followed, and an 11–0 aggregate thrashing of Jeunesse d'Esch in the UEFA Cup qualifying round set up the Celts for the first serious acid test of O'Neill's reign.

Was the new manager up to besting Rangers? Having been subjected to O'Neill's loquaciousness on several occasions, the author has no hesitation in saying that he considers the former law student to be the cleverest man in British football. His intelligence, his range of knowledge on a wide variety of subjects, his intuitive psychology and his occasional circumlocutions are the products of a lively and enquiring mind, and there's little doubt that, had he become a lawyer or followed any other walk of life, Martin O'Neill would have been a success. His passion for football is immense, and he had learned much while a player at Nottingham Forest from his manager, the great Brian Clough. As well as experience, brains and ambition, O'Neill had the courage of his convictions and the single-mindedness that all winners must possess. In short, he wanted to win and knew how to go about doing it, and Dermot Desmond and everyone at Celtic Park soon knew his standards were set very high – Desmond spoke about how one man could transform an organisation, and there was no doubt he meant O'Neill.

The manager had inherited the core of a team from Jansen, Venglos, and Barnes and Dalglish and had made only a couple of additions in the form of Valgaeren and Sutton, but in energising the likes of Stiliyan 'Stan' Petrov and Bobby Petta and reinvigorating

Paul Lambert, he had given Celtic virtually new players. Rangers, by contrast, seemed to be resting on their laurels and in the summer had bought 'only' the Dutch pair Fernando Ricksen and Bert Konterman plus Danish striker Peter Lovenkrands for a combined outlay of nearly £10 million – a paltry sum compared with Advocaat's first spending spree and only twice the amount that Dalglish and Barnes had wasted on the Brazilian 'internationalist' Rafael Scheidt, whose second name was consistently and aptly pronounced by most who saw him with the 'd' being silent.

The pre-match punditry was all about O'Neill's first Old Firm game. Could the man who had clearly rejuvenated the club now take things to a higher level? His biggest signing, Chris Sutton, certainly thought so: 'The important thing is to put Rangers in their place,' said the lanky one, who was obviously a big loss to the diplomatic corps.

On the morning of the match, neither side could catch Hibs, who had made a very good start to the season and were clear at the top on sixteen points, though they had played two games more than the Old Firm, who were level on twelve points. Few pundits gave Celtic much of a chance, despite Rangers missing three of their best players: defenders Craig Moore and Arthur Numan, and forward Michael Mols. The bookmakers still made Rangers the 6/5 favourites, and only the venerable Archie McPherson predicted both a Celtic win and perhaps lots of goals. 'The Rangers defence is an accident waiting to happen,' said Archie, but not in his wildest dreams could he have foreseen the damage Celtic were about to do to that shaky defence.

Paul Lambert recalled that the team was determined to show the new manager what they could do: 'When Martin was appointed, I thought he was someone who, having shown what he could do with Leicester, could achieve great success at a club the size of Celtic.

'He had brought in Chris Sutton and Joos Valgaeren and later would bring Neil Lennon and Alan Thompson and moulded us all together as a team. His man management was great, and his assistants, John Robertson and Steve Walford, were terrific to work with on the training ground.

'At that point in the season we were starting to come together as a side, and we really felt we could beat Rangers. Martin also gave us tremendous belief in ourselves and instilled a real will to win. We were all up for it, and the new guys like Chris and Joos couldn't wait.'

In goal for Celtic was Jonathan Gould. The back four of McNamara, Valgaeren, Stubbs and Mahé was fluid, with the two wing-backs intended to get upfield as often as possible. The midfield of Petrov, Lambert, Moravčik and Petta looked under-powered compared with Rangers, but the twin forward line of Sutton and Larsson was already established as the most potent in Scotland, each having scored three goals in the opening four league matches. Rangers fielded Klos, Ricksen, Konterman, Amoruso, Vidmar, Reyna, Ferguson, van Bronckhorst, McCann, Dodds and Wallace. The referee was Stuart Dougal, who may have anticipated an eventful day, but perhaps not in the way it turned out.

Parkhead was full to the brim, and the stadium, which had been completed the previous year, rocked with 60,000 fans enjoying the warm August sunshine. Celtic kicked off, and within seconds Moravčik was on the ball, sending a superb pass down the left wing to Bobby Petta. Though he was not always everyone's cup of tea during his time at Celtic, Petta was sometimes a sublime left-winger and not a bad bargain, as he had joined up at Parkhead on a Bosman-style free transfer. On this warm Sunday afternoon, he would play a vital part, not the least of which was winning the first corner after he was hauled down by Fernando Ricksen.

Moravčik curled in the corner, and Lorenzo Amoruso managed to beat Sutton in the air, but his clearing header went into the heart of his own penalty area and deflected off Stubbs into the path of Larsson. Unusually for the Swede, he lost his balance as he turned to shoot and succeeded only in poking the ball forward into the six-yard box, where Sutton was still lurking and gleefully smacked the ball home. In vain, the Rangers defenders appealed for offside, seemingly unaware that Billy Dodds had defended like a forward and stayed at his post to play Sutton onside. Exactly 51 seconds had been played. Parkhead erupted. After all the anticipation, O'Neill's new Celtic had come good inside a minute.

Such has been the developing legend of this match that most Celtic fans forget that it was not a one-sided slaughter at first. Rangers straight away came back strongly – too much so, as referee Dougal booked Dodds and Neil McCann for late tackles. The former also missed a clear chance from a Giovanni van Bronckhorst free kick, heading wide from close range.

With seven minutes gone, however, Celtic went further ahead. Again Petta attacked Ricksen, who conceded a corner that Moravčik again swung over into the danger area. Valgaeren, Stubbs and Larsson all made for the near post and were duly followed by Bert Konterman and Amoruso, which left a wide gap into which Petrov leaped to power home the header. Two up after seven minutes: the Celtic fans were in dreamland.

Less than five minutes later they were way beyond dreaming. Out on the left, Petrov and Petta battled to keep possession until the latter dinked a lovely little pass through to Moravčik. This time it was the turn of Rangers' other new Dutch defender, Konterman, to look silly. Moravčik barrelled in towards goal and had time to slip and fall and still get to his feet, with Konterman all at sea, before the Slovakian rolled the ball into the path of the inrushing Paul Lambert, who fired in an unstoppable right-foot shot from 15 yards. There was less than twelve minutes showing on the clock, and the Celts were three up – the Martin O'Neill era was well and truly under way.

'I could see the way the ball was moving around, and when Lubo got a hold of it I knew I had to get up in support,' said Lambert. 'His pass was perfection, and I knew the instant I hit it that it was going in.'

It was one-way traffic at that point, with Celtic superior in every department. A long clearance from Gould was picked up by Moravčik, and his clever through ball sent Larsson away. You would have bet your mortgage on him scoring, but Larsson tried to waltz round Stefan Klos, and the German goalkeeper managed to smother the ball. As you would expect of them, Rangers kept trying to come back, and after twenty-two minutes Advocaat took off the hapless Ricksen – the Dutchman had been roasted by Petta and actually looked physically ill – so that he could switch to a five-man midfield with the addition of Turkish player Tugay Kerimoglu.

Paul Lambert suffered a groin injury in a clash with Neil McCann and was taken off on a stretcher before returning, though he eventually succumbed and was replaced by Johan Mjällby after 34 minutes. 'The last thing I wanted to do was go off, but I just couldn't carry on,' said Lambert.

By that time Rod Wallace had begun to appear the most dangerous player in blue, and Gould had to look lively to save a shot from him. The competitive nature of the match was shown by the fact that Moravčik was booked for a foul on Barry Ferguson – the Slovakian was proving that he could battle a bit as well as play the smooth stuff.

Five minutes before half-time, Wallace beat Stubbs to the byline and sent in a deep cross that was met at the far post by Claudio Reyna. Gould saved his powerful downward header, but the goalkeeper's momentum took him and the ball possibly just over the line, the assistant giving the goal even though television evidence was not conclusive. The official redeemed himself a minute or so later when Barry Ferguson put Wallace through and the striker hammered in a left-foot shot that flew past Gould into the net, only to see the linesman's flag raised for offside. Replays showed that Wallace had just been onside when the ball was last played. As the clock ran down to the interval, Chris Sutton, who was outplaying Lorenzo Amoruso and Konterman, lobbed in a ball that Petta chased into the box. His snatched effort was well saved by Klos, and Larsson was going just too fast to control the rebound, the Swede shooting narrowly wide.

Leading 3–1 at half-time, Celtic still had to kill off the game, and after a nervy start to the second half Henrik Larsson intervened in the 50th minute with the goal that is regularly voted one of the best ever scored by Celtic in an Old Firm match, arguably second only to Murdo MacLeod's strike in the 1979 league-winning game. It started in route-one fashion. Gould took advantage of the fact that so many Rangers players had gone upfield looking for a crucial counter by belting the ball deep into the visitors' half, where Sutton chested it into the path of Larsson nearly 40 yards from goal.

Moving at lightning pace, Larsson outstripped Tugay and headed for goal. Konterman was the last line of defence, and as he stuck out a leg, Larsson performed a classic nutmeg to take the Dutchman out of the equation. Klos had come out of his goal and presented a formidable obstacle – well, formidable to anyone but Larsson. Without decelerating, Larsson simply scooped the ball up and over Klos for a goal of sublime quality. From the moment the ball left Gould's hands to the instant the ball crossed the line, just 11 seconds had elapsed. It was breathtaking stuff, and now the Celtic fans knew the three points were secured. More importantly, even if Hibs were in the lead in the SPL, there would be daylight between Celtic and Rangers early in what was surely going to be a crucial season.

It was all over, the home fans thought, but only for three minutes. With Celtic pushing up in search of more goals, in typical fashion, Rangers broke to the other end and Mahé clumsily felled Rod

Wallace for a dubious penalty that Dodds thumped beyond Gould. At 4–2, there was just the chance that Rangers could come back, and with Moravčik toiling after a knock, O'Neill replaced him with Tom Boyd, indicating, you would think, a more sensible defensive approach to preserve the lead.

Not a bit of it. Celtic just kept on pressing, and in the 62nd minute Johan Mjällby persevered manfully as Amoruso tried to bully him off the ball, the Rangers defender conceding a free kick out on the right wing. Petta's cross came whistling into the penalty area, where Larsson rose unchallenged to guide the ball past Klos with a glancing header. For a man who had broken a leg the previous season, the athleticism he showed was wholly admirable.

Credit to Rangers for continuing to try, Dodds sending a gilt-edged chance wide of the post. No credit at all to Barry Ferguson, who hacked down Stan Petrov and then earned a red card for a deliberate handball, which he compounded by throwing the ball away. To complete his felony, Ferguson made what is euphemistically called a 'hand sign' to the crowd on his way off the field, which got him into trouble with the SFA. Later that night, he was involved in an altercation with Celtic fans in Bothwell. It was not one of his best days.

Mark Burchill, who had come on as a substitute in the 5–1 victory in 1998 that featured in the previous chapter, again came on late, this time for Henrik Larsson: 'I was only on for about five minutes, but at least I can say I played in Celtic's two biggest defeats of Rangers for decades. The atmosphere was incredible that day – you couldn't hear yourself think.'

The pace of the game never let up, and the icing on the Celtic cake came with a fine sixth goal in the final minute. Petta put Mahé away down the left wing, and the Frenchman's low cross sliced across goal and through the befuddled defence to Sutton, who sidefooted home for his second and Celtic's sixth.

It capped a remarkable turnaround for Sutton, who had endured a miserable time at Stamford Bridge. His partnership with Larsson was sealed that day and would prove lethal for Celtic. The new boys who were supposed to be overawed by the Old Firm atmosphere – Petta, Valgaeren and Mjällby – performed as if the stage had been made for them. The sheer *joie de vivre* shown by the team as they carved up an admittedly poor Rangers defence transmitted confidence to the Celtic fans, who really now began to believe O'Neill's talk of a bright future.

O'Neill himself was determined not to get carried away. He told the press, 'It was fantastic. I can't think that you'll find a better atmosphere than that anywhere else in Europe. I didn't know where it was going to end. Even at 4–1, I was thinking there's still a long way to go. But our performance was immense.

'The players are all delighted, but there is no feeling of euphoria, because a few of them have been here a couple of years and they know not to get too carried away with anything.

'I'll be happy tonight and maybe tomorrow morning. But after that, I and the players will concentrate on the next game. The players have often been in the shadow of Rangers, so I don't think anyone is getting too excited about it.'

A week after the Demolition Derby, as it became known, Allan MacDonald resigned as chief executive, his greatest achievement being to sign Henrik Larsson to a long-term contract. He had also played his role in bringing O'Neill to Parkhead. For his part, the manager continued to build his team, bringing in Alan Thompson from Aston Villa, an unknown Frenchman called Didier Agathe and goalkeeper Rab Douglas from Dundee. All the time Celtic were piling up the points, though they exited the UEFA Cup at the hands of Bordeaux on 9 November.

Having gone unbeaten in the SPL from the start of the season, Celtic went to Ibrox Park on 26 November with a 12-point lead. For some reason, the side did not click, especially in defence, and with Alan Thompson sent off after an hour and Rangers buoyed up by the panic buy of Tore Andre Flo for the Scottish-record sum of £12 million, it was the turn of the Ibrox men to inflict a huge defeat – but 5–1 didn't read quite as well as 6–2.

That defeat had a silver lining, because it enabled O'Neill to go to the board and say that it proved he needed to make one more important signing: Neil Lennon. Paul Lambert had broken his shinbone, so reinforcements were necessary.

Lennon said, 'Like every other Celtic fan, I had watched the 6–2 game and was absolutely delighted with the score and was just disappointed I wasn't on the pitch in the hoops, as I could have been. Before Martin signed up, he asked me privately if I would consider joining him at Celtic Park, and I said of course I would. It just took a bit longer than we thought, and at least I missed the defeat at Ibrox.'

With 'the Lurgan Lion' in midfield, Celtic never looked back and went on a long unbeaten run that, as every Celtic fan knows, secured the club's first Treble since 1969. Rangers were defeated in a towsy CIS Insurance League Cup semi-final before Larsson's hat-trick secured the trophy against Kilmarnock. The championship itself was won in early April with the 1–0 defeat of St Mirren at Parkhead, Tommy Johnson clinching it with his last goal for the club, before the Celts went to Ibrox and demonstrated their superiority over Rangers, winning there for the first time in more than six years in a game dominated by Lubo Moravčik, who scored two great goals, with Larsson adding the other in a 3–0 rout. The Scottish Cup was duly lifted in May, McNamara and Larsson (twice) scoring in a 3–0 victory over Hibernian.

Those two goals by Larsson took his tally to 53 in all competitions, with his SPL tally of 35 goals in 38 matches winning him the Golden Boot award as top goalscorer in any European league. He was also both the Players' and Football Writers' Player of the Year, and that just a season after his leg break.

Manager of the year Martin O'Neill had won the Treble in his first season in charge. Not even Jock Stein had accomplished that feat. What glory lay ahead for the new Celtic? How much could a team inspired by O'Neill achieve? The fans dared to dream even of European glory again. How close Celtic would come to winning it . . . And it really all began on a sunny Sunday afternoon when the Rangers net bulged six times.

18

GREENWASH

8 MAY 2004
SCOTTISH PREMIER LEAGUE
CELTIC 1, RANGERS 0

The Celtic team that Martin O'Neill created has already gone down as one of the greatest sides in the club's history. From the outset, it was a team that battled hard and played football the Celtic way: strong at the back, the ball moved forward at pace, the goals scored any which way they came and the players all passionate about the club and about winning. Yet there was also a pragmatic side to O'Neill that was unusual for Celtic. They could often throttle back and choke a game if necessary, playing 'keepball', if only to conserve the strength of the relatively small number of players who featured in the first-team squad week in and week out.

O'Neill's first tumultuous season was followed by a title-winning season that was almost an anticlimax, if any year in which the championship is secured could be termed as such. New imports John Hartson and Bobo Baldé were soon fixtures in the side, while other incomers Momo Sylla and Steve Guppy were fine squad players. Club captain Tom Boyd's career was winding down, Alan Stubbs moved on to Everton after successfully battling testicular cancer, Mark Burchill signed for Portsmouth and Eyal Berkovic went on loan to Blackburn before signing for Manchester City, but otherwise the side had a settled look, with youngsters Shaun Maloney and Jamie Smith coming in occasionally to make an impact early in their careers.

With transfer windows and the SPL splitting into top six and bottom six for the last part of the season, Scottish football in the 'noughties' was considerably different from the previous decade. One thing had not changed, however, and that was the dominance of the Old Firm. The other half had got themselves a new manager, Alex McLeish, who had revitalised Hibs after their demotion in 1998 and who took over from Advocaat in December 2001. As he had done at Hibs, McLeish had an energising effect on Rangers, and 'Big Eck' undoubtedly made them a better team.

Old Firm matches were as keenly contested as ever. Paul Lambert recalled an incident in one match when he fell out with a friend in blue: 'I am good friends with goalkeeper Stefan Klos from the time we played together at Borussia Dortmund, and we used to socialise together with our wives. But in a match at Ibrox we had been awarded a penalty, and Stefan refused to give the ball back as I tried to get it. As an experienced professional player, you do make a conscious effort to keep your cool, but in the heat of an Old Firm match anything can happen, so we had a go at each other. We made up and were all pals again after the game.'

Neil Lennon's attitude to Rangers was that Celtic should stand up for themselves: 'Watching Old Firm matches on television, I saw that Rangers often intimidated Celtic, so I made sure that didn't happen any longer. It didn't make me popular with the Rangers fans, but the day that the Rangers fans stop booing me will be the day that I know I'm not doing my job.'

Nevertheless, Rangers were to prove a real threat, but the biggest disappointment for Celtic in 2001–02 was their exit from the Champions League at the group stage, Celtic gaining nine points – including a fabulous 4–3 victory over Juventus – yet just failing to qualify. The UEFA Cup defeat at the hands of Valencia on penalties after the second leg was also hard to take, but domestically it seemed another Treble was on, as the Celts seemed almost invincible.

Celtic simply tore through the SPL, losing only one match and drawing four as they amassed an incredible 103 points and a goal difference of plus 76. Larsson was again the talisman, notching 29 goals from 33 league matches. Under McLeish, Rangers proved the bugbear in the second half of the season, winning 2–1 in a hugely exciting CIS Insurance League Cup semi-final that Celtic could, and perhaps should, have won. Rangers went on to lift the trophy, beating Ayr United in the final, and then the Scottish Cup final between the two Old Firm sides was even more of a thriller, though again it was Celtic who lost out, Peter Lovenkrands scoring in the final minute for a 3–2 victory.

That match was Lubo Moravčik's last competitive game for Celtic, and he moved to Japan with the fervent good wishes and thanks of everyone at Parkhead. Japan figured prominently for two great Celts that summer, Johan Mjällby captaining Sweden and Henrik Larsson inspiring his country to a group-winning performance in the World Cup finals. The club having run up a fair amount of debt, there was little transfer activity at the time, with Ulrik Laursen from Hibs and goalkeeper Magnus Hedman from Coventry City the only arrivals.

The following season, Celtic won nothing. And everything. Everything, that is, if you believe in moral victories.

In a remarkable 11 months of football, Celtic recorded their best performance in European competition for 32 years; lost the SPL championship by a single goal on the last day; went out of the Scottish Cup to Inverness Caledonian Thistle owing to one of O'Neill's very rare misjudgements; and lost the CIS Insurance League Cup to Rangers in a controversial final won 2–1 by Alex McLeish's side.

The domestic season was completely overshadowed by an experience that can be summed up in one word: Seville. Celtic's extraordinary progression through the UEFA Cup to the final in the Spanish city was the stuff of legend. It began in some ignominy, however, with FC Basel of Switzerland putting Celtic out of the Champions League at the final qualifying stage. Parachuted into the UEFA Cup, which was not seen as much of a consolation, Celtic put up a string of incredible performances, including two 'Battle of Britain' victories over Blackburn Rovers and Liverpool, the latter coming in the quarter-final. As well as the two English clubs, Celtic beat FK Suduva, Celta de Vigo, and VfB Stuttgart on the road to the semi-final, each match bringing its own tensions and creating its own stories.

The semi-final against Boavista of Portugal did not start well, with the Portuguese side defending well for a 1–1 draw at Parkhead. They would need just a single goal to beat Celtic in the return leg, but instead it was the Bhoys who triumphed, Larsson pouncing in the 78th minute to put Celtic into the final against FC Porto.

Those of us who were in Seville on 21 May 2003 will never forget the experience. The only sad note that day was the scoreline, which read Porto 3, Celtic 2 after extra time. Players and fans wept at the conclusion of a remarkable match played in searing heat, Larsson's two goals giving Celtic the chance they so nearly took. José Mourinho's men denied the Celts with some fine goals of their own and, it must be said, cheating gamesmanship tactics that made stomachs turn.

Seville was the highlight of the season, indeed of the decade, for Celtic. That they finished 2002–03 trophy-less was a travesty of justice, and Martin O'Neill set about putting things right.

He bought only one player – Stephen Pearson from Motherwell – and allowed Steve Guppy, Bobby Petta, David Fernandez and Stephen Crainey to go or be loaned. At the beginning of the year, O'Neill had quietly acquired Slovakian international Stan Varga on a free from Sunderland, and in July he gave the big defender a two-year contract, despite the fact he only played once in the previous season. It would be yet another shrewd decision by O'Neill, who also promoted young Liam Miller into the first team and was rewarded with fine displays by the player, who had clearly benefited from a loan spell with Aarhus in Denmark after long-term injuries had blighted his early career. John Kennedy was another exciting youngster, and with Shaun Maloney, Ross Wallace and Craig Beattie also promising prospects, it looked as though Celtic had a decent blend of experienced and young players.

O'Neill and everyone at Celtic Park knew that season 2003–04 would be momentous for one principal reason. Henrik Larsson, now firmly ensconced as the King of Kings for Celtic fans, had made it clear that he would leave the club at the end of the season, his seventh in the hoops. He would be 32 by then and had a hankering to sample life elsewhere before returning to his beloved Helsingborg in Sweden, where it had all begun for him. Throughout his final months at Celtic, the media were full of 'will he go or will he stay' stories, but anyone who was aware of the player's steely determination would have known that he could not be persuaded to carry on, no matter how much he loved the club.

There is simply not enough space in this book to charter the sheer footballing genius of Larsson. Suffice to say that in 2002, when Celtic polled their fans to find the club's greatest all-time XI, the team was named as Ronnie Simpson, Danny McGrain, Tommy Gemmell, Bobby Murdoch, Billy McNeill, Bertie Auld, Jimmy Johnstone, Paul McStay, Kenny Dalglish, Henrik Larsson and Bobby Lennox. For him to be up there alongside seven Lisbon Lions and McGrain, McStay and Dalglish, and be compared to Jimmy McGrory, as Larsson often was, says everything about the Swede's place in the Celtic pantheon. Add his incredible record for Sweden and you have a genuine world-class footballer, perhaps the only one to play in Scotland in the past decade or so.

Neil Lennon said, 'He will always be remembered for his goalscoring feats, but he was much more than a striker. He would pop up in midfield or in defence if needed – he covered so much yardage. It helped that he was super fit when he had to come back from a broken leg and broken jaw.

'But I knew he would leave. When Henrik made his mind up to do something, he always did it.'

Larsson's final season was not going to pass without him putting his stamp all over it, and so it proved. For the second time in three years, Celtic utterly romped away with the SPL title. Though Rangers challenged for a couple of months, by Christmas the league was so embarrassingly one-sided that if it had been a boxing match the referee would have called it off in January – indeed some bookmakers paid out on Celtic as league winners that early.

The only disappointment in the first half of the season was in December, when Hibs beat Celtic 2–1 in the CIS Insurance League Cup, ending the hopes of a domestic Treble. It was the first domestic defeat since April and came just eight days after a controversial late penalty awarded to Olympique Lyonnais saw Celtic exit the Champions League at the end of the group stage. Still, there was always the UEFA Cup again.

Larsson was a goal machine, but other players such as Chris Sutton and John Hartson grabbed their share, while Stan Petrov and Alan Thompson were always dangerous from midfield and big Stan Varga grabbed his share from dead-ball situations.

After Celtic set a British record of twenty-five consecutive league victories, Motherwell ending that with a 1–1 draw in March, matters home and abroad came to a head in the space of ten days in April. After Celtic's stunning single-goal aggregate defeat of Barcelona, their fellow Spaniards Villarreal provided the opposition in the UEFA Cup quarter-final, and after a 1–1 draw in Glasgow, Villarreal were the better team in Spain and went through with a 2–0 victory. Victory for Celtic over Livingston in the Scottish Cup semi-final was sandwiched between those two European ties before Celtic went to Rugby Park – scene of their heartbreaking 4–0 win that had not been enough to win the previous season's championship – and defeated Kilmarnock 1–0 with a goal from Petrov. Perhaps embarrassingly for the SPL, the six–six split was still another game away, and Celtic had gone thirty-two matches unbeaten.

O'Neill used the remaining league matches to plan ahead by giving youngsters and fringe players some experience, and that was one reason why the 77-match-unbeaten-at-home record fell against Aberdeen a week after the title was sealed. Dunfermline Athletic also notched a victory as Celtic started to coast. A sprightly young midfielder with blinding pace and control called Aiden McGeady, a product of the Celtic youth system, was handed his debut against Hearts and scored Celtic's goal in a 1–1 draw, while a chunky defender called Stephen McManus played a handful of games at left-back.

The end of the season was all about Henrik Larsson, and such was the emotion surrounding his departure and the special elements he himself brought to his parties that fans were left wondering who wrote his scripts. For surely no one other than a screenwriter or dramatist could have imagined what the Swede would do in his final matches for Celtic.

It was another player who would clinch victory in the final Old Firm match of the season. The Ne'erday Derby might well have been chosen for this book, since it involved a magnificent 3–0 win at Parkhead that effectively finished Rangers' challenge for the league, such as it was. It also established a record 18th successive derby win for Celtic and added to the earlier narrow 1–0 victory in the league at Ibrox.

As luck would have it, the Old Firm were drawn together in the Scottish Cup quarter-finals in early March, and with the Double very much in their sights Celtic made it a hat-trick of seasonal victories over the old enemy, winning a poor game by a single goal to nil. The fourth encounter between the teams was back at Ibrox and represented the last lingering chance for Rangers to chip away at Celtic's lead, which stood at a massive 16 points on the morning of the game. It was 19 points at full-time, goals from Larsson and Alan Thompson, against a late counter by Steven Thompson, giving Celtic a record fifth successive victory over Rangers.

'That was one of my best matches at Ibrox,' said Neil Lennon.

'We had to work hard, but at the end we were much the better team, and it showed. The looks on the faces of the Rangers players said it all. They knew the title was ours.'

The league duly won, the stage was set for a monumental Old Firm occasion. Never before had Celtic beaten their greatest rivals five times in one season. To 'greenwash' the men in blue would prove once and for all that Celtic had been by far the dominant team in Scotland in that season 2003–04 and would give O'Neill's band a unique place in Celtic's history.

It was some team that season: up front, Larsson, Sutton and Hartson were usually used in combination, or sometimes all three together, though injuries to the latter two saw them out of the team at times. In goals, O'Neill could use young David Marshall, hero against Barcelona, or Rab Douglas, both of them full Scotland internationals. The centre-backs Bobo Baldé, Johan Mjällby and Stan Varga often formed a back three in a 3–5–2 formation and must have been unique in world football, as all three had captained their national teams – Guinea, Sweden and Slovakia respectively. Joos Valgaeren was not the force he had been but helped out on occasion, while young Stephen McManus and John Kennedy seemed the future for Celtic, until the latter was cruelly and permanently damaged by a Romanian thug during his international debut in March 2004.

Didier Agathe, bought from Hibs for just £50,000, was possessed of blinding speed and made the right wing-back position seem easy, while Jackie McNamara was the ideal utility player, capable of playing right or left in defence or midfield and, like his father, Jackie senior, not afraid to join in the attack. Petrov was the motor in midfield, a box-to-box player who scored a useful number of goals. Alan Thompson and Stephen Pearson shared the duties on the left, and a crop of youngsters such as McGeady, Smith and Wallace was on call to help out when needed.

As tigerish on the field as he is gentlemanly off it, Neil Lennon was that most misunderstood and yet valuable of creatures, the perfect holding midfielder. Every Celtic team should have a Lennon. He could break up attacks single-handedly, keep Celtic in possession by doing the simple things well and often sent in the telling pass that started a scoring move. His work off the ball was crucial to the success of O'Neill's side, while his very presence on the field made sure the opposition knew they would get no easy ride.

Lennon's background in his native Northern Ireland made him a Celtic supporter from childhood, but, as he revealed in his autobiography, he might well have signed for Rangers as a young teenager had it not been for that club's bar on Catholic players at the time.

Distraught at having to end his Northern Ireland international career after sectarian death threats, Lennon showed immense courage in overcoming depressive illness in his time at Leicester and Celtic. That he decided to talk about his illness openly has been widely acknowledged as a great contribution to combating the stigma attached to mental illness in this country.

In season 2003–04, Lennon was often seen at his best, doing the hard work that allowed Petrov, Thompson and the rest of the midfield to go up and support Larsson and whoever was alongside him. The final Old Firm match against Rangers was a case in point, as no one in the hoops worked harder for victory that day.

History was in the offing for Celtic on what was a truly momentous day in the club's record as part of the Old Firm. They had not won six successive league matches against Rangers since 1914, and their last seasonal 'greenwash' had been in 1971–72 when they won four times against Rangers, twice in the league and twice in the League Cup. Only once before had either half of the Old Firm beaten their rivals five times in one season, Rangers achieving that feat in 1963–64.

It was epoch-making stuff, potentially, and both sets of fans were anxious to see what would transpire. Yes, the league was already won, but there is no such thing as a meaningless Old Firm match, and the chance to make history, or avoid it being made at your team's expense, was a real spur for the players.

Neil Lennon recalled, 'We all knew we had a chance to set a new record, and it just added to the atmosphere in the build-up to the game. We had won the league, but now we could make a bit of history, and Martin and all the squad were up for it.'

Forty years after the five-victory bluewash, the Celtic team sent out by O'Neill that Saturday to rewrite the record books was in 3–5–2 formation. Marshall was in goals; Varga, Baldé and McNamara were at the back; Agathe, Petrov, Lennon, Pearson and Thompson were the middle five, with Agathe and Pearson doing much of the wing-back running; and Larsson and Sutton were up front again, Hartson being injured and the former playing in his last-ever Old

Firm game – how the Rangers fans would be glad to see the back of him.

Knowing he was enduring a trophy-less season, McLeish concentrated on youth and started his team as follows: Klos, Hutton, de Boer, Khizanishvili, Vanoli, Burke, Ricksen, Arteta, Hughes, Mols and Thompson. The referee was Hugh Dallas, Scotland's best whistler of the day but someone whom the Celtic support felt was not entirely amenable to the hoops.

Three minutes into the match and that particular piece of paranoia appeared to have some justification. Stan Varga seemed to get his head on a Thompson free kick for what he claimed as the opening goal, though it may have come off Zurab Khizanishvili. Dallas was having none of it, however, awarding Rangers a free kick for what looked more like a 50–50 tussle between Larsson and Frank de Boer.

Rangers enjoyed a spell of pressure, but they could not take advantage of corner kicks against the giant Celtic central pair of Baldé and Varga. Larsson's 15th-minute free kick showed that the Swede was anxious to score in his final Old Firm game, but the effort from 20 yards went straight to Klos, who then foiled Chris Sutton.

Neil Lennon and Fernando Ricksen had a wee spat after 35 minutes, as Lennon recalled: 'I don't know what it was about Fernando, but he always seemed to lose the plot when he was playing us. But I was not going to let him get away with anything.'

The temperature inside Parkhead went up a degree or two, and Rangers came close with a Stephen Hughes shot that was deflected by Petrov. Hughes's next effort was also deflected wide, and from Mikel Arteta's corner de Boer sent in an effort that Marshall parried away. The young goalkeeper was nearly caught out by Mols shortly afterwards but recovered to foil Steven Thompson in the act of scoring. Mols again looked set to pull the trigger when Baldé arrived and robbed him with a stunningly accurate tackle.

Rangers started the second half brightly, but slowly Celtic began to turn the screw, the difference in sheer class telling as first Varga and then Petrov came close, the latter foiled by a fine Klos save. A rash of yellow cards followed as tempers began to fray, both sides receiving three bookings in total.

After an hour, Celtic should have taken the lead when Petrov latched onto Larsson's cross shot but fired into the side netting.

A Thompson free kick was well held by Klos, who also tipped a Sutton header over the bar. Klos then defied Larsson, punching his header clear and then just holding another effort from the departing superstar, though the Celtic fans shouted that the German had got the ball over the line.

It was not to be Larsson's day as he squandered a golden chance seven minutes from time. As the Celtic fans continued to sing their champions' ditties, the scoreline of 0–0 loomed large, especially after Sutton missed a couple of chances and Steven Thompson headed wide of Marshall's goal.

In the final minute, Marshall decided on the direct approach and launched a long one into the Rangers half, where Sutton headed the ball in to Larsson. Creating the 'assist' that he so often did, Larsson turned the ball in to Sutton's path, and the big Englishman held off de Boer before despatching, from 23 yards, a lovely curling chip shot over Klos and into the top corner of the goal. It was a magnificent strike and worthy of winning any game.

Neil Lennon said, 'Chris and Henrik had done it so many times before that we should never have been surprised. We also never gave up, not till the final whistle, so in many ways that goal was typical of that time at Celtic. It was actually my favourite win over Rangers, and I was involved in plenty of them.'

There was no time for Rangers to come back, and in all honesty they looked utterly shattered. The greenwash had been achieved, and another chapter in Celtic's history had been written.

Another truly great chapter in that history then drew to a close. On 16 May, Henrik Larsson played his last competitive home match against Dundee United and was made captain for the day. He produced an ending that only he could conjure up, scoring two late goals to secure a 2–1 victory. The tears flowed as he left the scene, and they were not just in Larsson's eyes.

He topped that performance with a quite incredible end to his competitive time at Celtic, bagging a double as Celtic came from a goal down to beat a battling Dunfermline Athletic 3–1 in the Scottish Cup final. It only remained for him to take a final emotional bow in his testimonial match against Seville, won 1–0 with a Sutton goal.

Thus ended the Celtic career of one of the greatest footballers ever to wear the hoops. In just seven years he had scored 242 goals to sit behind only Jimmy McGrory and Bobby Lennox in the all-time scorers list for Celtic. He plainly adored the supporters that had made his time at Parkhead so special, and in turn the fans hailed him as the King of Kings. He has started a new career in management in Sweden, so maybe one day Henrik Larsson will return to Parkhead in a new guise. Until then, only gilded memories of his genius must suffice.

19

BEING UNDER PRESSURE IS A
WORRYING THING

27 APRIL 2008
SCOTTISH LEAGUE PREMIER DIVISION
CELTIC 3, RANGERS 2

All things must pass. Not many people thought Martin O'Neill would manage Celtic for the rest of his life, and even before season 2004–05 he had been tempted to look at the managership of Leeds United but wisely stayed away from that poisoned chalice. Any time a big managerial job came up anywhere in Europe, however, his name was linked to it, and the Celtic fans surmised that one day he would surely be tempted by a bigger club, perhaps of the calibre of Manchester United or the Milan clubs.

In the end his departure was not caused by ambition but by his deep love for his wife, Geraldine. Following her diagnosis with lymphoma, O'Neill rightly took time off to care for her at the beginning of season 2004–05, and the strain showed on his face for the rest of the season as Celtic underperformed in comparison with previous years, though they won the first Old Firm match to extend the league-victory sequence to a record seven.

Apart from a draw in Barcelona, the Champions League was a disaster, and Celtic were out of Europe completely before Christmas, not helped by Henrik Larsson scoring for his new club at Parkhead – the least-celebrated goal against Celtic ever seen. The League Cup saw Rangers triumph after removing the Celts in an early round. With Craig Bellamy arriving on loan and making an instant impact in the January, the SPL should have been wrapped up by April, and that looked to be the case when Celtic went to Ibrox and won 2–1, with goals from Petrov and Bellamy. It gave O'Neill a record of 16 wins in 20 league matches against Rangers.

Neil Lennon remembered one gesture at the end of the 0–2 loss at Ibrox in November 2004 that meant a great deal to him, as he had suffered constant abuse in his time at Celtic: 'When Martin came out onto the pitch and went over with me to our fans, he was basically saying that he had had enough of listening to what I had to go through.

'But the point is that I thrived on that abuse. All it ever did was make me try even harder for Celtic. And it meant that every game we won against Rangers was one to relish. But I can tell you, every one that you lose hurts for a very long time.'

Rangers had also had a fine season, and in the last round of matches Celtic still needed a draw to lift the title but succumbed to two very late goals by Scott McDonald as Motherwell won 2–1, allowing Rangers to take the flag in dramatic fashion with a 1–0 win over Hibs. It was the ultimate sickener, and many people pointed out that one more goal in 2003 and three more minutes of a clean sheet against Motherwell would have seen Martin O'Neill and his successor Gordon Strachan lead Celtic to eight titles in a row.

On 25 May, a date that is usually celebrated by Celtic fans because of the Lisbon connection, it was announced that Martin O'Neill would be leaving Celtic after that weekend's Scottish Cup final against Dundee United. He intended to care for Geraldine full-time during her illness. Most fans were bereft but recognised that O'Neill and his family had a much bigger fight on their hands than mere football.

Celtic had dismissed Rangers earlier in the Scottish Cup, and though the team looked tired, an early Alan Thompson free kick was enough to secure the seventh and last trophy of O'Neill's tenure. The scenes as he lifted the Cup and saluted the fans were highly emotional, and credit should go to those United fans who joined in the applause. Fortunately, Geraldine O'Neill survived, and Martin was able to return to football 15 months later as manager of Aston Villa.

It was the end of one era and the beginning of another as Gordon Strachan arrived to manage Celtic. Once the bane of Celtic's life as a player, the wee ginger-haired midfielder inspiring many an Aberdeen performance, Strachan had successfully managed Southampton, though his earlier spell at Coventry City had ended with them being relegated. He was best known to fans for his media punditry and pawky sense of humour – he was once asked by a reporter for a quick word and replied 'velocity'.

Strachan's first season in charge started disastrously with the humiliating 0–5 defeat at the hands of Artmedia Bratislava. Yet in the return leg, in which Celtic came within an ace of making history – they would have been the only team in fifty years of European competition to come back from five down – the signs were evident of a grinding winning mentality as the Celts won 4–0, which was not enough to keep them in Europe.

The new manager wanted to put his own stamp on the team and brought in Japanese midfielder – and superstar in his own country – Shunsuke Nakamura, Polish goalkeeper Artur Boruc and fellow Pole Maciej Zurawski, and Paul Telfer and Dion Dublin from England, but arguably the best decision he made was to make Neil Lennon captain.

Lennon said, 'Jackie McNamara had just announced that he was leaving, which was a real shock, and I was on holiday in Portugal thinking about what to do myself when Gordon called and asked me to stay on as captain. In my first press conference as captain I said we would win the league. I meant it, too.'

The wisdom of Strachan's decision was questioned, to put it mildly, by a vitriolic press when Lennon was sent off for arguing with referee Stuart Dougal after a 1–3 defeat at Ibrox early in the season. 'Looking back, I regret what happened, maybe not completely, but I do regret it,' said Lennon.

In the return fixture at Parkhead in November, Celtic won 3–0 and went three points clear at the top of the SPL. They would not look back.

The addition of Roy Keane in January inspired Celtic to greater heights, though his debut was a terrible loss to Clyde in the Scottish Cup. With Lennon driving the team onfield and Nakamura providing real class, the league became a procession. Celtic then won the first trophy of Strachan's managership in March by beating Dunfermline Athletic 3–0 in the CIS Insurance League Cup final.

That final became known as 'Jinky's Final', the greatest of all Celtic players having finally succumbed to motor neurone disease on 13 March, just six days earlier. The team all wore Johnstone's number seven on their shorts and unveiled T-shirts in his honour after full-time.

Neil Lennon spoke for the team in those days: 'When people here speak about playing the Celtic way, I think they are talking about Jimmy. He was entertaining, exciting and pretty fearless as well. We've lost a talismanic figure.'

No tribute, however, could ever be fulsome enough for Jinky. He was the greatest.

Strachan's Celtic then added the SPL title, again before the six–six split, by beating Hearts 1–0 in early April. Roy Keane retired at the end of that season, and John Hartson and Stiliyan Petrov left shortly afterwards. Alan Thompson did not fit into Strachan's plans and left during the 2006–07 season, while Bobo Baldé mysteriously disappeared from view. Only Neil Lennon remained of the core of Martin O'Neill's team, but new players like Gary Caldwell, Lee Naylor, Dutch internationalist Jan Vennegoor of Hesselink, former Ranger – and now back there – Kenny Miller, Evander Sno, Jiří Jarošík, Mark Wilson, Darren O'Dea, Derek Riordan and Thomas Gravesen came in and made varying degrees of impact.

Over at Ibrox Alex McLeish paid the price of failing to take even second place in the league, Hearts becoming the only team in SPL history to split the Old Firm at the top. McLeish was replaced by Frenchman Paul Le Guen, and many pundits predicted this would be the turning point for Rangers. That was indeed true, because in the following season they at least got back up to second again as Celtic cruised to the Double.

Neil Lennon recalled, 'Le Guen was just the wrong choice for Rangers, and a few of us thought that would be the case as soon as he was appointed. I only recently was told that I actually had more league wins at Ibrox than Paul le Guen.'

The highlight of 2006–07 for Celtic was a remarkable Champions League night at Parkhead when Celtic defeated Manchester United 1–0 with a brilliant trademark Nakamura free kick. It was the first time that the club had qualified from the group stages of the Champions League. Not even O'Neill had managed that, and Strachan had also put one over on his old boss Sir Alex Ferguson.

Celtic then gave AC Milan a scare before exiting the tournament. Otherwise it was a domestic canter, the league secured with four games to play and the Scottish Cup won, albeit with a poor showing, by a 1–0 defeat of Dunfermline Athletic, the goal scored by loan signing Jean-Joël Perrier Doumbé.

That was Neil Lennon's last game as a player. The Celtic captain had been paid his own unique tribute in his last home match against Aberdeen a fortnight previously, the fans recognising his seven and a half seasons of unswerving commitment to the club. He left with five league medals, three Scottish Cup medals, two League Cup medals and the honour of being the first man to captain Celtic to the later stages of the Champions League. 'I wanted to go out on a high,' said Lennon, 'and winning a second title as captain seemed an appropriate time to leave.'

Joining Nottingham Forest, the Lurgan Lion would not be away for too long, however.

The first two seasons of Strachan's managership had seen Celtic saunter to successive SPL titles. The third season would be anything but easy and would involve one of the greatest comebacks in the club's long history.

Walter Smith had stabilised Rangers in the second half of the 2006–07 season, and along with Ally McCoist the new management threatened to get the other half of the Old Firm into a challenging position, which they duly did. They proved their competitiveness in the first Old Firm match of the season in October. With Stephen 'Mick' McManus installed as captain and new signings Scott McDonald, Massimo Donati and future captain Scott Brown all featuring, the Celts went down 0–3 and somehow also managed to set another record: no fewer than nine Celtic players were booked by referee Mike McCurry.

For the second year running in the Champions League, Celtic surprised one of the giants of Europe, beating AC Milan 2–1 on yet another unforgettable night at Parkhead before going on to qualify for the later stages once again. Old foes Barcelona would put Celtic out in the round of 16, but given the disparate resources available to Celtic, compared with those of the biggest European clubs, the Bhoys were truly punching way above their weight.

Exiting the CIS Insurance League Cup and the Scottish Cup to Hearts and Aberdeen respectively, only the Scottish Premier League remained for Celtic.

The season had been tragically interrupted by the death of former Celt Phil O'Donnell. While playing for Motherwell against Dundee United on 29 December, O'Donnell collapsed and died from heart failure. One of the most popular people in football, O'Donnell's passing was marked with many tributes, and both the Ne'erday Derby and Celtic's next match against Motherwell were postponed as a mark of respect.

Behind the scenes at Parkhead, another tragedy was developing. Tommy Burns had already been treated once for skin cancer, but the melanoma had returned, and this time there would be no recovery for the much-loved former player and manager. Celtic's fans learned how serious Burns's condition was only when Neil Lennon was recalled as first-team coach in late March, less than a year after leaving Parkhead.

Celtic were chasing Rangers for most of the season, and before Lennon returned, the Ibrox club looked to have effectively secured the championship on the last weekend in March, when they beat Celtic 1–0 at home. Rangers were now six points clear and had a game in hand, and with Celtic having only eight matches to play, all looked lost.

Any small chance of Celtic retaining the league looked to be thoroughly gone a week later on 5 April, when Motherwell came to Parkhead and won with the only goal of the match despite having former Ranger Bob Malcolm sent off after 50 minutes.

All was not completely lost, however. Rangers had been going well in the UEFA Cup and Scottish Cup, and for various reasons they had built up a backlog of fixtures – replays in the Scottish Cup and matches postponed from earlier in the season meant that, if they reached the UEFA and Scottish Cup finals, the Ibrox club faced a punishing schedule of 17 matches in 51 days. They were already looking tired, and two of their final nine SPL matches would be against Celtic, both of them at Parkhead. It could have been worse. The SPL obligingly agreed to add four days to the season if Rangers reached the UEFA Cup final, despite official protests by Celtic.

The prize for the league winners was also very great: automatic entry to the lucrative group stages of the Champions League. When Rangers could only draw 3–3 with Dundee United on 6 April, it looked as though a miracle could happen, but most Celtic fans knew that their heroes were having considerable difficulty scoring goals and felt that the league was lost, not least because Rangers could lose the two matches against Celtic and still take the title if they won all their remaining matches.

With Strachan and Lennon driving them on, Celtic went to Fir Park and took revenge on Motherwell. Even though the team did not play well, they ground out a comfortable 4–1 victory, and Jan Vennegoor of Hesselink helped himself to two goals.

Paul Hartley had joined his former Hearts colleague Steven Pressley in Celtic's ranks on the last day of the transfer window in January 2007, and after an indifferent first year at Parkhead he was now coming into his own. Barry Robson had signed from Dundee United on that last day of the previous January's transfer window too, and now these two hard workers bossed the midfield tough stuff, allowing McGeady and Nakamura the freedom to attack that was to prove vital in the coming weeks. Behind them German international Andreas Hinkel was frequently impressive at right-back. Strachan had the tools to do the job – with Lennon growling at his side, surely the two fiery redheads could spark Celtic to something wonderful?

'Gordon was determined that we would all give everything and then a bit more,' said Lennon. 'We were going to fight to the last whistle of the last game, if necessary, and we knew that we had two home games against Rangers to help turn things round.'

The stage was set for an utterly crucial Old Firm encounter, and it was a toss-up whether this match or the later Old Firm game of that season made the top 20. If Celtic lost at Parkhead on Wednesday, 16 April, the league really was over, as Rangers by then had two games in hand. Not surprisingly, the game turned out to be a classic of the Old Firm variety: nervy players, scything tackles, controversy in spades and almost unendurable tension for the Celtic fans.

There was also a goal of supreme quality, and thankfully it came for Celtic. After 20 minutes of thunderous exchanges, including Barry Robson smashing Christian Dailly into obscurity, Gary Caldwell chipped a pass forward to Nakamura, who had drifted into the centre of the Rangers half. The Japanese maestro almost miscontrolled the pass with his left foot, the ball going forward and fortunately sitting up nicely for him. A few quick steps and Nakamura let fly from 28 yards with his left, the ball swerving and dipping and completely deceiving Allan McGregor in the Rangers goal.

It was a wondrous strike, as good as any Nakamura had scored, and set up Celtic to dominate the rest of the half, McGregor saving from Scott McDonald before Stephen McManus came to the rescue for Celtic with a pinpoint late tackle foiling Jean-Claude Darcheville in the act of scoring.

Walter Smith decided to go for broke and sent on Nacho Novo for Kirk Broadfoot at the interval. The Spaniard, who just loved to score against Celtic, struck ten minutes into the half with a fine shot across Artur Boruc into the far corner of the net.

Back came Celtic, and McGregor injured himself making a needless save from McDonald, referee Kenny Clark having already blown for an infringement. The Rangers keeper limped on and was clearly struggling when Nakamura unleashed a thunderbolt that beat the goalkeeper and seemed netbound until Carlos Cuéllar instinctively threw up a hand and diverted the ball onto the crossbar. Rangers' best player of the season was shown the red card, and Celtic now had a gilt-edged chance to seal the points from the penalty spot.

Up stepped Scott 'Skippy' McDonald, and normally his low shot to the goalkeeper's left would have found the net. McGregor was in the form of his life, and despite his injury he flung himself to the left and pushed the shot onto the post before gathering the ball at the second attempt. McGregor went off a few minutes later, replaced by Neil Alexander.

As the 90 minutes came and went, it looked like season over for Celtic, but in the third minute of injury time, Caldwell sent a hopeful cross to the back post, where McDonald found unknown inches to rise and head the ball across the goal to where Vennegoor of Hesselink was waiting to head home a truly dramatic winner.

At full-time, the tensions erupted and harsh words between captains Stephen McManus and Barry Ferguson led to a brawl that was really more handbags than anything. David Weir of Rangers and Celtic's Gary Caldwell both raised their hands, however, and were shown red cards.

Gary Caldwell said, 'Feelings were running high, obviously, and when it kicked off Davie and I ended up being the scapegoats. I thought it was unfair on both of us because it was nothing too serious.'

The pressure was now telling on Rangers. The following weekend saw them go to Perth and display exhaustion at times in a 1–1 draw with St Johnstone. They were not much better in the first leg of their UEFA Cup semi-final, a goalless draw against Fiorentina, before they returned to Parkhead for the match that would surely determine the outcome of the SPL.

The Celts had beaten Aberdeen 1–0 the previous weekend to go top of the table for the first time that season, albeit with Rangers having two games in hand. A point was not good enough for Celtic – only victory would do.

'Everyone knew that we just had to win,' said Lennon. 'That is always the case with Celtic – only winning is acceptable. But we needed to win that Old Firm game more than any other I've been involved in.'

Celtic's team was a 4–4–2 formation as follows: Boruc; Hinkel, Caldwell, McManus and Naylor; Nakamura, Hartley, Robson and McGeady; Vennegoor of Hesselink and McDonald. On the bench were Scott Brown and Georgios Samaras, the Greek internationalist who was on loan from Manchester City and who had scored some vital goals.

With McGregor still injured, Rangers fielded this team: Alexander, Broadfoot, Dailly, Weir, Papac, Whittaker, Hemdani, Ferguson, Davis, Novo, Cousin. Darcheville was rested, Cuéllar was suspended and there was no place for Kris Boyd, who had scored both his side's goals in the victory – on penalties – over Dundee United in the previous month's CIS Insurance League Cup Final. He would notch another double in the Scottish Cup final win over Queen of the South and end the season with 25 goals in all, but none of them was against Celtic, as for some reason manager Walter Smith seemed to think Boyd was not up to Old Firm competition.

Gary Caldwell said, 'At that time when they played us, or played in Europe, Rangers usually left only one up front. People were giving them stick for the system they were playing, but it was effective, and you can't argue with that. It was hard to break down, and I can tell you it was frustrating to play against them. So you had to be ready for their method and be patient.'

Rangers swept into the attack from the start and won a corner. Daniel Cousin shot from 12 yards, but Artur Boruc reacted well to punch the ball away. Celtic replied to that early scare with the best possible answer: a goal.

In the fourth minute, Andreas Hinkel punted a long one to just outside the box, where Jan Vennegoor of Hesselink outjumped both Christian Dailly and Kirk Broadfoot to head the ball into the path of strike partner McDonald. The Rangers players and fans claimed for offside, but replays later showed that the Australian was just about level with the last Rangers man when the ball left

Vennegoor of Hesselink's head. Assistant referee Tom Murphy was in line with the move and called it correctly, allowing McDonald to steady himself and coolly blast the ball low past Neil Alexander before setting off on a lap of honour that seemed to go round half the stadium.

The Celtic fans sat back to enjoy what would surely be a blistering performance by the Bhoys, but Rangers had other thoughts. Outraged at not getting an offside decision at McDonald's goal, they charged upfield, and Celtic conceded too many free kicks as the Light Blue pressure mounted. From one of them, Saša Papac curled in a cross that Dailly headed just past the post, though the referee had already whistled for a Celtic free kick. It was a bad omen – with 17 minutes on the clock, Steven Davis sent in a corner that seemed to come off the back of Davie Weir's head and tricked Boruc, who only flapped at the ball on its way into the net. The 37-year-old Weir had collided with Caldwell in scoring his goal, and his face soon swelled up – a small price to pay for his first goal against Celtic.

Celtic were clearly rattled, and Barry Robson saw a yellow card for a lunging tackle on Ferguson. The Rangers captain then blasted into the penalty area a shot that struck Caldwell on the arm, the referee correctly ruling that there had been no deliberate handball. Some 12 minutes after Rangers' first goal, the Celtic fans were almost in despair. Another Davis corner from the right wing found Cousin in space, and the Gabon internationalist made no mistake with his header for what was also his first goal against Celtic. Not since 1993 had Celtic come from behind to win an Old Firm match – surely now the dream was over.

Down from the stands poured an unremitting cacophony of noise as the Celtic fans tried desperately to lift the team. Hartley and Robson had not been able to impose themselves in midfield as usual, the former showing his frustration with a crude tackle on Ferguson that earned him a booking, but Aiden McGeady slowly but surely began to exert his own special influence. He was giving Broadfoot a torrid time, and after one run he fired in a cross that Dailly only just reached before McDonald. The minutes before half-time were all Celtic, with McGeady to the fore.

In the 43rd minute, McGeady probed the defence once again and this time played a short pass to McDonald, standing just inside the box on the Celtic left. As Dailly moved to close him down,

McDonald whirled and shot, the ball looping off Dailly's foot and up and over Alexander. McDonald rightly claimed the goal and nearly made it a hat-trick just before half-time with an effort that went just wide. After 45 minutes of hugely entertaining stuff, it was all-square, and both sides had everything to play for in the second half.

That half was barely five minutes old when Rangers suffered a real blow. They had already seen McDonald go close and Vennegoor of Hesselink be robbed of a sitter by Broadfoot when David Weir, the veteran rock in their defence, left the field injured. His replacement was Amdy Faye, the Senegalese player who was on loan from Charlton Athletic and who had only played a handful of games for Rangers, the last of them in October. A few minutes after Faye's arrival, Vennegoor of Hesselink gave him a warm introduction with a serious crunching boot at midriff height, for which the Dutchman was booked, as had Lee Naylor been a few minutes earlier for a foul on Nacho Novo.

Sensing that their opponents were now weaker at the back, Celtic began a series of attacks without creating many clear chances. Darren O'Dea and Georgios Samaras came on for the injured Stephen McManus and Vennegoor of Hesselink respectively, the latter coming off to avoid a second booking and suspension. Still there was no breakthrough, and as the clock showed the 70-minute mark the Celtic fans were more than a little anxious.

They need not have worried. Paul Hartley lobbed a long pass towards the penalty area, and McDonald took off. Just as McDonald entered the box, the flailing Kirk Broadfoot came from behind and flattened the Australian rugby-style. It was a clear penalty, and referee Thomson swithered about sending Broadfoot off before deciding that Faye might have got back to stop McDonald's 'clear goalscoring opportunity' as the law states. A booking was therefore deemed sufficient.

Winning the tussle with Samaras to take the kick, Barry Robson's penalty-taking style was like the man himself: direct and no nonsense. Alexander dived to his left, but the ball went low down the middle and into the net. Celtic had indeed come from behind, and having begun to dominate play, they looked set to go on and win, but still the tension was at boiling point.

A Robson corner struck the post at one end while substitute Jean-Claude Darcheville was only just foiled by Caldwell at the other. The closing minutes saw Celtic come close to adding a fourth, Dailly handling a Robson cross in the penalty box – accidental, ruled referee Thomson – and McGeady shooting high. In the third minute of injury time, Steven Whittaker completely lost the plot and booted Nakamura. Having already been booked, Whittaker had to go, and his red card meant he would miss Rangers' next game against Hibs.

The final whistle saw amazing scenes of jubilation among the Celtic support. As the shell-shocked Rangers team and their fans made their exit, the Parkhead tannoy system crackled with a very appropriate song: the old David Bowie and Queen hit 'Under Pressure'. Very naughty of the DJ, but the Celtic fans loved it, and they also loved Artur Boruc unveiling his 'God Bless the Pope' T-shirt. Having received a Fiscal's caution less than two years previously for laughing at Rangers fans – definitely not for making the sign of the cross, of course – Boruc might have been well advised not to go seeking controversy again, but at least 'the Holy Goalie' was careful this time not to flaunt anything directly at the Rangers supporters, though he and every Celt was laughing inside.

Neil Lennon said, 'In my experience, Old Firm games define you as a player with either team, and they define your reputation with the fans, as they will always hark back to particular matches and talk about players or goals or incidents from them. That match defined that Celtic team as fighters, and I really felt that we could go on and win the league.

'We knew other teams had to take points off Rangers, but they were under severe pressure at the time, and I thought there might be some reaction in their ranks.'

In the space of 12 days, Celtic had turned things around. A hard-fought 2–1 victory away to Motherwell then put the Celts eight points clear at the top, but Rangers still had four games in hand. Though Celtic had the better goal difference, it still required two of the other top six to take at least two points each off Rangers for the title to go to Parkhead. The pressure on Rangers was unrelenting, and they cracked.

Hibs and Motherwell duly obliged, with draws either side of Rangers losing the UEFA Cup final to Zenit St Petersburg in Manchester. The rioting of the Rangers fans shown around the world hardly helped the atmosphere within the Ibrox club, and on the final day of the season, Thursday, 22 May, Rangers had to travel to Pittodrie knowing that Celtic were now favourites for the title.

The Celts had beaten Hibs 2–0 on 11 May, but four days later came the news that Celtic and the football world had been dreading. At the age of 51, Tommy Burns died of cancer. The passing of this huge figure in the club's recent history was mourned by everyone who knew this good and decent man and brought about a temporary lull in the usual Old Firm rivalry as fans of both teams marked his untimely death. His great friends Walter Smith and Ally McCoist acted as pallbearers at his funeral, and the tributes to Burns from Rangers fans showed that, on occasion, all the sadder aspects of the Old Firm can be set aside. Perhaps one day that will happen permanently.

Tommy's death and the funeral two days before the last matches of season 2007–08 were shattering events, but Celtic were not brittle and did not break.

Lennon said, 'The whole football club was desperate to win it for Tommy. Even though we knew his death was inevitable, we were all devastated, and there were a lot of tears flowing, with Gordon really badly upset. We already knew how much we missed having Tommy around the place, and now that would be permanent. But we came together as a club and pulled ourselves together for one last game.'

On the Thursday evening at Tannadice Park, Jan Vennegoor of Hesselink scored the only goal of the match. Simultaneously, at Pittodrie a tired and dejected Rangers lost 0–2, and even though they would go on to beat Queen of the South and win the Scottish Cup, the air of huge disappointment around Ibrox was palpable.

Celtic were champions by three clear points, and the miracle that had seemed so unlikely only a month previously had occurred. It seemed only fitting that the championship had been achieved in tribute to the great spirit that was Tommy Burns.

20

SETTING MATTERS STRAIGHT

15 MARCH 2009
COOPERATIVE INSURANCE LEAGUE CUP FINAL
CELTIC 2, RANGERS 0

Having won the SPL title on the last day of the 2007–08 season, Celtic unfurled the league flag on the first day of the 2008–09 season. Showing why he had been a populist politician as well as a genuine fan, club chairman Dr John Reid set aside tradition and, with a gesture that was greatly welcomed by the supporters, invited Mrs Rosemary Burns, widow of Tommy, to carry out the ceremony instead of himself.

It was one of the few things that the club got exactly right in a topsy-turvy season. Another was victory in the Cooperative Insurance Cup, the latest name for the Scottish League Cup.

Until this match, Celtic had not beaten Rangers in a cup final at Hampden in 20 years. The two sides had met in two League Cup finals, those of 1990–91 and 2002–03, when Rangers won 2–1 on both occasions. The Scottish Cup finals of 1998–99 and 2001–02 had been won by Rangers 1–0 and 3–2 respectively, and you had to go back to 1989 and Celtic's 1–0 victory in the Scottish Cup final courtesy of a Joe Miller goal to find the last time the Bhoys had triumphed in an Old Firm final.

Not even a third title in a row could convince the entire Celtic support that Gordon Strachan was the right man for the manager's job. The hangover from his Celtic-baiting time at Aberdeen was still prevalent almost 25 years on, and though many more fans were warming to him, the man himself seemed slightly less in love with the job after the death of Tommy Burns, an event that had deeply affected him.

Neil Lennon was carrying on as coach and had plenty time to observe Strachan and appreciate his work: 'I never understood those who wanted Gordon out. Who could have done a better job in such circumstances? He was under pressure from day one because Martin O'Neill was always going to be a hard act to follow, but having had the chance to work closely with Gordon as a member of his backroom staff, I saw the effort he put in along with assistant manager Garry Pendrey. They left nothing to chance, and their attention to detail really impressed me.'

There was not a lot of money to spend, however. Georgios Samaras's loan was converted to a permanent signing, young Marc Crosas came from Barcelona, Dutch centre-back Glenn Loovens was signed from Cardiff City and Paddy McCourt came from Derry City, but the biggest transfer news – apart from the constant rumours surrounding the possible departures of Artur Boruc and Aiden McGeady – was the return of Shaun Maloney after an unhappy spell at Aston Villa. No fewer than ten players were either allowed to leave or were loaned out, while Evander Sno was transferred to Ajax in his native Netherlands and Derek Riordan went back to Hibs. Rangers' financial problems were not yet the everyday currency of the back pages, however, and while Carlos Cuéllar had been transferred to Aston Villa, they had made several signings, including Kenny Miller, Pedro Mendes, Andrius Velička, Madjid Bougherra and Kyle Lafferty.

The first Old Firm match of the season gave an indication of the roller-coaster months ahead. Former Celt Kenny Miller's two goals were the key to Rangers' 4–2 win at Parkhead in a bad-tempered game that saw both teams reduced to ten men. The reverse hardly seemed to matter – well, not too much – as Celtic promptly went on to get a run of 12 successive SPL victories by the end of November. Unfortunately there had been no victories at all in the Champions League, with draws at home to Manchester United and Aalborg the only points gained. After Hibs brought the league leaders' winning streak to an end, the Celts finally won a Champions League match, beating Villarreal 2–0, though the match was meaningless, as the Spaniards had already qualified, and Celtic were out of Europe altogether, joining Rangers, who had been ignominiously dismissed by Lithuanian club Kaunas at the start of the season.

The second Old Firm league game, on 27 December, was a cracker from a Celtic viewpoint. Celtic's record at Ibrox had been poor in the previous three years, and Rangers were unbeaten at home in 2008.

Not many fans were relishing the match, but Neil Lennon was: 'It was my first visit there as part of the coaching team, and I enjoyed being back. I know it sounds crazy, but I loved playing at Ibrox. The playing surface was usually good, and the intensity of the atmosphere always brought out the best in me. I'd actually been to the stadium as a lad when Rangers were showing interest in me, but to go back as a player for Celtic and win there was just a dream.

'It was quite funny what used to happen. When we got there, the rest of the squad always got off the bus and moved inside and opened the windows so they could hear the boos when I got off. That's not changed.

'I never missed a single Old Firm match while I was playing for Celtic, and I came out well ahead with eighteen wins, five draws and ten defeats – and I can't believe we lost ten.'

Gordon Strachan had devised a new strategy for the match. Playing a containing game and hitting on the counter, Celtic achieved an unexpected and memorable victory, Scott McDonald grabbing the only goal of the game just before the hour mark. It put Celtic seven points clear at the top of the SPL, and thoughts of a Treble were being entertained. Strachan had again shown he could outwit Walter Smith. He would do so one more time that season.

The first leg of the Treble would be the League Cup. Victories over Livingston and Kilmarnock set up a semi-final clash with Dundee United at Hampden in late January. Craig Levein's side were going well, and Celtic had taken notice, signing their goalkeeper Lukasz Zaluska on a pre-contract deal that would see him join up at Parkhead in the summer. Celtic's interest in Willo Flood, the Irish midfielder, was also well known, and it was rumoured that he would sign within hours.

It turned out to be an absolutely enthralling match. Played on a pitch that resembled a ploughed field, Celtic should have had it won by full-time, though United competed well. Flood and Zaluska, it should be said, did their level best to thwart their future employers. In extra time, Celtic threw everything at United, and Samaras hit the bar, but after 120 minutes of consistently exciting play, a penalty shoot-out ensued.

Player after player scored, until the scoreline stood at 8–8. Boruc and Zaluska then saved the kicks of Lee Wilkie and Glenn Loovens before the two goalkeepers scored against each other. Incredibly, with just the two misses, each player in each team had taken part, and the rota began again. Scott McDonald made his safe before Willo Flood stepped up and fired his shot over the bar to make the final score 11–10 for Celtic.

In quite extraordinary and indeed record-setting fashion – it was Celtic's highest-ever score in a penalty shoot-out – the Bhoys had made it to the final. Having missed the penalty, Flood duly joined Celtic a couple of days later. No one suggested that the Irishman had done anything other than his professional duty for United.

Gary Caldwell recalled that his plea after the semi was simple: 'We all wanted the Hampden pitch relaid so we could have a final against Rangers that everyone would be proud of.'

By the time that final came round, the Treble dream was already dead. After hammering St Mirren 7–0 in early March, in their very next match Celtic were put out of the Scottish Cup by the same team. That inconsistency was beginning to tell in the SPL, too, but the title was still Celtic's to lose, as they remained ahead of Rangers following a dire goalless draw at Parkhead.

Apart from the seven against St Mirren, goals had been hard to come by, but there was consolation in the form of players like Scott Brown and Gary Caldwell, who had recovered from a nervy start to his Parkhead career.

Caldwell said that Strachan's loyalty was a telling factor: 'People will always have opinions, and sometimes they don't like you. But the manager stuck by me, and hopefully I repaid that loyalty.'

The squad all knew that Old Firm finals, contrary to the 1960s and 1970s, were quite rare creatures in the 1990s and 2000s.

Caldwell said, 'I remember we were talking about the possibility of an Old Firm League Cup final even before the Dundee United semi-final and how long it had been since the last one.

'It was in 2003, but it was so long ago that few players that played in that match were still around. We were going to ask Neil Lennon about it – but then we remembered he got sent off in it.'

Lennon had no doubts about the importance of the final: 'It was a massive game in itself, and I was well aware that I had been on the losing side twice in the only two Old Firm cup finals during my playing career at Celtic. Most people thought it would give the winner a psychological advantage in the run-in to the league title, the race being as close as the previous year's at that point. But for days before it, Gordon and Walter Smith kept saying the League Cup would have no bearing on the outcome of the league. They were still saying that after the final, and they were right.'

It was also a clever move to try to get both squads motivated for the final as a trophy-chance in itself. Strachan also had a surprise card to play with the line-up, dropping underachieving strikers Samaras and Vennegoor of Hesselink to the bench and putting Scott McDonald on his own up front, though Aiden McGeady was instructed to get forward at every chance. Celtic's team was Boruc, Hinkel, Loovens, McManus, O'Dea, Caldwell, Nakamura, Brown, Hartley, McGeady and McDonald.

Rangers had the following line-up: McGregor, Whittaker, Weir, Broadfoot, Papac, Davis, McCulloch, Ferguson, Mendes, Miller and Lafferty. They, too, played with a single striker, former Celt Kenny Miller. Madjid Bougherra was a telling late call-off for them, forcing Broadfoot into central defence. Again, the only place for top scorer Kris Boyd was on the bench. The referee was Dougie McDonald, who would have a relatively quiet time, at least until the final seconds of the game.

Once again, as with the semi-final, it was a match Celtic should have won in regulation time. With both sides competing fiercely from the off, the match was fairly even at first. The newly laid pitch began to cut up straight away, but then some of the football was of the agricultural variety, too.

Celtic began to control things as Rangers were seemingly determined to play a containing game and created little threat, while Scott Brown, Shunsuke Nakamura and above all Aiden McGeady gradually began to show what they could do. In truth, however, for most of the first hour both sides were trying to cancel each other out. The tackles flew in, Andreas Hinkel becoming the first of four Celtic players to be booked with an unnecessarily tough tackle on Kyle Lafferty.

Clear-cut chances were few and far between in an absorbing but not high-quality first half. The best were created by Celtic just before the half-hour, with Scott Brown firing just over from 25 yards and then sclaffing a Nakamura cross over the bar after Glenn Loovens had sent a header just wide, again from a cross by the Japanese midfielder. It took until two minutes before half-time for

Rangers to create their first real chance, Artur Boruc saving well from Kyle Lafferty's volley.

Boruc gave the Celtic fans a near heart attack five minutes into the second period. Steven Davis had just missed from distance when Boruc collected a pass back from Stephen McManus and tried to play it around Lafferty, eventually conceding a throw-in as the Northern Irishman threatened.

Walter Smith sent on Nacho Novo for Kenny Miller, but it was Celtic who looked the fresher side, McGeady coming into his own as the match wore on. The Rangers fans had once sung the dire 'Famine Song' and thrown potatoes at the player who chose to represent the Republic of Ireland instead of Scotland. Now it was his turn to carve the Rangers defence into chips.

With Scott Brown and Nakamura also pressing forward, clearly besting Barry Ferguson et al., McGeady began to run directly at Steven Whittaker, Davie Weir and Kirk Broadfoot, who did not appreciate what was happening to them.

McGregor did well to save a 'Nakamura Special' free kick before Darren O'Dea came forward and headed the subsequent corner over the bar. He had enjoyed the experience, however, and showed he could be a threat at set-pieces.

A Loovens effort from Paul Hartley's 71st-minute corner was cleared off the line by Pedro Mendes, and then Hartley made way for Samaras, which allowed McGeady to go more to the wing. With no chances coming Rangers' way, Walter Smith finally decided to beef up their attack, sending on Kris Boyd for Lafferty in 78 minutes. Boyd had one chance to win it in normal time but couldn't reach Ferguson's chip.

In the first minute of extra time, Celtic raised their game and won the match. Whittaker fouled McDonald on Celtic's right and up stepped who else but Nakamura to whip in one of his bending free kicks. Up for the set-piece as usual, young Darren O'Dea outjumped everyone and headed into the net, with McGregor beaten. Ironically, had Lee Naylor been fit, O'Dea probably would not have been playing.

The Celtic end became a seething mass of green and white, but there was still 28 minutes or so left, and when McDonald shot wide and Samaras over-egged the pudding and failed to put away a golden chance, the fans began to wonder if Rangers might just come back and force penalties – those of us who attended the semi-final wondered if our hearts could stand another such shoot-out.

There was a comical moment when Neil Lennon and Barry Ferguson clashed off the field as the Rangers captain and Celtic coach went for the ball out of play. 'Just a wind up,' recalled Lennon, but the Celtic fans hailed him for his spirit.

With some more brilliant wing play, McGeady set up McDonald, but the striker's shot was deflected wide. As the seconds wound down, McGeady launched one last attack and broke through into the penalty box, where Kirk Broadfoot hauled him down. It was a clear penalty, and even though it was now in injury time, referee McDonald applied the letter of the law and sent Broadfoot off. There was no sympathy for the Rangers man from the Celtic cohorts, needless to say.

McGeady got a hold of the ball and, with supreme confidence, buried it behind McGregor. There was just enough time for the restart before Dougie McDonald blew the full-time whistle. The League Cup was Celtic's for the 14th time, and the green and white brigade celebrated long and loud. At the end, Rangers' dismay and frustration at their own poor performance was shown by Barry Ferguson, who booted the ball into the Celtic crowd.

Gary Caldwell had completed a clean sweep of domestic honours. His view was that Gordon Strachan's tactics had worked and had made all the difference: 'We had been struggling to create chances and score goals, and it was the manager who decided to move things around a bit, which is always a risk in a cup final. It worked very well, you have to say. We really should have won before extra time, but I just felt that, the longer the game went on, the better we were looking. I thought we had played well for long spells, and we struggled a bit in the second half but came strong again.'

Gary Caldwell also understood the significance of the victory: 'It was always great to win against Rangers; it was great for the fans. I was just six years old when Celtic last beat Rangers in a cup final at Hampden, so it's good to know that we are now a part of the club's history.'

For Neil Lennon, the feeling of victory was every bit as good as it had been when he was a player: 'The real pressure is always on the players to perform, but as a coach you do feel part of the achievement. Everyone at Celtic knows that beating Rangers is always important, and it always will be. To be a part of a victory over them in a cup final is doubly sweet. We'd like many more.'

That cup final day was to be the sole high point as the season petered out dismally for Celtic. The goals dried up as the team developed even more inconsistency. By the gloomy end, Rangers were champions by four points from Celtic, and two days later Gordon Strachan resigned. Rangers also went on to complete the Double, beating Falkirk 1–0 in the Scottish Cup final to bring them within one of Celtic's record haul of thirty-four Scottish Cups.

The Tony Mowbray era – more like an interval – came and went, and that's all that's to be said about the latest unhappy season. At the time of writing, in the summer of 2010, that League Cup victory over Rangers remains the latest final to feature Celtic. It is also the latest trophy won by the club.

Notice the word 'latest' and not 'last'. For it is inconceivable that Celtic will not win more trophies, and they will certainly encounter Rangers FC many, many more times in the hopefully endless battle between the two members of the Old Firm.

It is still the greatest derby in the world, and now that you know just some of the history as seen from Celtic's viewpoint, you realise why it is that, even if, please God, all the tawdry associations that have grown up around the Old Firm were to be removed, these two clubs would still have a rivalry second to none.

We would have it no other way. Bring on the Rangers!